ENGLISH AS WE SPEAK IT IN IRELAND

The life of a people is pictured in their speech

PATRICK WESTON JOYCE

(By permission of Dr. P. Dwyer-Joyce)

P W Joyce

ENGLISH AS WE SPEAK IT IN IRELAND

with an introduction by
TERENCE DOLAN

WOLFHOUND PRESS

36178

This edition © 1979 Wolfhound Press
Introduction © 1979 Terence Dolan
Portrait by permission of Dr. P. Dwyer-Joyce

First published 1910

ISBN 0 905473 27 2

Wolfhound Press
98 Ardilaun
Portmarnock County Dublin

Printed and bound in Great Britain by
REDWOOD BURN LIMITED
Trowbridge & Esher

CONTENTS

Portrait   frontispiece

Introduction by Terence Dolan   vi

P. W. Joyce's Preface   xxxvii

   I.   Sources of Anglo-Irish Dialect   1

  II.   Affirming, Assenting, and Saluting   9

 III.   Asserting by Negative of Opposite   16

 IV.   Idioms Derived from the Irish Language   23

  V.   The Devil and his 'Territory'   56

 VI.   Swearing   66

VII.   Grammar and Pronunciation   74

VIII.   Proverbs   105

 IX.   Exaggeration and Redundancy   120

  X.   Comparisons   136

 XI.   The Memory of History and of Old Customs   143

XII.   A Variety of Phrases   185

XIII.   Vocabulary and Index   209

     Alphabetical List of Persons who sent
     collections of Dialectical Words and Phrases   353

INTRODUCTION[1]

This famous and distinguished book has long been out of print. Its author's life spanned the years 1827-1914, which saw Catholic emancipation, the Great Famine, emigration, the institution of primary schools, and the political movements instituted by O'Connell and his followers, all of which affected in one way or another the relative currency of English and Irish. The fourth of eight brothers, Patrick Weston Joyce was born into a farming family in Ballyorgan, a small village in the extreme south of Co. Limerick, only two miles from the boundary with Co. Cork. His father, Garrett, a man of many talents, well merited his nickname 'the Scholar': he was a skilled musician, a very fine speaker, powerful in argument and, according to his son Michael, 'his taste for poetry was so great and his retentiveness so vast that he could repeat the poems of the *Iliad* and *Odyssey* with but very few mistakes.' (Incidentally, he is probably disguised as 'Garrett Barry' in an anecdote on pp. 314-15 of this book.) Garrett's father, Robert, known among his compères as 'Roibeárd an Gaeilgeoir', had settled down in Glenosheen, a mile west of Ballyorgan, on a piece of land which came to him through his marriage to a certain Anne Howard in 1783. Garrett married Elizabeth O'Dwyer (1795-1872), daughter of John O'Dwyer of Glendara. According to Michael Joyce, John 'was an only son and in order that he should be accomplished, he was sent to school to some university [sic] in Dublin, where he spent three years.' Later he met and fell in love with a young Protestant girl, Mary Rosaleen Weston, who had been attending a dancing academy at Kilfinane, about four miles north of Glenosheen. Her father, Major Weston, was furious at her marriage to someone of different religion and class (though it is to be noted on this point that, according to Professor Dwyer-Joyce, the Dwyers had been known as 'Lords of Kilnamanagh' and would not have recognised the Westons as in any way superior to themselves). The story ends well, because when the major was at last induced, with the help of Captain Oliver, a local landlord, to meet his son-in-law, he was, in the words of Michael Joyce, 'so highly pleased with O'Dwyer for his splendid appearance and fascinating manners, that he at once acknowledged him', and Mary later became a

See page XXVI for footnotes.

Catholic. Patrick added her surname to his own in later life, and his brother Robert (the second of the brothers to achieve distinction — as an author and composer (he wrote, for instance, 'The Boys of Wexford')) added their mother's surname to his. Robert Dwyer-Joyce was a committed Fenian, and spent most of his working life as a doctor in Boston in America, but died in Patrick's house in Rathmines in 1883.

Patrick was brought up speaking both Irish and English and received his early education in hedge-schools in Fanningstown, Kilmallock, Galbally, and Mitchelstown. His experience in them enabled him to leave us the incomparable, first-hand description of them which occurs later in this book [149 ff].[2] He benefited so much from this training that when he was only about eighteen years old he was appointed as a teacher by the Commissioners of National Education and very shortly became principal of the Model School in Clonmel, Co. Tipperary. In 1856 the Government selected for training fifteen teachers, of whom Joyce was one, to reorganize the National School System and he was succeeded as principal of Clonmel school by his brother Robert, whose studies he had supervised. In 1856 he married a member of a rich Protestant family, Caroline, daughter of Lieutenant John Waters of Baltinglass, and they had three sons and two daughters. In 1861 he was awarded a B.A. by Trinity College, Dublin, and proceeded M.A. in 1864. The same college conferred an LL.D. on him in 1870. By this time his outstanding abilities had already begun to be recognised. He was elected to membership of the Royal Irish Academy in 1863 and was a member of Council from 1884 to 1895. In 1865 he became a member of the Royal Society of Antiquaries in Ireland, of which he was president from 1906 to 1908. His final appointment before retirement, as Principal of the Board of Education Training College in Marlborough Street, Dublin, extended from 1876 to 1893. The twenty-one years which he enjoyed after his retirement were spent most productively with publication after publication flowing from his pen till he died at his house, Barnalee, Rathmines, 7 January, 1914.

He had already published a number of books before he retired and the full bibliography of his writings shows the range of his interests and studies, e.g., *Handicraft for Handy People: plain instructions on choice and use of tools, carpentry, &c.* with illustrations. By an amateur mechanic, [i.e. P. W. Joyce himself] (1886); *Irish Peasant Songs* (1906); *Old Celtic Romances,* trans.

from the Gaelic (1879); *A Grammar of the Irish Language* (1879); *A Short History of Ireland to 1608* (1893); *The Origin and History of Irish Names of Places* (1869-1913). The Joyce family recall him as a very witty conversationalist, excellent company, and a scholarly man who did not suffer fools gladly.

English as We Speak it in Ireland was first published in two editions in 1910, with a third edition in 1920. The book is full of information, both relevant and irrelevant for HE[3] studies, which is presented in a readable, enthusiastic way almost as a continuous narrative, with a strong prejudice in favour of the integrity of both Irish and Anglo-Irish culture. It is at times a dictionary of sayings, an anthology of proverbs, a diary of folklore, as well as being a collection of Hiberno-Englishisms. Consequently, the selection is very eclectic and the chapter headings, which include such items as 'The Devil and his "Territory" ' and 'The Memory of History and Old Customs', indicate an eccentric division of the material. After his chapter on 'Redundancy and Exaggeration', the next chapter ('Comparisons') begins with the statement that 'some of the items in this chapter would fit very well in the last; but this makes no matter; for good punch drinks well from either dandy or tumbler'. At the outset he disarmingly writes that 'this is essentially a subject for popular treatment, and accordingly I have avoided technical and scientific terms: they are not needed'. As we shall see in the bibliographical essay which concludes the introduction to this reissue, the study of the dialect has become much less amateurish since Joyce's day.

He was ideally suited to write this type of book and it clearly reflects his main interests — the Irish and English languages (passim), the educational system (see the celebrated section on hedge-schools [149 ff]. Irish music and song [113, 129, 336, etc.] place-names (e.g., Gorey [70], Knockanaffrin [144], etc.), and local history (passim). He derives his material from a variety of sources — his memory, his reading, and the replies from the correspondents listed at the end of this book. Unfortunately, the scholarly value of the book suffers from the haphazard nature of his references, and also from the constant anecdotalism arising from his extraordinarily associative mind: for instance, after one story he goes on to say 'for they had wireless telegraphy there long before Mr. Marconi's Irish mother was born' [59]. The

reader must be prepared for a considerable degree of inconsis-
tency in his treatment of the subject. Sometimes he does not
explain the reasons for significantly HE usages (e.g., on 'bold' he
merely says 'applied to girls and boys in the sense of "forward" ',
without indicating that Ir. *dána* means 'bold' or
'forward' [219] Elsewhere he omits to give the Ir. word which
explains a specific usage (e.g., 'the likes of', [286], Ir.
leithéid). Sometimes, he indicates pronunciation (e.g., 'twould
be no har-um', [16]), often not. Frequently he omits to give
derivations of words (e.g., 'mitch', 'thole'). There is doubt about
some of his explanations (e.g., 'chook chook', [234], which he
associates with Ir. *tiuc*, 'come', whereas the *English Dialect
Dictionary* places it in the West of England (see EDD under
Chook)). This is not to say that we should have no confidence
in his explanations — he is, for instance, supported by the
Oxford English Dictionary for his note on 'Cess' (see *OED*
under *Cess* sb.5), as also on Hobby (see *OED* under *Hobby* sb.
sb. 1). All in all, his book is of great interest for the study of
HE, of local history (e.g., 'a Kilmallock fire' [107], 'porter-
meal' [304]), as well as of general native Irish culture
'Banshee', Leprachaun', 'Come-all-ye', etc.). We shall now go
through the book, chapter by chapter, indicating their
respective usefulness for the study of HE. Chapters IV and VII
will be dealt with last because they are the most important.

Chapter I distinguishes three main sources of the HE dialect:
1. the Irish language (including Irish influence on pronunciation ('thrue', 'de books', 'dozhen', etc.), and on vocabulary
('galore', 'shamrock', 'whiskey', 'bother', 'blarney',
'smithereens')); 2. Old English (giving rise to such conservative
pronunciations as 'tay' for 'tea', 'sevare' for 'severe', etc.) and
Scottish (the latter being 'confined to Ulster while the remnants
of the Elizabethan English are spread all over Ireland'); 3. 'the
gradual growth of dialect among our English-speaking people'.
He also presents a short sketch of the history of the HE dialect.
Chapter II includes a list of expressions 'Affirming, Assenting,
and Saluting' which notes, among other things, what happens
as a result of the absence of 'yes' and 'no' in Irish — thus the
emphatic, affirmative answer to 'This is a real wet day' would be
'I believe you'. Other expressions discussed include the common
idiom represented by 'He hit me with his stick, so he did'. In
Chapter III he considers the germane topic of 'Assertion by

Negation of Opposite' (e.g., 'Where do you keep all your money?': 'Oh, indeed, it's not much I have' – Ir. *Ní móran atâ agum*). Chapter V lists a host of expressions in which 'The Devil and his "Territory" ' figures, and includes this interesting note on *yerra* or *arrah* (Ir. *aire*): 'The old people didn't like our continual use of the word; and in order to deter us we were told that *Yerra* or *Arrah* was the name of the devil's mother' [62]. Chapter VI on 'Swearing', includes a list of what he calls 'blank cartridges' ('begob', 'begor', 'dang it', etc.) as well as an explanation of the important expression 'the dear knows' [69]. Chapter VIII includes many general proverbs as well as some more interesting local ones (e.g., ' "You might as well go to hell with a load as with a pahil " . . . A *pahil* or *paghil* is a bundle of anything (Derry)' [108]; 'Why you're *as grand as Mat Flanagan with the cat*' [118] – this last is so localized as to have only distant interest with the general reader).

Chapter IX, 'Exaggeration and Redundancy', includes such distinctive HE features as 'kilt' meaning 'pretty badly hurt', 'murthered entirely' meaning 'really badly hurt', 'destroyed' characterizing 'any trifling damage easily remedied' [123-4], and 'killed dead', for which he cites comparison with Ir. *marbh gan anam* [132]. Chapter X has many non-HE examples (e.g., ' . . . as poor as a church mouse', 'put that in your pipe and smoke it'), again with an admixture of very localized ones (e.g., 'I'm a man in myself like Oliver's bull' [142]), and relevant HE ones (e.g., 'his heart is as low as a *keeroge's* kidney', (Ir. *ciar + óg*) [143]. Chapter XI presents a fascinating collection of descriptions and stories under the heading of 'Memories of History and Old Customs', beginning with a shrewd exposition of the terms 'Church, Chapel, and Scallan' [143 ff], and moving on to his treatment of the hedge-schools [149 ff], dealing with their history and development, the activities of the pupils and masters, and with what was taught in them. As we have seen, Joyce was peculiarly well-equipped to write on them because he received his own early education in them. He describes the original and well-named 'hedge-schools', and then instances some of the *ad hoc* locations (barns, etc.) in which they were held when things got easier. This chapter is so rich in social history that it is impossible to summarize, and the reader is drawn on through an immensely attractive range of topics, including the jig 'Rattle the hasp', Tent pot, *Beltane*,

tenaigin, the legal classification of animals, his explanation of
the expression 'paying on the nail' [183], and 'Oliver's
Summons' [184] (how the local landlord near his home got
men to do his work for him). This chapter is remarkably
digressive, but it conditions the reader for the next chapter
('A Variety of Phrases'), which is even more so, and takes in
such varied pieces of information as the idea that 'pigs can see
the wind' [193], pious expressions such as 'God help me'
[195], Charles Macklin's invention of the expression 'she looks
as if butter wouldn't melt in her mouth' [198], and a notable
instance of misplacing – 'I got a bite in the leg of a dog' [204].
Chapter XII, 'A Variety of Phrases', is very random, and
includes some gratuitous explanations for easily comprehensible
expressions (e.g., 'He is down in the mouth' [193]; 'I wouldn't
put it past him' [300]). The final section of the book, Chapter
XIII, 'Vocabulary and Index', contains many non-HE entries,
as well as substantially relevant ones such as 'Brogue', 'Cess',
'Ditch/Dyke', 'Great' (= intimate), 'Learn' (= teach), 'Lief',
'Likes', 'Mad/Angry', 'Quit', 'Raumaush/Raumaish', and
'Shaughraun'.

Chapters IV and VII, entitled respectively 'Idioms Derived
from the Irish Language' [23-55] and 'Grammar and Pronunciation' [74-104], are seminal studies of topics which later scholars
have tackled in much greater detail and, it must be said, in a
much more orderly fashion. In Chapters IV Joyce's principal
interests include the construction exemplified in 'I am in my
standing'; the word *ann* and its reflex in HE ('in it', [25]);
the distinctive use of prepositions in HE [26 ff] (e.g., 'he lost
my knife on me' (Ir. *air*); 'I'll break your head for you' (Ir.
ag)); idiomatic expressions using the word *head* 'to denote the
cause, occasion, or motive of anything' [32]; rhetorical
questions of the type 'Who should come up to me in the fair but
John' which are used to make an assertion [33]; the pronouns
'myself', 'himself', etc. [33]; constructions like 'He interrupted
me and *I writing* my letters' and 'How could you expect Davy
to do the work and *him* so very sick', leading to an explanation
of such expressions as 'Them are the boys' ("iad" is in some
Irish constructions correctly used as a nominative (cf. *é* and *í*)
[35]); the conjunction 'the way' representing Ir. *amhlaidh* or
caoi [35 ff]; the word 'itself' (Ir. *féin* = 'even' 'itself') [36-7];
'the time' used as a conjunction instead of 'when' (Ir. *an uair*)

[37]; the use of 'show' instead of 'give/hand' (e.g., 'show me
that knife' [37-8]; 'that' (Ir. *go*) placed in front of wishes or
prayers (e.g., 'That you may soon get well' [38]); direct translations from Irish (e.g., 'it's a fine day that' (Ir. *is breagh an lá é
sin*) [40]; 'the full of' (Ir. *lán*) [41]; 'at all' (Ir. *idir*) [43]; 'it
is equal to me' (Ir. *is cuma liom*) [43]; duplication of prepositions, e.g., 'the dog got in under the bed' [44]; 'you'll get your
death' (cf. *fuair sé bás*) [45]; the 'narrative infinitive' (i.e.,
beginning a story without a finite verb, e.g., 'To get (= I got)
into the heart of the fair' [45-6]; 'This is herself, sir' [46]; 'I
have no Irish' [47]: *Ní 'l Gaodhlainn agum*; 'on foot' [47];
'nough' shortened from 'enough' (used in HE with a possessive
pronoun) [48]; 'for' used before an infinitive (e.g., 'for to make a
coat') [51]; the almost total absence of 'whose', because 'the
people . . . do not know how to use it' — hence such combinations as 'there's a man that his wife leaves him whenever she
pleases' [52]; 'kind father for him' [= 'He is of the same kind as
his father') [53].

The first section of Chapter VII, on Grammar, includes the
usage of 'will' in preference to 'shall' [74-77]; irregular past
tenses of verbs ('slep', 'crep', etc.) [77-8]; the imperative with
'let' [81]; the increased use of the definite article in HE [82-3];
HE equivalents to standard English perfect and pluperfect ('I have
finished my work', 'I had finished my work') [84-6]; the consuetudinal tense ('do be') [86]; the pronominal plurals ('yous,
yez, yiz') [88]; adjectives used as adverbs (e.g., 'This is a *cruel*
wet day') [89-90]; the diminutive suffix *een, in* [90-91]. The
second section, on Pronunciation, [91 ff] describes the conservative elements in HE pronunciation ('sea' pronounced as 'say'
[91]; 'er' pronounced as 'ar' (cf. Dryden rhyming 'certain' and
'parting') [93]. Joyce goes on to note the placing of 'a very
short obscure vowel' between consonants ('firm' pronounced
'ferrum') [96]; other distinctive pronunciations such as 'ould'
for 'old' [99], the omission of final *d* after *l* and *n* ('an' for 'and')
[100], the pronunciation of short *e* before *n* and *m* and sometimes in other positions (thus giving rise to confusion over 'pen'
meaning 'pin' or 'pen'), different accentuation, as in 'ex-cel-
lent, commit-tee', etc. [101], the pronunciation of the vowel *i* as
oi in Tipperary ('foine day') [102], archaic survivals such as the
pronunciation of 'oblige' as 'obleege' (cf. Pope rhyming 'besieged'
and 'obliged') [103], the tendency to shorten words ('garner'

for 'gardener', 'Carnal' for 'Cardinal') [103], and, finally, other
variant pronunciations such as 'me' for 'my', 'be' for 'by', 'sperrit'
for 'spirit', and 'merricle' for 'miracle'.

Having described the virtues and vices of Joyce's book we can
move on to a summary description and evaluation of the main
scholarly studies of HE, taking into account the external and
the linguistic history of the period from the Norman invasions
onwards, the vocabulary, syntax, and distinctive pronunciation
of HE, the significantly different features of the Ulster dialects,
and the application of the study of the language of HE to Anglo-
Irish writing.
    In an eminently readable paper,[4] E. J. Curtis presents evidence
for his claim that 'French, English and Irish were the three rivals
for linguistic supremacy in medieval Ireland' [235], traces the
'brief flowering' of French in Ireland, and goes on to describe
the fortunes of English from the Conquest onwards, pointing out
its survival in various urban pockets (e.g., Kilkenny, the scene of
the Kyteler case) up to the fourteenth century, and then its
gradual collapse in most inland areas in the face of the 'revival of
the native race', until by the sixteenth century only two areas
could be counted as predominantly English speaking (the Pale,
and the baronies of Forth and Bargy in Wexford) [246]. The
resurgence of Irish in spite of futile legislation such as the
Statutes of Kilkenny of 1366 (written in French) would have
continued unabated were it not for the Tudor plantations. Curtis
takes the story from the twelfth century to the sixteenth, and it
may be taken up in Alan Bliss's chapter on 'The English language
in early modern Ireland' in *A New History of Ireland* (vol. III)[5],
in which he describes some of the salient features of two dialects
which survived from the medieval period (Fingall, and the Forth
and Bargy), and discusses the nature and value of surviving
evidence about the kind of English used in the towns. This is to
be found mainly in the non-standard spellings used to represent
the speech of Irish characters in Elizabethan and Jacobean plays.[6]
In addition he points out the very interesting clues which Swift
gives about the language of planters in *Polite Conversation*
(1738), and about other features of HE in a work which survives
both in conversational form under the title *A Dialogue in
Hybernian Stile between A and B* and in the form of a letter
under the title *Irish Eloquence*.[7] The chapter concludes with an

excellent summary of what happened to the spoken English in Ireland after the medieval period. Finally, the student should read Seán de Fréine's article on 'The dominance of the English Language in the nineteenth century'.[8] This looks back to the 'language situation at the end of the eighteenth century' which 'was not all that different geographically from what it was in the year 1700. There was a certain amount of give and take in the territories occupied by the two languages' [73].

After familiarizing himself with the external history, the reader may turn to more linguistically biased studies, beginning with J. J. Hogan's distinguished book.[9] He sets out to deal with 'both the Outer History of English in Ireland — its fortunes as a spoken tongue, its area of use, its use in literature — and its Inner History — its grammar and linguistic development', and he works on the assumption that both 'the Inner history and the Outer history are inseparable'. His book is divided into four parts: I. Outline of the History of English in Medieval Ireland, followed by an Appendix covering the Dialects of Fingall (with reference to 'the Irish Hudibras') [39 ff] and of Forth and Bargy (with reference to the texts in Poole's Glossary) [44 ff]; II. Summary of the Grammatical Features of Medieval Anglo-Irish; III. Outline of the History of Modern Anglo-Irish; IV. Phonology of Modern Anglo-Irish. This excellent little book ends with a series of specimens demonstrating HE works of different periods starting with Friar Michael of Kildare's Hymn (c. 1300) and finishing with an excerpt from the Congratulatory address in the dialect of Forth presented to the Earl Mulgrove, Lord Lieutenant of Ireland, at Wexford in 1836.

Hogan's book should be read in conjunction with P. L. Henry's 'A Linguistic Survey of Ireland: Preliminary Report',[10] which begins with a historical section indicating the fortunes of the English Language in Ireland up to 1600: the linguistic resurgence of the natives in the fourteenth century and the decreasing use of English, with the exception of the two rural areas of 'Fingall (the coastal stretch from Dublin to Skerries) and the baronies of Forth and Bargy in South Wexford'. There follows a discussion of medieval HE with particular reference to the Kildare poems (c. 1300) and their affinities with the language of Forth and Bargy. He gives a chart aiming to give 'some idea of the relative consistency of Leinster' HE [69] (with evidence from the Kildare poems, Dublin municipal records, and literature in the Forth dialect, which he describes as 'a mosaic of archaic E[nglish] and of Ir[ish] in which N[orman] F[rench], Flemish and Welsh features are still discernible' [75]. Next he provides a brief analysis of the phonology, vocabulary, and syntax of selected specimens of the Forth dialect. The second section of his study includes a very interesting account of the methodology required for researching and recording features of HE and the accompanying problems (e.g., whether phonological or lexical criteria should be given precedence). He goes on to list the features of sixteenth- and seventeenth-century English which have been retained in HE, and presents many examples of distinctive HE idioms and constructions (e.g., use of the definite article ('the measles', 'the cold', etc.), tense and aspect in the verbal system, prepositions, subordination (e.g., 'I saw him an' I (me) goin' to town'). Towards the end of his study Henry discusses what he calls 'the primary dialect boundary': North and South.

We shall move on to vocabulary and syntax. A year before Joyce's book was first published, Mary Hayden and Marcus Hartog published a most informative, readable paper on 'The Irish Dialect of English: Its Origins and Vocabulary' [11]which they divided into three sections, the first two dealing mainly with vocabulary (I. 'Survivals of Tudor and Stuart English words that have disappeared from S[tandard] E[nglish] . . .'; II. 'Peculiarities due to Gaelic Influence' (borrowings of both Irish words and of Irish idioms). In Section III they tackle what they call 'Solecisms that have arisen from imperfect assimilation of the alien tongue'. The archaic survivals outlined in Section I [777-782] include such items as 'mich', 'message' (= errand), 'till' (= in order that), 'for to' (to indicate an infinitive of purpose), 'hunt' (= to send about one's business), as well as new formations like 'Come all ye' and miscellaneous words like 'gossoon' ('probably the French "Garçon" which came into I[rish] E[nglish] through the Irish language'). In section II [782-785, 933-941] under borrowings of words from Irish they include 'gob', 'crubeen', 'barmbrack', 'garron' (= horse, nag), 'shanty', 'galore', 'mooley' (hornless cow < Ir. *mael* = bare), 'arrah'/'yerrah' (Ir. *ara* = truly), 'gombeen', 'pishog', 'bucalaun' (ragwort), and finally 'hybrid diminutives' such as 'girleen', 'dogeen', etc. The section on idioms borrowed from Irish begins with aspects of the HE verbal system ('I am after writing a letter', 'He fell out of his standing', etc.), and goes on to discuss the love of periphrasis in Irish speech, the consequences of there being no 'yes' or 'no' in Irish, and the use of the auxiliary 'do' in the present continuous tense of verbs ('does be wanting to shave'). There follows an interesting section on the perfect tense in HE, tracing parallels between the absence in Irish of 'have' and the Latin construction *est mihi liber* (lit. 'there is a book to me' = I have a book). Next comes treatment of the prepositions (including the *dativus incommodi*: 'I broke his stick on the master'), the definite article ('He had *the* fever'), and reflexive pronouns. In the final part of their paper]941-947] Hayden and Hartog deal with solecisms: the use of 'on' in expressions of time ('on tomorrow', 'on today', etc.), the imperative with 'let', and the distinctive use of the word 'right' ('He had a right to do a thing!'). Later they deal with what they call 'dyslexicology' (= 'that misuse of the dictionary which consists of acting on the assumption that all words are synonymous directly or by metaphor in the one language are necessarily synonymous in the other') – hence, Ir. *féin* ('even', 'self'), *cogar* ('whisper', 'listen': e.g., 'Whisper, father, are you going to Kilkenny today?'), *siar* ('west', 'behind').

J. M. Clark's major study of HE vocabulary [12] begins with a general Introduction to the subject working on the premise that 'it was not the English of London, but that of the Pale that ousted out Erse' [4], and that 'for a thoroughly reliable account of the Irish peasantry and idiomatic specimens of their speech, we must turn to writers like Griffin, Croker and Kickham, who represent the counties of Limerick, Cork and Tipperary respectively' [8]. In Section IV he outlines 'the general character of Anglo-Irish', and specifies the main areas of difference between it and standard English: pronunciation, vocabulary, accent, accidence, and syntax. In Section V, on pronunciation, he states that his main interest is to consider 'the way in which Erse on one hand and Elizabethan English on the other have left their traces on the Anglo-Irish vocabulary' [14], and deals with such features as the values of *t* and *d* before *r*, the aspiration of *p* and *b*, the substitution of *t* or *d* for *th*, the change of *s* to *sh* before *p*, *t* and *k*, the palatalization of *l*, the change of slack $\breve{e}$ to tense $\breve{i}$ before nasals, and the dropping of final *d* after *n*, and then moves on to vowels. In Section VI [19-25] he instances the general tendency of HE to shift the accent towards the end of the word (hence, 'excéllent', 'necéssary', etc.); 'some Elizabethan features' such as the use of adverbs without the ending -*ly* (e.g.,

'She played beautiful'); archaic plural endings (e.g., 'Horses *wears* shoes'); the ending *-in* for *-ing* in the present participle; the new personal pronoun formation with *ye/you* singular, and *yez, yiz, youz* in the plural; the ascription of masculine or feminine pronouns to inanimate objects (note the absence of neuter gender in modern Irish); syntactical features such as the preference for *will* over *shall* in HE; the use of 'like' adverbially in the sense of 'as it were' (e.g., 'A long dry cave or underground cellar *like*'); and *nor* used in the same sense as the comparative conjunction 'than'.

Then, with due reference to the work of Hayden and Hartog, van Hamel, and P. W. Joyce, Clark presents a concise account of the use of characteristically distinct tenses in HE (e.g., 'Some people *do be very* cute', 'He *has* his mind *made up* . . .', 'Now I would not *be after saying* . . .', 'Is it raving you are?'); the omission of the relative pronoun in adjective clauses; the retention of the direct word-order in indirect questions (e.g., 'She asked me did I ever see . . .'); the ubiquitous use of *and* as a conjunction in subordinate clauses (e.g., 'The voice of the whipper-in, and he shouting out . . .'). He ends the section with a brief mention of such idioms as 'the full of', 'itself' (= 'even') and the ethic dative ('on him', Ir. *air,* etc.).

Section VII [25-32] concerns 'Celtic Loans': e.g., the pregnant use of black (Ir. *duibh,* e.g., 'black Protestant'), technical words ('cleeve', 'kish', 'loy', 'sugawn', etc., all from Irish), geographical terms (e.g., 'inch', 'lough', 'slob' (Ir. *slab,* mire), shipping terms (e.g., 'curragh', 'pookawn'), botanical and zoological terms (e.g., Ir. *ceanabhan,* bog-cotton) miscellaneous words (e.g., *shebeen, gossoon, cosher, dun, ogham*), terms of endearment (e.g., *agra, ma bouchal,* etc.), diminutives (e.g., *boreen, kippeen* (Ir. *cipín,* a short stick), *crubeen, keeroge* (Ir. *ciaróg,* 'beetle')), diminutives of hybrid formation (e.g., 'bullockeen', 'houseen', 'poteen', 'Jackeen'), terms of abuse (e.g., 'bosthoon' (Ir. *bastún,* 'good-for nothing fellow'), 'omadhaun' and 'oonshugh' (fool, masculine and feminine respectively), 'angishore' (Ir. *aindeiseoir,* 'wretch), *etc., Irish words which have become* HE slang (e.g., 'mouth'/'gob'); miscellaneous ejaculations and interjections (e.g., 'Musha' or 'wisha' (Ir. *má is eadh*), 'arrah' or 'yerrah' (Ir. *ara*)), and terms denoting superstitions (e.g., 'pisrogue' (Ir. *piseog*), 'meeraw' (Ir. *miorath*).

Section VIII [32-39] features 'Old English Survivals' which are no longer used in Standard English: e.g., 'crack', which originally meant 'a lively lad' in Elizabethan English, 'to mitch', 'mering' (boundary); and words which retain a meaning now lost in England, e.g., 'put away' (divorce), 'mind' (notice), 'slip' (boy or girl), 'quit' (vb. = 'leave'), 'beholden' (obliged), 'stout' (strong), etc.

Section IX [39-43] begins with a short and not very helpful digression on what constitutes the evolution of dialect survivals — the way that 'words . . . at one time perfectly correct . . . have now sunk down to the level of dialect words' (e.g., 'man' in the sense of husband, 'gripe' (ditch), 'renege' (jilt, renounce), 'handsel' (earnest money), which Clark suggests may have survived because of its resemblance to Ir. *airgead láimhe* (money of hand).

The final section [43-48] covers Dialect Loans (e.g., Scottish or Northern English 'skelp' (strike), 'oxter' (armpit), 'clocking' (sc. hens), 'grand' (excellent, fine)), Slang, and New Formations (both new creations and independent developments of meaning: 'blarney' (cajoling talk), foreign derivatives such as Scandinavian 'haggard' (stock garden or kitchen garden), and new hybrids with -y (e.g., 'mountainy', etc.)).

A valuable account of HE syntax was published by A. G. van Hamel, [13] who identifies obvious Hiberno-Englishisms in selected works of Yeats and Synge and compares them with their Irish equivalents, for which he cites an Irish grammar prepared by the Christian Brothers (Dublin, 1906). In the first section [275-279] he deals with constructions with the verb *to be* present tense: 'I'm thinking it's dead he is surely'; past tense: 'Wasn't I telling you it was for that I called to him'; imperative: 'Be taking your rest'; infinitive: 'I'd be putting a little stitch in my old coat'; the English present perfect tense, which takes two forms in Irish (both reflected in HE): (i) 'He's after dying on me', and (ii) 'I have the letter written', which has an interesting development from the *tá agam* construction because of the absence of the verb 'to have' in Irish. In this connexion he makes the significant point that 'a sentence like "I have my door painted" would mean quite a different thing in Irish and in Anglo-Irish'. The fact that the verb is given first position in Irish leads to such formations as 'It's not shining at all they are', which allow considerable freedom in emphasizing one part of a sentence rather than another. He goes on to discuss assertions phrased as questions, on

the pattern of 'Who now has it ordered but the Lord
Lieutenant?', and the habitual tense of HE reflecting the Irish
bídhim, etc. (e.g., 'They do be cheering').

In the second section [279-281] van Hamel considers 'Other
idiomatic constructions': the use in HE of the infinitive in place
of the verbal noun found in Irish (e.g., 'It is a pity he not to
awaken at this time'); indirect questions in HE which, following
Irish, in contrast to standard English, are constructed with the
same order as direct questions (e.g., 'I don't know is it here she
is coming?'); the frequency of the conditional mood in HE,
again reflecting Irish usage, but not Standard English (e.g., 'It
would be best to put it out, whatever way it would be (= could
be) put out'; and finally the imperative with 'let you'.

The third section [281-284] begins with the most important
point that 'the lack of a few common verbs − in the first place
of the verb "to have" ' causes Irish to make much greater use of
prepositions than, for instance, English. In many constructions
HE reflects Irish usage: Ir. *ar,* which lies behind such expressions
as 'And the fret lies on me', 'He's after dying on me'; Ir. *do,*
which is reflected in expressions such as 'It is true for you'; Ir.
tar éis, which influences the formation of the present perfect
tense of HE (see above), and is also reflected in such expressions
as 'He is after death'; Ir. *tar,* giving sentences like 'I taught him to
recognise stones beyond angels'; Ir. *le* (now more usually *ag*)
'used to denote the agent or cause with passive verbs' (e.g., 'I'ld
have been . . . eaten with crows . . .').

Section 4 [284-285] deals with conjunctions, which are not
employed as frequently in Irish as in English, both because of the
tendency to use the verbal noun and through the ubiquitous use
of 'and' (Ir. *agus*) in substitution for the more specific range of
subordinate conjunctions ('when', 'because', 'although', 'which')
used in Standard English (e.g., 'It was raining and I coming
home'). As an alternative to temporal clauses headed by *and,* HE
often has 'the time' (representing Ir. *an nuair > nuair*), giving such
expressions as 'And this morning, the time he was going off . . .'.
The Standard English conjunctions used for heading result
and purpose clauses are often exchanged for 'the way' (Ir. *ionnus
go, i gcaoi go, i slighe go,* e.g., 'Smooth the sheet the way it was
lying').

Section 5 [286-289] instances twelve idiomatic expressions
with their Irish equivalents; 'in it' (Ir. *ann*); 'enough' (always

preceded by a possessive pronoun in Irish: e.g., *a dhothain*);
'the full of' (e.g., Ir. *lán na míosa*); 'self' used as an equivalent to
'so' or 'even' — cf. also *himself, herself,* meaning the master/
mistress of the house (Ir. *é féin, í féin*); 'the like of' (Ir. *leithéid*);
'that length' meaning 'as far as, as long as' (Ir. *fad*); 'right' (Ir.
ceart) used as an adjective or noun (e.g., 'You'd have a right to
be minding . . .'); 'to have a call' (Ir. *cáll*) used in such expressions
as 'You'll have no call to complain'; 'from this out' (Ir. *as so
amach*); 'west, back, backward' (Ir. *siar*); 'not long, meaning
'soon' (Ir. *ní fada*); 'the year that's gone' meaning 'last year' (Ir.
an bhliadhain seo a ghaibh tharainn). In his final section
[289-291] van Hamel deals with six words literally translated
from Irish: 'master/woman of the house' (Ir. *fear tighe, bean
tighe*); 'share' used substantively (Ir. *cuid*, e.g., 'your share of
trouble'); 'black' meaning 'fatal, accursed' (Ir. *dubh*); 'let on'
meaning 'pretend, feign' (e.g., *leigim orm*); 'destroyed', meaning
'very much tired, fatigued, exhausted' (Ir. *sáruighthe, claoidte,
silte*); 'shut of' meaning 'apart from, separate from' (Ir. *druidhte*).

The only major study so far published of a specifically
delimited area of HE is P. L. Henry's 'study of the rural dialect of
Anglo-Irish spoken in Cloongreghan, in the hinterland of the
village of Cootehall, some seven miles from Boyle in Co.
Roscommon'.[14] He divides his study into three parts covering
Phonology, Accidence, and Syntax, followed by a Glossarial
Index, and consistently gives phonetic transcriptions of HE
phrases and expressions accompanied by the Irish bases where
necessary (e.g., 'as the man says', cf. Ir. *mar deir an fear*) [116].
This fine book is packed with information, but it is presented in a
labyrinthine fashion. Fortunately Henry's aims and the
significance of his findings have been sympathetically expounded
in a substantial review-article on the book by E. G. Quinn,[15] who
also furnishes us with a brief survey of some of the earlier studies
of HE. The student of HE literature will find Part III of Henry's
book particularly useful (on the Substantival System, the Verbal
System, and Coordination and Subordination). Of major
importance are his comprehensive presentation of the evidence
for the varieties of the 'it's' construction ('It's flat it was', 'It's
what it'll grow', etc.: [192 ff]) and the section on word order
[201 ff].

We should recognize the linguistic distinctiveness of Ulster,
and G. B. Adams has done much to establish our knowledge of

the dialect. In an excellent paper entitled 'An Introduction to the Study of Ulster Dialects',[16] he says that Ulster English may be defined as 'that variety of Irish-English to which both Scottish and English dialects have contributed, though this would exclude the speech of some areas in the south-west of the province where the Scottish element was lacking' [5]. He first roughly identifies four types of English spoken in Ulster (1. 'the various dialects spoken in different localities by the mass of the rural and urban population'; 2. 'the fairly well defined regional type of pronunciation and idiom which in Ulster, as in other parts of the British Isles, has been evolved among the educated classes'; 3. 'a small minority of Ulster people who . . . speak naturally "standard" Southern English or a close approximation to it'; 4. 'the English spoken by those people whose native language is Irish' [2]. He then sketches the history of the settlements in Ulster, working on the assumption that 'the modern English dialects of Ulster are derived from the English of the seventeenth-century settlers from England and, even more, from Scotland' [5]. He treats grammar and intonation briefly, before going on to his main task — to describe the phonetics of his own speech (which he hopes is fairly representative of 2 above) and that of the local Belfast dialect.

To familiarize himself with HE as represented in Anglo-Irish literature the reader may consult John Garvin's perceptive article on 'The Anglo-Irish Idiom in the works of Major Irish Writers',[17] outstanding among whom is Synge whose recent centenary stimulated several important studies. For our purpose the most recommendable of these is Alan Bliss's felicitous and sensitive appraisal of 'The Language of Synge',[18] which begins with a brief historical sketch of the English language in Ireland, traces its representation in writing from Swift onwards, and notes that 'the first use of Anglo-Irish as a literary medium was made by Douglas Hyde in 1890, when in his *Beside the Fire* he published a series of folk-tales in the original Irish, and accompanied them with a translation into Anglo-Irish' [36-37]. Synge's developing use of HE vocabulary and syntax is analysed and exemplified, with some significant observations about his syntactical inaccuracies (e.g., in '. . . tell me *if* it's cold he is', [48] which wrongly represents HE idiom where 'this use of *if* is unknown, and the indirect question has exactly the same form as a direct question' [47]. More recently, Declan Kiberd, in his impressive analysis of the bene-

ficial effects which Synge's 'manoeuvre' of the two languages
(Irish and English) [88] had on his writings, has presented a
powerful set of arguments in favour of his claim that Synge had a
genius for translation, and that the excellence of his Irish scholarship and knowledge of the language is reflected in his use of the
HE dialect. [18a]

The fullest study of the use made of the HE dialect in Anglo-
Irish literature was published by a Japanese scholar.[19] In absolute
contrast to Joyce's vaguely structured account of HE, Taniguchi's
exhaustive treatment of what he calls 'Artistic Representation of
Irish English' (i.e., in the works of Anglo-Irish writers,
Edgeworth, O'Flaherty, Synge, etc.) is very precisely organised;
Section I — Parts of Speech: Noun; Pronouns; Adjectives,
Adverbs and Articles; Verbs; Conjunctions and Prepositions;
Section II — Sentence Structures; The construction 'And +
subject + predicate without verb' (with a rich variety of examples
covering the whole range of subordinate clausal substitutions,
e.g., time: '. . . I got married then, and *I holding* out till I was
forty'); The construction 'It is . . .'; Anacoluthia; Repetition and
Redundance; Afterthought (following on from his opening
statement that 'the Irish are much inclined to add words, phrases,
clauses in an extra-position as a kind of afterthought after the
subject and predicate have been expressed'; Reported Questions;
Complicated Sentence Structures; Final Remarks on sentence
structures of Irish English; Section III — Sounds and Spelling:
Introduction; Consonants; Vowels; Addition, Loss and Metathesis
of Sounds; Accent. He follows all this with a singularly helpful
recapitulary chapter [256-265] detailing everything he has
covered so far. This is followed by a substantial Appendix‾
entitled 'Studies on the Structure of the Dialogue in Synge's
Plays' (dealing with such specific features as the 'high average of
syllables in a sentence', the 'differences in prose rhythm between
Standard English and Synge's Irishism', etc.), and finally with a
series of scansions, e.g., the last forty nine sentences of *In the
Shadow of the Glen.* The book concludes with a full bibliography ('List of Novels and Plays in which Irish English is used or
Irishmen Represented', 'Miscellaneous Works regarding Ireland
and Irish English' (in two parts), 'List of Novels and Plays Written
by American or British Writers in Other Dialects', 'Principal
Works on Grammar, Language, Phonetics, and Rhetoric,
Consulted (in 2 parts), and an excellent Index.

He makes over thirty references to Joyce's book which, as we have seen, sacrifices methodology to readability. If the reader of Joyce's book bears Tanaguchi's headings in mind under the general headings of vocabulary, the structure of the sentence, the verbs, idiomatic usages, and pronunciation, he will be able to distinguish and recognise the main features of HE outlined in the present book.

The reader will have to engage in much cross-checking if he wishes to build up a composite picture of striking phenomena in HE. For instance, Joyce's section on propositions [26 ff] should be compared with those of Hayden and Hartog [938 ff] and of van Hamel [281 ff]. His list of vocabulary should be checked against those of Hayden and Hartog, Clark, and van Hamel [289 ff]. Joyce's interesting note on the word 'brogue' [225] and that by Hayden and Hartog [785] should be reconsidered in the light of Bliss's definitive identification of its derivation.[20] Joyce's short note on the imperative with 'let' [81] should be cross-checked with Bliss's full statement in his major study of four distinctive features of HE; [21] similarly Joyce's lengthy entry on the word 'bother' [221] should be compared with Bliss's article on 'Bother' and 'Pother'; [22] and Bliss's account of the HE use of *do* as a consuetudinal auxiliary ('he does be', etc.) [23] should be used to supplement Joyce's note [86].

To get some idea of the contraction in the currency of Irish and the corresponding increase in the use of English, the reader should consult linguistic maps: Seán de Fréine's Language Map of Ireland, c. 1800 [78]; the two maps showing the relative density of Irish speakers in 1851 and 1891; [24] T. W. Freeman's maps showing 'the distribution of the language in 1926 and 1936',[25] and Henry's map showing the decline of the Gaeltacht since 1925.[26] The reader should also consult Wagner's Linguistic Atlas, at the beginning of which he claims that his material 'will also show the influence which English exercised on Irish during the past hundred years' [X.A.].[27] For Ulster, reference should be made to G. B. Adams' two maps.[28] Those interested in the dialect of Forth and Bargy should consult Poole's Glossary, the studies published by Hogan, Henry, and O'Muirithe, Bliss's introductory remarks and the new edition of Poole's Glossary by Dolan and O'Muirithe.[29]

All these studies in greater or lesser detail demonstrate that the linguistic history of the language reflects the external history of the country, which may be summarized as follows:

1167 onwards	Arrival of the Anglo-Normans in Ireland
1366	Statutes of Kilkenny
14th century	Gaelic Revival
1460s	Definition of the Pale as the counties of Louth, Meath, Dublin and Kildare
1494-5	Poyning's Parliament
1536-7	Reformation of Parliament (forbidding intermarriage, insisting on use of English language and dress, etc.)
1549-57	Plantation of Laois and Offaly
1560	Act of Supremacy (English the language of the Prayer Book)
1586-92	Plantation of Munster
1601	Battle of Kinsale
1609	Plantation of Ulster (NB. Scottish immigrants from the western isles living there already)
1649-50	Cromwell's campaigns in Ireland; confiscations ('to hell or Connaught')
1690	Battle of the Boyne
1691	Siege of Limerick
1695	Introduction of Penal Legislation against Catholics
1780 onwards	Easing of the Penal Laws
1800	Act for the Legislative Union of Ireland with Great Britain
1808	Beginning of O'Connell's rise to leadership (using English as his medium of communication)
1831	Introduction of a system of Primary Education (with English as the medium for instruction; *bata scóir* for discouraging Irish)
1840s	Efforts made by the Established Church to preach through Irish (making an unholy association for the Irish language in the minds of the intended proselytes)
1845-8	Famine (staggering losses among the poorest, Irish-speaking section of the

	population)
19th century	Emigration (English seen to be the
(throughout)	language for advancement)

Although this list of dates oversimplifies and thus conceals the rich complexities of Irish history since the millenium, it provides a handy chronological framework for appreciating the time-scale covered in Joyce's book. His evidence recreates and cele-brates the lifestyle and linguistic resources of the Irish people during the period, as the maps and list of dates show, in which the English language came to prevail in Ireland. He offers us an exuberant account of his contemporaries which is, in the best sense of the word, a gallimaufry of sayings; at times it resembles the transcription of a tape-recorded survey that has not been fully edited and processed. Herein lies the unique linguistic and historical value of this book: Joyce does precisely what the motto promises — he pictures the life of the people through their speech.

T. P. Dolan

University College, Dublin
July, 1979

1 My thanks to Professor A. J. Bliss for letting me have his preliminary notes on Joyce's life, and to Professor Patrick Dwyer-Joyce for allowing me access to books which belonged to his grandfather, P. W. Joyce, and to the Joyce family papers which are in his possession. Of particular help was the short family pedigree dated 6 October, 1898, prepared by Michael Joyce, brother of P. W., which survives in typescript. The present book furnishes many details about its author's life; see also the absorbing paper by Mannix Joyce [no relation] on 'The Joyce Brothers of Glenosheen', *The Capuchin Annual* (1969), 257-287.

2 Henceforth page numbers will be given in square brackets.

3 'HE' will be used as the abbreviation for Hiberno-English, and 'Ir.' for Irish.

4 E. Curtis, "The Spoken Languages of Medieval Ireland", *Studies* VIII (1919), 234-54.

5 Alan Bliss, "The English language in early modern Ireland" in *A New History of Ireland*, ed. T. W. Moody, F. X. Martin, F. J. Byrne, III: Early Modern Ireland 1534-1691 (Oxford: The Clarendon Press, 1976), pp. 546-560. See also Bliss's article on "The Emergence of Modern English Dialects in Ireland", which forms the first chapter of Diarmaid O'Muirithe (ed.) *The English Language in Ireland*, The Thomas Davis Lecture Series (Dublin and Cork: The Mercier Press, 1977), henceforth cited as 'O'Muirithe'.

6 Alan Bliss, *Spoken English in Ireland 1600-1740, Representative Texts Assembled and Analysed* by Alan Bliss (Dublin: The Cadenus Press and The Dolmen Press, 1979). This will become the classic exposition of the twenty-seven texts selected.

7. See Alan Bliss (ed.) *A Dialogue in Hybernian Stile Between A & B, & Irish Eloquence* by Jonathan Swift (Dublin: The Cadenus Press, 1977).

8 Seán de Fréine, "The Dominance of the English Language in the Nineteenth Century" in O'Muirithe, pp. 71-87.

9 Jeremiah J. Hogan, *The English Language in Ireland* (Dublin: The Educational Company of Ireland, 1927).

10 P. L. Henry, "A Linguistic Survey: Preliminary Report", *Lochlann* I (Oslo, 1958), 49-208.

11 Mary Hayden and Marcus Hartog, "The Irish Dialect of English: Its Origins and Vocabulary", *Fortnightly Review* LXXXV (1909), 775-785, 933-947.

12   James Midgley Clark, *The Vocabulary of Anglo-Irish* (Saint-Gall: Handels-Hoshschule. Siebzehnter and achzenter Jahresbericht, etc., 1917).

13   A. G. van Hamel, "On Anglo-Irish Syntax", *Englische Studien* XLV (1912), 272-292.

14   P. L. Henry, *An Anglo-Irish dialect of north Roscommon* (publ. by the Department of English, University College, Dublin, 1957).

15   E. G. Quin, "Irish and English", *Hermathena* XCIII (1959), 26-37.

16   G. B. Adams, "An Introduction to the Study of Ulster Dialects", *Proceedings of the Royal Irish Academy* LII, sect. C (1948), 1-26. See also Adams's less technical paper on "The Dialects of Ulster', in O'Muirithe, pp. 56-70.

17   John Garvin, "The Anglo-Irish Idiom in the Works of Major Irish Writers" in O'Muirithe, pp. 100-114.

18   Alan J. Bliss, "The Language of Synge" in *J. M. Synge Centenary Papers 1971*, ed. Maurice Harmon (Dublin: The Dolmen Press, 1972), pp. 35-62.

18a   Declan Kiberd, *Synge And The Irish Language* (London: Macmillan, 1979). See especially chaps. 3 ('Scholar and Translator') and 8 ('Anglo-Irish as a Literary Dialect: The Contribution of Synge').

19   Jiro Taniguchi, *A Grammatical Analysis of Artistic Representation of Irish English with a Brief Discussion of Sounds and Spelling* (Tokyo: Shinozaki Shorin, 1972).

20   Bliss, *Spoken English in Ireland*, pp. 269-70.

21   A. J. Bliss, "Languages in Contact: Some Problems of Hiberno-English", *Proceedings of the Royal Irish Academy* LXXII, Section C, 1972, 72-5.

22   Alan J. Bliss, " 'Bother' and 'Pother' ", *Notes & Queries*, new series XXV, no. 6 (December, 1978), 536-540.

23   Bliss, "Languages in Contact", pp. 75-81.

24   Included by Brian O'Cuiv at the end of his *Irish Dialects and Irish-Speaking Districts* (Dublin: Dublin Institute for Advanced Studies, 1971).

25   T. W. Freeman, *Ireland: A General and Regional Geography* (London: Methuen, second edition, revised, 1960), p. 167.

26   Henry, "A Linguistic Survey", p.55.

27   Heinrich Wagner, *Linguistic Atlas and Survey of Irish Dialects,* vol. I, Introduction, 300 maps (Dublin: Dublin Institute for Advanced Studies, 1958).

28   Adams, "Introduction", p. 3; "Dialects of Ulster" in O'Muirithe, p. 70.

29   Poole's Glossary, ed. William Barnes (1867); Hogan [44 ff] ; Henry, "Linguistic Survey" [75 ff]; O'Muirithe, "The Anglo-Normans and their English Dialect of South-East Wexford", in O'Muirithe, pp. 37-55; Bliss, "The English Language in early modern Ireland", *New History of Ireland* vol. III, pp. 547-549; *Poole's Glossary, with some pieces of Verse of the Old Dialect of the English Colony in the Baronies of Forth and Bargy, County of Wexford,* newly edited by T. P. Dolan and Diarmaid O'Muirithe (Wexford: The Uí Cinsealaigh Historical Society, 1979).

ENGLISH AS WE SPEAK IT
IN IRELAND

BY

P. W. JOYCE, LL.D., T.C.D., M.R.I.A.

One of the Commissioners for the Publication of the Ancient Laws of Ireland

Late Principal of the Government Training College, Marlborough Street, Dublin

Late President of the Royal Society of Antiquaries, Ireland

THE LIFE OF A PEOPLE IS PICTURED IN THEIR SPEECH.

LONDON: LONGMANS, GREEN, & CO.

DUBLIN: M. H. GILL & SON, LTD.

1910

PREFACE.

THIS book deals with the Dialect of the English Language that is spoken in Ireland.

As the Life of a people—according to our motto—is pictured in their speech, our picture ought to be a good one, for two languages were concerned in it—Irish and English. The part played by each will be found specially set forth in Chapters IV and VII ; and in farther detail throughout the whole book.

The articles and pamphlets that have already appeared on this interesting subject—which are described below—are all short. Some are full of keen observation ; but very many are mere lists of dialectical words with their meanings. Here for the first time—in this little volume of mine— our Anglo-Irish Dialect is subjected to detailed analysis and systematic classification.

I have been collecting materials for this book for more than twenty years; not indeed by way of constant work, but off and on as detailed below. The sources from which these materials were directly derived are mainly the following.

First.—My own memory is a storehouse both of idiom and vocabulary ; for the good reason that from childhood to early manhood I spoke— like those among whom I lived—the rich dialect

b

of Limerick and Cork—and indeed to some
extent speak it still in the colloquial language of
everyday life.

I have also drawn pretty largely on our Anglo-
Irish Folk Songs of which I have a great
collection, partly in my memory and partly on
printed sheets; for they often faithfully reflect
our Dialect.

Second.—Eighteen years ago (1892) I wrote a
short letter which was inserted in nearly all the
Irish newspapers and in very many of those
published outside Ireland, announcing my intention to write a book on Anglo-Irish Dialect, and
asking for collections of dialectical words and
phrases. In response to this I received a very
large number of communications from all parts
of Ireland, as well as from outside Ireland, even
from America, Australia, and New Zealand—all
more or less to the point, showing the great and
widespread interest taken in the subject. Their
importance of course greatly varied; but many
were very valuable. I give at the end of the
book an alphabetical list of those contributors:
and I acknowledge the most important of them
throughout the book.

Third.—The works of Irish writers of novels,
stories, and essays depicting Irish peasant life in
which the people are made to speak in dialect.
Some of these are mentioned in Chapter I.,
and others are quoted throughout the book as
occasion requires.

Fourth.—Printed articles and pamphlets on the special subject of Anglo-Irish Dialect. Of these the principal that I have come across are the following :—

'The Provincialisms of Belfast. and Surrounding District pointed out and corrected,' by David Patterson. (1860.)

'Remarks on the Irish Dialect of the English Language,' by A. Hume, D.C.L. and LL.D. (1878.)

'A Glossary of Words in use in the Counties of Antrim and Down,' by Wm. Hugh Patterson, M.R.I.A. (1880)—a large pamphlet—might indeed be called a book.

'Don't, Pat,' by 'Colonel O'Critical': a very good and useful little pamphlet, marred by a silly title which turns up perpetually through the whole pamphlet till the reader gets sick of it. (1885.)

'A List of Peculiar Words and Phrases at one time in use in Armagh and South Donegal': by D. A. Simmons. (1890.) This List was annotated by me, at the request of Mr. Simmons, who was, at or about that time, President of the Irish National Teachers' Association.

A Series of Six Articles on *The English in Ireland* by myself, printed in 'The Educational Gazette'; Dublin. (1890.)

'The Anglo-Irish Dialect,' by the Rev .William Burke (an Irish priest residing in Liverpool); published in 'The Irish Ecclesiastical Record' for 1896. A judicious and scholarly essay, which I have very often used.

'The Irish Dialect of English; its Origins and
Vocabulary.' By Mary Hayden, M.A., and Prof.
Marcus Hartog (jointly): published in 'The
Fortnightly Review' (1909: April and May).
A thoughtful and valuable essay. Miss Hayden
knows Irish well, and has made full use of her
knowledge to illustrate her subject. Of this
article I have made much use.

Besides these there were a number of short
articles by various writers published in Irish
newspapers within the last twenty years or so,
nearly all of them lists of dialectical words used
in the North of Ireland.

In the Introduction to the 'Biglow Papers,'
Second Series, James Russell Lowell has some
valuable observations on modern English dialectical words and phrases derived from Old
English forms, to which I am indebted for much
information, and which will be found acknowledged through this book: for it touches my
subject in many places. In this Introduction
Mr. Lowell remarks truly :—' It is always worth
while to note down the erratic words or phrases
one meets with in any dialect. They may
throw light on the meaning of other words, on
the relationship of languages, or even history
itself.'

Of all the above I have made use so far as
served my purpose—always with acknowledgment.

Fifth. For twenty years or more I have kept
a large note-book lying just at my hand; and

whenever any peculiar Irish-English expression, or anything bearing on the subject, came before me—from memory, or from reading, or from hearing it in conversation—down it went in the manuscript. In this way an immense mass of materials was accumulated almost imperceptibly.

The vast collection derived from all the above sources lay by till early last year, when I went seriously to work at the book. But all the materials were mixed up—*three-na-haila*— 'through-other'—and before a line of the book was written they had to be perused, selected, classified, and alphabetised, which was a very heavy piece of work.

A number of the Irish items in the great 'Dialect Dictionary' edited for the English Dialect Society by Dr. Joseph Wright were contributed by me and are generally printed with my initials. I have neither copied nor avoided these—in fact I did not refer to them at all while working at my book—and naturally many—perhaps most— of them reappear here, probably in different words. But this is quite proper; for the Dialect Dictionary is a book of reference—six large volumes, very expensive—and not within reach of the general public.

Many of the words given in this book as dialectical are also used by the people in the ordinary sense they bear in standard English; such as *break*:—'Poor Tom was broke yesterday' (dialect: dismissed from employment): 'the bowl fell on the flags and was broken in pieces' (correct English): and *dark*: 'a poor dark man' (dialect: blind): 'a dark night' (correct English).

This is essentially a subject for popular treatment; and accordingly I have avoided technical and scientific details and technical terms: they are not needed.

When a place is named in connexion with a dialectical expression, it is not meant that the expression is confined to that place, but merely that it is, or was, in use there.

P. W. J.

Dublin: *March*, 1910.

ENGLISH AS WE SPEAK IT IN IRELAND.

CHAPTER I.

SOURCES OF ANGLO-IRISH DIALECT.

OUR Anglo-Irish dialectical words and phrases are derived from three main sources :—

First : the Irish language.

Second : Old English and the dialect of Scotland.

Third : independently of these two sources, dialectical expressions have gradually grown up among our English-speaking people, as dialects arise everywhere.

In the following pages whenever a word or a phrase is not assigned to any origin it is to be understood as belonging to this third class :—that is so far as is known at present; for I have no doubt that many of these will be found, after further research, to be either Irish-Gaelic or Old English. It is to be also observed that a good many of the dialectical expressions given in this book as belonging to Ireland may possibly be found current in England or in Scotland or in both. But that is no reason why they should not be included here.

Influence of Irish.

The Irish language has influenced our Irish-English speech in several ways. To begin with : it

B

has determined the popular pronunciation, in certain combinations, of three English consonants, *t, d,* and *th,* but in a way (so far as *t* and *d* are concerned) that would not now be followed by anyone even moderately well educated. The sounds of *English t* and *d* are not the same as those of the *Irish t* and *d* ; and when the people began to exchange the Irish language for English, they did not quite abandon the Irish sounds of these two letters, but imported them into their English, especially *when they came before r.* That is why we hear among the people in every part of Ireland such vulgarisms as (for *t*) *bitther, butther, thrue* ; and (for *d*) *laddher* (ladder), *cidher* (cider), *foddher,* &c. Yet in other positions we sound these letters correctly, as in *fat, football, white; bad, hide, wild,* &c. No one, however uneducated, will mispronounce the *t* and *d* in such words as these. Why it is that the *Irish* sound is retained before *r* and not in other combinations—why for instance the Irish people sound the *t* and *d* incorrectly in *platter* and *drive* [platther, dhrive] and correctly in *plate* and *dive*—is a thing I cannot account for.

As for the English *th,* it may be said that the general run of the Irish people never sound it at all ; for it is a very difficult sound to anyone excepting a born Englishman, and also excepting a small proportion of those born and reared on the east coast of Ireland. It has two varieties of sound, heard in *bath* and *bathe* : and for these two our people use the Irish *t* and *d,* as heard in the words given above.

A couple of centuries ago or more the people had another substitute for this *th* (in *bathe*) namely *d,* which held its place for a considerable time, and this sound was then considered almost a national characteristic; so that in the song of 'Lillibulero' the English author of the song puts this pronunciation all through in the mouth of the Irishman :—'*Dere* was an ould prophecy found in a bog.' It is still sometimes heard, but merely as a defect of speech of individuals :—'*De* books are here : *dat* one is yours and *dis* is mine.' Danny Mann speaks this way all through Gerald Griffin's 'Collegians.'

There was, and to a small extent still is, a similar tendency—though not so decided—for the other sound of *th* (as in *bath*) :—'I had a hot *bat* this morning ; and I remained in it for *tirty* minutes': 'I *tink* it would be well for you to go home to-day.'

Another influence of the Irish language is on the letter *s*. In Irish, this letter in certain combinations is sounded the same as the English *sh*; and the people often—though not always—in similar combinations, bring this sound into their English :— 'He gave me a blow of his *fisht*'; 'he was *whishling* St. Patrick's Day'; 'Kilkenny is *sickshty* miles from this.' You hear this sound very often among the more uneducated of our people.

In imitation of this vulgar sound of *s*, the letter *z* often comes in for a similar change (though there is no such sound in the Irish language). Here the *z* gets the sound heard in the English words *glazier*, *brazier* :—'He bought a *dozhen* eggs'; ''tis *drizzhling* rain'; 'that is *dizhmal* news.'

The second way in which our English is influenced by Irish is in vocabulary. When our Irish forefathers began to adopt English, they brought with them from their native language many single Irish words and used them—as best suited to express what they meant—among their newly acquired English words ; and these words remain to this day in the current English of their descendants, and will I suppose remain for ever. And the process still goes on—though slowly—for as time passes, Irish words are being adopted even in the English of the best educated people. There is no need to give many examples here, for they will be found all through this book, especially in the Vocabulary. I will instance the single word *galore* (plentiful) which you will now often see in English newspapers and periodicals. The adoption of Irish words and phrases into English nowadays is in great measure due to the influence of Irishmen resident in England, who write a large proportion—indeed I think the largest proportion—of the articles in English periodicals of every kind. Other Irish words such as *shamrock, whiskey, bother, blarney*, are now to be found in every English Dictionary. *Smithereens* too (broken bits after a smash) is a grand word, and is gaining ground every day. Not very long ago I found it used in a public speech in London by a Parliamentary candidate—an Englishman ; and he would hardly have used it unless he believed that it was fairly intelligible to his audience.

The third way in which Irish influences our English is in idiom : that is, idiom borrowed from the Irish language. Of course the idioms were transferred about the same time as the single words of the vocabulary. This is by far the most interesting and important feature. Its importance was pointed out by me in a paper printed twenty years ago, and it has been properly dwelt upon by Miss Hayden and Professor Hartog in their recently written joint paper mentioned in the Preface. Most of these idiomatic phrases are simply translations from Irish ; and when the translations are literal, Englishmen often find it hard or impossible to under-stand them. For a phrase may be correct in Irish, but incorrect, or even unintelligible, in English when translated word for word. Gerald Griffin has pre-served more of these idioms (in 'The Collegians,' 'The Coiner,' 'Tales of a Jury-room,' &c.) than any other writer ; and very near him come Charles Kickham (in 'Knocknagow'), Crofton Croker (in 'Fairy Legends') and Edward Walsh. These four writers almost exhaust the dialect of the South of Ireland.

On the other hand Carleton gives us the Northern dialect very fully, especially that of Tyrone and eastern Ulster ; but he has very little idiom, the peculiarities he has preserved being chiefly in voca-bulary and pronunciation.

Mr. Seumas MacManus has in his books faithfully pictured the dialect of Donegal (of which he is a native) and of all north-west Ulster.

In the importation of Irish idiom into English, Irish writers of the present day are also making their influence felt, for I often come across a startling Irish expression (in English words of course) in some English magazine article, obviously written by one of my fellow-countrymen. Here I ought to remark that they do this with discretion and common sense, for they always make sure that the Irish idiom they use is such as that any Englishman can under-stand it.

There is a special chapter (iv) in this book devoted
to Anglo-Irish phrases imported direct from Irish ;
but instances will be found all through the book.

It is safe to state that by far the greatest number
of our Anglo-Irish idioms come from the Irish
language.

Influence of Old English and of Scotch.

From the time of the Anglo-Norman invasion, in
the twelfth century, colonies of English and of Welsh-
English people were settled in Ireland—chiefly in the
eastern part—and they became particularly numerous
in the time of Elizabeth, three or four centuries
ago, when they were spread all over the country.
When these Elizabethan colonists, who were nearly
all English, settled down and made friends with the
natives and intermarried with them, great numbers
of them learned to use the Irish language ; while
the natives on their part learned English from the
newcomers.   There was give and take in every place
where the two peoples and the two languages mixed.
And so the native Irish people learned to speak
Elizabethan English—the very language used by
Shakespeare ; and in a very considerable degree the
old Gaelic people and those of English descent retain
it to this day.   For our people are very conservative
in retaining old customs and forms of speech.   Many
words accordingly that are discarded as old-fashioned
—or dead and gone—in England, are still flourishing
—alive and well—in Ireland.   They are now regarded
as vulgarisms by the educated—which no doubt they
are—but they are vulgarisms of respectable origin,

representing as they do the classical English of Shakespeare's time.

Instances of this will be found all through the book ; but I may here give a passing glance at such pronunciations as *tay* for *tea*, *sevare* for *severe*, *desaive* for *deceive* ; and such words as *sliver*, *lief*, *afeard*, &c. —all of which will be found mentioned farther on in this book. It may be said that hardly any of those incorrect forms of speech, now called vulgarisms, used by our people, were invented by them ; they are nearly all survivals of usages that in former times were correct—in either English or Irish.

In the reign of James I.—three centuries ago—a large part of Ulster—nearly all the fertile land of six of the nine counties—was handed over to new settlers, chiefly Presbyterians from Scotland, the old Catholic owners being turned off. These settlers of course brought with them their Scotch dialect, which remains almost in its purity among their descendants to this day. This dialect, it must be observed, is confined to Ulster, while the remnants of the Elizabethan English are spread all over Ireland.

As to the third main source—the gradual growth of dialect among our English-speaking people—it is not necessary to make any special observations about it here ; as it will be found illustrated all through the book.

Owing to these three influences, we speak in Ireland a very distinct dialect of English, which every educated and observant Englishman perceives the moment he sets foot in this country. It is most marked among our peasantry ; but in fact none of us are free from it, no matter how well educated.

This does not mean that we speak bad English; for it is generally admitted that our people on the whole, including the peasantry, speak better English— nearer to the literary standard—than the corresponding classes of England. This arises mainly— so far as we are concerned—from the fact that for the last four or five generations we have learned our English in a large degree from books, chiefly through the schools.

So far as our dialectical expressions are vulgar or unintelligible, those who are educated among us ought of course to avoid them. But outside this a large proportion of our peculiar words and phrases are vivid and picturesque, and when used with discretion and at the right time, give a sparkle to our conversation; so that I see no reason why we should wipe them out completely from our speech so as to hide our nationality. To be hypercritical here is often absurd and sometimes silly.

I well remember on one occasion when I was young in literature perpetrating a pretty strong Hibernicism in one of my books. It was not forbidding, but rather bright and expressive : and it passed off, and still passes off very well, for the book is still to the fore. Some days after the publication, a lady friend who was somewhat of a pedant and purist in the English language, came to me with a look of grave concern—so solemn indeed that it somewhat disconcerted me—to direct my attention to the error. Her manner was absurdly exaggerated considering the occasion. Judging from the serious face and the voice of bated breath, you might almost imagine that I had committed a secret murder and that she had come to inform me that the corpse had just been found.

CHAPTER II.

AFFIRMING, ASSENTING, AND SALUTING.

THE various Irish modes of affirming, denying, &c., will be understood from the examples given in this short chapter better than from any general observations.

The Irish *ni'l lá fós é* [neel law fo-say : it isn't day yet] is often used for emphasis in asseveration, even when persons are speaking English; but in this case the saying is often turned into English. 'If the master didn't give Tim a tongue-dressing, *'tisn't day yet'* (which would be said either by day or by night): meaning he gave him a very severe scolding. 'When I saw the mad dog running at me, if I didn't get a fright, *neel-law-fo-say.*'

'I went to town yesterday in all the rain, and if I didn't get a wetting *there isn't a cottoner in Cork*' : meaning I got a very great wetting. This saying is very common in Munster ; and workers in cotton were numerous in Cork when it was invented.

A very usual emphatic ending to an assertion is seen in the following :—' That horse is a splendid animal *and no mistake.*'

'*I'll engage* you visited Peggy when you were in town' : i.e. I assert it without much fear of contradiction : I warrant. Much in the same sense we use *I'll go bail* :—' I'll go bail you never got that money you lent to Tom': 'An illigant song he could sing I'll go bail' (Lever): 'You didn't meet your linnet (i.e. your girl—your sweetheart) this evening I'll go bail' (Robert Dwyer Joyce in 'The Beauty of the Blossom Gate ').

'I'll hold you' introduces an assertion with some emphasis: it is really elliptical: I'll hold you [a wager: but always a fictitious wager]. I'll hold you I'll finish that job by one o'clock, i.e. I'll warrant I will—you may take it from me that I will.

The phrase 'if you go to that of it ' is often added on to a statement to give great emphasis, amounting almost to a sort of defiance of contradiction or opposition. 'I don't believe you could walk four miles an hour ': ' Oh don't you : I could then, or five if you go to that of it ' : ' I don't believe that Joe Lee is half as good a hurler as his brother Phil.' ' I can tell you he is then, and a great deal better if you go to that of it.' Lowry Looby, speaking of St. Swithin, says :—' He was then, buried more than once if you go to that of it.' (Gerald Griffin : ' Collegians ' : Munster.)

'Is it cold outside doors ? ' Reply, 'Aye is it,' meaning ' it is certainly.' An emphatic assertion (after the Gaelic construction) frequently heard is ' Ah then, 'tis I that wouldn't like to be in that fight.' ' Ah 'tis my mother that will be delighted.'

' What did he do to you ? ' ' He hit me with his stick, *so he did*, and it is a great shame, so it is.' ' I like a cup of tea at night, so I do.' In the South an expression of this kind is very often added on as a sort of clincher to give emphasis. Similar are the very usual endings as seen in these assertions :—' He is a great old schemer, *that's what he is* ' : ' I spoke up to the master and showed him he was wrong—*I did begob.*'

I asked a man one day: ' Well, how is the young doctor going on in his new place ?' and he replied ' Ah, how but well '; which he meant to be very emphatic: and then he went on to give particulars.

A strong denial is often expressed in the following way : ' This day will surely be wet, so don't forget your umbrella ' : ' What a fool I am ' : as much as to say, ' I should be a fool indeed to go without an umbrella to-day, and I think there's no mark of a fool about me.' ' Now Mary don't wait for the last train [from Howth] for there will be an awful crush.' ' What a fool I'd be ma'am.' ' Oh Mr. Lory I thought you were gone home [from the dance] two hours ago ' : ' What a fool I am,' replies Lory (' Knocknagow '), equivalent to ' I hadn't the least notion of making such a fool of myself while there's such fun here.' This is heard everywhere in Ireland, ' from the centre all round to the sea.'

Much akin to this is Nelly Donovan's reply to Billy Heffernan who had made some flattering remark to her :—' Arrah now Billy what sign of a fool do you see on me ? ' (' Knocknagow.')

An emphatic assertion or assent : ' Yesterday was very wet.' Reply :—' You may say it was,' or ' you may well say that.'

' I'm greatly afeard he'll try to injure me.' Answer: —' 'Tis fear *for* you ' (emphasis on *for*), meaning ' you have good reason to be afeard ' : merely a translation of the Irish *is eagal duitse.*

'Oh I'll pay you what I owe you.' ''Tis a pity you wouldn't indeed,' says the other, a satirical reply, meaning ' of course you will and no thanks to you for that ; who'd expect otherwise?'

'I am going to the fair to-morrow, as I want to buy a couple of cows.' Reply, 'I know,' as much as to say 'I see,' 'I understand.' This is one of our commonest terms of assent.

An assertion or statement introduced by the words ' to tell God's truth ' is always understood to be weighty and somewhat unexpected, the introductory words being given as a guarantee of its truth :—' Have you the rest of the money you owe me ready now James ? ' ' Well to tell God's truth I was not able to make it all up, but I can give you £5.'

Another guarantee of the same kind, though not quite so solemn, is ' my hand to you,' or ' I give you my hand and word.' ' My hand to you I'll never rest till the job is finished.' ' Come and hunt with me in the wood, and my hand to you we shall soon have enough of victuals for both of us.' (Clarence Mangan in Ir. Pen. Journ.)

> ' I've seen—and here 's my hand to you I only say
> what 's true—
> A many a one with twice your stock not half so proud
> as you.' (CLARENCE MANGAN.)

' Do you know your Catechism ? ' Answer, ' What would ail me not to know it ? ' meaning ' of course I do—'twould be a strange thing if I didn't.' ' Do you think you can make that lock all right ? ' ' Ah what would ail me,' i.e., ' no doubt I can—of course I can ; if I couldn't do that it would be a sure sign that something was amiss with me—that something ailed me.'

' Believe Tom and who'll believe you ': a way of saying that Tom is not telling truth.

An emphatic 'yes' to a statement is often expressed in the following way :—' This is a real wet day.' Answer, ' I believe you.' ' I think you made a good bargain with Tim about that field.' ' I believe you I did.'

A person who is offered anything he is very willing to take, or asked to do anything he is anxious to do, often answers in this way :—' James, would you take a glass of punch ?' or ' Tom, will you dance with my sister in the next round ?' In either case the answer is, ' Would a duck swim ?'

A weak sort of assent is often expressed in this way:—'Will you bring Nelly's book to her when you are going home, Dan ?' Answer, ' I don't mind,' or ' I don't mind if I do.'

To express unbelief in a statement or disbelief in the usefulness or effectiveness of any particular line of action, a person says ' that's all in my eye,' or ' 'Tis all in my eye, Betty Martin—O ' ; but this last is regarded as slang.

Sometimes an unusual or unexpected statement is introduced in the following manner, the introductory words being usually spoken quickly :—' *Now do you know what I'm going to tell you*—that ragged old chap has £200 in the bank.' In Derry they make it—' Now listen to what I'm going to say.'

In some parts of the South and West and North-west, servants and others have a way of replying to directions that at first sounds strange or even disrespectful :—' Biddy, go up please to the drawing-room and bring me down the needle and thread and stocking you will find on the table.' ' That will do ma'am,' replies Biddy, and off she goes and brings them. But this is their way of saying ' yes ma'am,' or ' Very well ma'am.

So also you say to the hotel-keeper :—' Can I have breakfast please to-morrow morning at 7 o'clock?' ' That will do sir.' This reply in fact expresses the greatest respect, as much as to say, ' A word from you is quite enough.'

' I caught the thief at my potatoes.' ' No, but did you ?' i.e., is it possible you did so ? A very common exclamation, especially in Ulster.

' Oh man ' is a common exclamation to render an assertion more emphatic, and sometimes to express surprise :—' Oh man, you never saw such a fine race as we had.' In Ulster they duplicate it, with still the same application :—' Oh man-o-man that's great rain.' ' Well John you'd hardly believe it, but I got £50 for my horse to-day at the fair.' Reply, ' Oh man that's a fine price.'

' Never fear ' is heard constantly in many parts of Ireland as an expression of assurance :—' Now James don't forget the sugar.' 'Never fear ma'am.' ' Ah never fear there will be plenty flowers in that garden this year.' ' You will remember to have breakfast ready at 7 o'clock.' 'Never fear sir,' meaning ' making your mind easy on the point—it will be all right.' *Never fear* is merely a translation of the equally common Irish phrase, *ná bi heagal ort.*

Most of our ordinary salutations are translations from Irish. *Go m-beannuighe Dia dhuit* is literally

'May God bless you,' or 'God bless you' which is a usual salutation in English. The commonest of all our salutes is 'God save you,' or (for a person entering a house) 'God save all here '; and the response is 'God save you kindly' ('Knocknagow'); where *kindly* means 'of a like kind,' 'in like manner,' 'similarly. Another but less usual response to the same salutation is, 'And you too,' which is appropriate. ('Knocknagow.') 'God save all here' is used all over Ireland except in the extreme North, where it is hardly understood.

To the ordinary salutation, 'Good-morrow,' which is heard everywhere, the usual response is 'Good-morrow kindly.' 'Morrow Wat,' said Mr. Lloyd. 'Morrow kindly,' replied Wat. ('Knocknagow.') 'The top of the morning to you' is used everywhere, North and South.

In some places if a woman throws out water at night at the kitchen door, she says first, 'Beware of the water,' lest the 'good people' might happen to be passing at the time, and one or more of them might get splashed.

A visitor coming in and finding the family at dinner :—'Much good may it do you.'

In very old times it was a custom for workmen on completing any work and delivering it finished to give it their blessing. This blessing was called *abarta* (an old word, not used in modern Irish), and if it was omitted the workman was subject to a fine to be deducted from his hire equal to the seventh part of the cost of his feeding. (*Senchus Mór* and 'Cormac's Glossary.') It was especially incumbent on women to bless the work of other women. This custom, which is more than a thousand years old, has

descended to our day ; for the people on coming up
to persons engaged in work of any kind always say
' God bless your work,' or its equivalent original in
Irish, *Go m-beannuighe Dia air bhur n-obair.* (See my
' Social History of Ancient Ireland,' II., page 324.)

In modern times tradesmen have perverted this
pleasing custom into a new channel not so praise-
worthy. On the completion of any work, such as a
building, they fix a pole with a flag on the highest
point to ask the employer for his *blessing*, which
means money for a drink.

CHAPTER III.

ASSERTION BY NEGATIVE OF OPPOSITE.

ASSERTIONS are often made by using the negative of
the opposite assertion. ' You must be hungry now
Tom, and this little rasher will do you no harm,'
meaning it will do you good. An old man has tired
himself dancing and says :—' A glass of whiskey will
do us no harm after that.' (Carleton.) A lady occupy-
ing a furnished house at the seaside near Dublin
said to the boy who had charge of the premises :—
' There may be burglars about here ; wouldn't it be
well for you to come and close the basement shutters
at night ? ' ' Why then begob ma'am *'twould be no
har-um.*' Here is a bit of rustic information (from
Limerick) that might be useful to food experts :—

> ' Rye bread will do you good,
>   Barley bread *will do you no harm,*
> Wheaten bread will sweeten your blood,
>   Oaten bread will strengthen your arm.'

This curious way of speaking, which is very general among all classes of people in Ireland and in every part of the country, is often used in the Irish language, from which we have imported it into our English. Here are a few Irish examples; but they might be multiplied indefinitely, and some others will be found through this chapter. In the Irish tale called ' The Battle of Gavra,' the narrator says :—[The enemy slew a large company of our army] 'and that was no great help to us.' In ' The Colloquy,' a piece much older than ' The Battle of Gavra,' Kylta, wishing to tell his audience that when the circumstance he is relating occurred he was very young, expresses it by saying [at that time] ' I myself was not old.'

One night a poet was grossly insulted : ' On the morrow he rose and he was not thankful.' (From the very old Irish tale called ' The Second Battle of Moytura ' : Rev. Celt.)

Another old Irish writer, telling us that a certain company of soldiers is well out of view, expresses it in this way :—*Ní fhuil in cuire gan chleith*, literally, ' the company is not without concealment.'

How closely these and other old models are imitated in our English will be seen from the following examples from every part of Ireland :—

' I can tell you Paddy Walsh is no chicken now,' meaning he is very old. The same would be said of an old maid :—' She's no chicken,' meaning that she is old for a girl.

' How are your potato gardens going on this year ? ' ' Why then they're not too good '; i.e. only middling or bad.

A usual remark among us conveying mild approval

is ' that's not bad.' A Dublin boy asked me one day :—
' Maybe you wouldn't have e'er a penny that you'd
give me, sir ? ' i.e., ' Have you a penny to give me ? '
' You wouldn't like to have a cup of tea, would you ? '
An invitation, but not a cordial one. This is a
case of ' *will you* was never a good fellow ' (for which
see Vocabulary).

' No joke ' is often used in the sense of ' very
serious.' ' It was no joke to be caught in our boat
in such a storm as that.' ' The loss of £10 is no joke
for that poor widow.'

> ' As for Sandy he worked like a downright demolisher—
> Bare as he is, yet *his lick is no polisher*.'
>
> (THOMAS MOORE in the early part of his career.)

You remark that a certain person has some fault,
he is miserly, or extravagant, or dishonest, &c. : and
a bystander replies, ' Yes indeed, and 'tisn't to-day
or yesterday it happened him '—meaning that it
is a fault of long standing.

A tyrannical or unpopular person goes away or
dies :—' There's many a dry eye after him.' (Kildare.)

' Did Tom do your work as satisfactorily as Davy ? '
' Oh, it isn't alike ' : to imply that Tom did the work
very much better than Davy.

' Here is the newspaper ; and 'tisn't much you'll
find in it.'

' Is Mr. O'Mahony good to his people ?' ' Oh, indeed
he is no great things ' : or another way of saying it :—
' He's no great shakes.' ' How do you like your new
horse ? ' ' Oh then he's no great shakes '—or ' he's

not much to boast of.' Lever has this in a song :—
'You think the Blakes are no great shakes.' But I
think it is also used in England.

A consequential man who carries his head rather
higher than he ought :—' He thinks no small beer of
himself.'

Mrs. Slattery gets a harmless fall off the form
she is sitting on, and is so frightened that she
asks of the person who helps her up, 'Am I
killed?' To which he replies ironically—' Oh there's
great fear of you.' (' Knocknagow.')

[Alice Ryan is a very purty girl] ' and she doesn't
want to be reminded of that same either.' (' Knocknagow.')

A man has got a heavy cold from a wetting and
says: 'That wetting did me no good,' meaning 'it did
me great harm.'

' There's a man outside wants to see you, sir,' says
Charlie, our office attendant, a typical southern
Irishman. ' What kind is he Charlie? does he look
like a fellow wanting money?' Instead of a direct
affirmative, Charlie answers, ' Why then sir I don't
think he'll give you much anyway.'

' Are people buried there now?' I asked of a man
regarding an old graveyard near Blessington in
Wicklow. Instead of answering ' very few,' he
replied : ' Why then not too many sir.'

When the roads are dirty—deep in mire—' there's
fine walking overhead.'

In the Irish Life of St. Brigit we are told of a
certain chief :—' It was not his will to sell the bondmaid,' by which is meant, it was his will *not* to sell
her.

So in our modern speech the father says to the son :—' It is not my wish that you should go to America at all,' by which he means the positive assertion :—' It is my wish that you should not go.'

Tommy says, ' Oh, mother, I forgot to bring you the sugar.' ' I wouldn't doubt you,' answers the mother, as much as to say, ' It is just what I'd expect from you.'

When a message came to Rory from absent friends, that they were true to Ireland :—

' " My *sowl*, I never doubted them " said Rory of the hill.' (Charles Kickham.)

' It wouldn't be wishing you a pound note to do so and so ' : i.e. ' it would be as bad as the loss of a pound, or it might cost you a pound. Often used as a sort of threat to deter a person from doing it.'

' Where do you keep all your money ? ' ' Oh, indeed, *it's not much 1 have* ' : merely translated from the Gaelic, *Ní mórán atâ agum.*

To a silly foolish fellow :—' There's a great deal of sense outside your head.'

' The only sure way to conceal evil is not to do it.'

' I don't think very much of these horses,' meaning ' I have a low opinion of them.'

' I didn't pretend to understand what he said,' appears a negative statement; but it is really one of our ways of making a positive one :—' I pretended not to understand him.' To the same class belongs the common expression ' I don't think ' :—' 1 don't think you bought that horse too dear,' meaning ' I think you did not buy him too dear '; ' I don't think this day will be wet,' equivalent to ' I think it will not be wet.'

Lowry Looby is telling how a lot of fellows attacked Hardress Cregan, who defends himself successfully :—' Ah, it isn't a goose or a duck they had to do with when they came across Mr. Cregan.' (Gerald Griffin.) Another way of expressing the same idea often heard :—' He's no sop (wisp) in the road' ; i.e. ' he's a strong brave fellow.'

' It was not too wise of you to buy those cows as the market stands at present,' i.e. it was rather foolish.

' I wouldn't be sorry to get a glass of wine,' meaning, ' I would be glad.'

An unpopular person is going away :—

> ' Joy be with him and a bottle of moss,
> And if he don't return he's no great loss.'

' How are you to-day, James ? '

' Indeed I can't say that I'm very well ' : meaning ' I am rather ill.'

' You had no right to take that book without my leave'; meaning ' You were wrong in taking it—it was wrong of you to take it.' A translation of the Irish *ní cóir duit*. ' A bad right' is stronger than ' no right.' ' You have no right to speak ill of my uncle' is simply negation :—' You are wrong, for you have no reason or occasion to speak so.' ' A bad right you have to speak ill of my uncle : ' that is to say, ' You are doubly wrong ' [for he once did you a great service]. ' A bad right anyone would have to call Ned a screw ' [for he is well known for his generosity]. (' Knocknagow.') Another way of applying the word—in the sense of *duty*—is seen in the following :—A member at an Urban Council

meeting makes an offensive remark and refuses to
withdraw it : when another retorts :—' You have a
right to withdraw it '—i.e. ' it is your duty.'   So :—
' You have a right to pay your debts.'

'Is your present farm as large as the one you
left ? '   Reply :—' Well indeed it doesn't want much
of it.'   A common expression, and borrowed from
the Irish, where it is still more usual.   The Irish
beagnach (' little but ') and *acht ma beag* (' but only
a little ') are both used in the above sense (' doesn't
want much '), equivalent to the English *almost*.

A person is asked did he ever see a ghost.   If his
reply is to be negative, the invariable way of expressing it is : ' I never saw anything worse than
myself, thanks be to God.'

A person is grumbling without cause, making out
that he is struggling in some difficulty—such as
poverty—and the people will say to him ironically :
' Oh how bad you are.'   A universal Irish phrase
among high and low.

A person gives a really good present to a girl :—
' He didn't affront her by that present.'   (Patterson :
Antrim and Down.)

How we cling to this form of expression—or
rather how it clings to us—is seen in the following
extract from the Dublin correspondence of one of the
London newspapers of December, 1909 :—' Mr. ——
is not expected to be returned to parliament at the
general election '; meaning it *is* expected that he will
not be returned.   So also :—' How is poor Jack Fox
to-day ? '   ' Oh he's not expected ' ; i.e. not expected to
live,—he is *given over*.   This expression, *not expected*, is
a very common Irish phrase in cases of death sickness.

CHAPTER IV.

IDIOMS DERIVED FROM THE IRISH LANGUAGE.

IN this chapter I am obliged to quote the original Irish passages a good deal as a guarantee of authenticity for the satisfaction of Irish scholars : but for those who have no Irish the translations will answer equally well. Besides the examples I have brought together here, many others will be found all through the book. I have already remarked that the great majority of our idiomatic Hibernian-English sayings are derived from the Irish language.

When existence or modes of existence are predicated in Irish by the verb *tá* or *atá* (English *is*), the Irish preposition *in* (English *in*) in some of its forms is always used, often with a possessive pronoun, which gives rise to a very curious idiom. Thus, ' he is a mason ' is in Irish *tá sé 'n a shaor*, which is literally *he is in his mason* : ' I am standing ' is *tá mé a m' sheasamh*, lit. *I am in my standing*. This explains the common Anglo-Irish form of expression :—' He fell on the road out of his standing ' : for as he is ' in his standing ' (according to the Irish) when he is standing up, he is ' out of his standing ' when he falls. This idiom with *in* is constantly translated literally into English by the Irish people. Thus, instead of saying, ' I sent the wheat thrashed into corn to the mill, and it came home as flour,' they will rather say, ' I sent the wheat *in corn* to the mill, and it came home *in flour*.' Here the *in* denotes identity : ' Your hair is in a wisp '; i.e. it *is* a wisp: ' My eye is in whey in my head,' i.e. it *is* whey. (John Keegan in Ir. Pen. Journ.)

But an idiom closely resembling this, and in some respects identical with it, exists in English (though it has not been hitherto noticed—so far as I am aware) —as may be seen from the following examples :— ' The Shannon . . . rushed through Athlone *in* a deep and rapid stream (Macaulay), i.e. it *was* a deep and rapid stream (like our expression ' Your handker-chief is in ribbons ').

' Where heaves the turf *in* many a mouldering heap.'
(GRAY's ' Elegy.')

' Hence bards, like Proteus, long in vain tied down,
Escape *in* monsters and amaze the town.'
(POPE: ' Dunciad.')

'The bars forming the front and rear edges of each plane [of the flying-machine] are always *in* one piece' (Daily Mail). Shelley's 'Cloud' says, 'I laugh *in* thunder' (meaning I laugh, and my laugh *is* thunder. ' The greensand and chalk were continued across the weald *in* a great dome.' (Lord Avebury.)

' Just to the right of him were the white-robed bishops *in a group*.' (Daily Mail.) ' And men *in* nations' (Byron in ' The Isles of Greece') : ' The people came *in* tens and twenties' : ' the rain came down *in* torrents' : ' I'll take £10 *in* gold and the rest *in* silver' : ' the snow gathered *in* a heap.' ' The money came [home] sometimes *in* specie and sometimes *in* goods ' (Lord Rothschild, speech in House of Lords, 29th November, 1909), exactly like ' the corn came home *in* flour,' quoted above. The

preceding examples do not quite fully represent
the Irish idiom in its entirety, inasmuch as the
possessive pronouns are absent.   But even these
are sometimes found, as in the familiar phrases,
'the people came *in their* hundreds.'   'You are
in your thousands' [here at the meeting], which is
an exact reproduction of the Gaelic phrase in the
Irish classical story :—*Atá sibh in bhur n-ealaibh,*
' Ye are swans ' (lit. ' Ye are in your swans ').

When mere existence is predicated, the Gaelic *ann*
(*in it*, i.e. ' in existence ') is used, as *atá sneachta ann,*
' there is snow ' ; lit. ' there is snow *there*,' or ' there
is snow *in it*,' i.e. in existence.   The *ann* should be
left blank in English translation, i.e. having no
proper representative.   But our people will not let it
go waste; they bring it into their English in the form
of either *in it* or *there*, both of which in this construction carry the meaning of *in existence.*   Mrs.
Donovan says to Bessy Morris :—' Is it yourself
that's *in it*? ' (' Knocknagow '), which would stand in
correct Irish *An tusa atá ann?*   On a Sunday one
man insults and laughs at another, who says, ' Only
for the day that's *in it* I'd make you laugh at the
wrong side of your mouth ': ' the weather that's
in it is very hot.'   ' There's nothing at all *there*
(in existence) as it used to be ' (Gerald Griffin :
' Collegians ') : ' this day is bad for growth, there's
a sharp east wind *there*.'

I do not find this use of the English preposition *in*
—namely, to denote identity—referred to in English
dictionaries, though it ought to be.

The same mode of expressing existence by *an* or
in is found in the Ulster and Scotch phrase for

to be alone, which is as follows, always bringing in the personal pronoun:—' I am in my lone,' ' he is in his lone,' ' they are in their lone '; or more commonly omitting the preposition (though it is always understood) : ' She is living her lone.' All these expressions are merely translations from Gaelic, in which they are constantly used; ' I am in my lone' being from *Tá me am' aonar,* where *am'* is ' in my' and *aonar,* ' lone.' *Am' aonar seal do bhiossa,* ' Once as I was alone.' (Old Irish Song.) In north-west Ulster they sometimes use the preposition *by* :—' To come home by his lone ' (Seumas Mac Manus). Observe the word *lone* is always made *lane* in Scotland, and generally in Ulster ; and these expressions or their like will be found everywhere in Burns or in any other Scotch (or Ulster) dialect writer.

Prepositions are used in Irish where it might be wrong to use them in corresponding constructions in English. Yet the Irish phrases are continually translated literally, which gives rise to many incorrect dialect expressions. Of this many examples will be found in what follows.

' He put lies *on* me '; a form of expression often heard. This might have one or the other of two meanings, viz. either ' he accused me of telling lies,' or ' he told lies about me.'

' The tinker took fourpence *out of* that kettle,' i.e. he earned 4*d.* by mending it. St. Patrick left his name *on* the townland of Kilpatrick : that nickname remained *on* Dan Ryan ever since.

' He was vexed *to* me ' (i.e. with me): ' I was *at* him for half a year' (with him); ' You could find no fault *to it* ' (with it). All these are in use.

'I took the medicine according to the doctor's order, but I found myself nothing the better *of it*.' 'You have a good time *of it*.' I find in Dickens however (in his own words) that the wind 'was obviously determined to make a night *of it*.' (See p. 10 for a peculiarly Irish use of *of it*.)

In the Irish poem *Bean na d-Tri m-Bo*, 'The Woman of Three Cows,' occurs the expression, *As do bhólacht ná bí teann*, 'Do not be haughty *out of* your cattle.' This is a form of expression constantly heard in English :—'he is as proud as a peacock *out of* his rich relations.' So also, 'She has great thought *out of* him,' i.e. She has a very good opinion of him. (Queen's Co.)

'I am without a penny,' i.e. I haven't a penny : very common : a translation from the equally common Irish expression, *tá me gan pinghín*.

In an Irish love song the young man tells us that he had been vainly trying to win over the colleen *le bliadhain agus le lá*, which Petrie correctly (but not literally) translates 'for a year and for a day.' As the Irish preposition *le* signifies *with*, the literal translation would be '*with* a year and *with* a day,' which would be incorrect English. Yet the un-educated people of the South and West often adopt this translation ; so that you will hear such expressions as 'I lived in Cork *with* three years.'

There is an idiomatic use of the Irish preposition *air*, 'on,' before a personal pronoun or before a personal name and after an active verb, to intimate injury or disadvantage of some kind, a violation of right or claim. Thus, *Do bhuail Seumas mo ghadhar orm* [where *orm* is *air me*], 'James struck my dog

on me,' where *on me* means to my detriment, in
violation of my right, &c.   *Chaill sé mo sgian orm*;
he lost my knife *on me.'*

This mode of expression exists in the oldest Irish
as well as in the colloquial languages—both Irish
and English—of the present day.   When St. Patrick
was spending the Lent on Croagh Patrick the
demons came to torment him in the shape of great
black hateful-looking birds : and the Tripartite Life,
composed (in the Irish language) in the tenth century, says, 'The mountain was filled with great sooty-
black birds *on him'* (to his torment or detriment).
In 'The Battle of Rossnaree,' Carbery, directing his
men how to act against Conor, his enemy, tells them
to send some of their heroes *re tuargain a sgéithe ar
Conchobar,* 'to smite Conor's shield *on him.'*   The
King of Ulster is in a certain hostel, and when his
enemies hear of it, they say :—' We are pleased
at that for we shall [attack and] take the hostel
on him to-night.' (Congal Claringneach.)   It occurs
also in the *Amra* of Columkille—the oldest of all—
though I cannot lay my hand on the passage.

This is one of the commonest of our Anglo-Irish
idioms, so that a few examples will be sufficient.

' I saw thee . . . thrice *on Tara's champions* win the goal.'
(FERGUSON : 'Lays of the Western Gael.')

I once heard a grandmother—an educated Dublin
lady—say, in a charmingly petting way, to her little
grandchild who came up crying :—' What did they
do to you on me—did they beat you on me ? '

The Irish preposition *ag*—commonly translated
'for' in this connexion—is used in a sense much
like *air*, viz. to carry an idea of some sort of injury

to the person represented by the noun or pronoun.
Typical examples are: one fellow threatening another
says, ' I'll break your head *for you* ' : or ' I'll soon
settle his hash for him.'   This of course also comes
from Irish ; *Gur scoilt an plaosg aige,* ' so that he
broke his skull *for him* ' (Battle of Gavra) ; *Do
ghearr a reim aige beo,* ' he shortened his career for
him.' ('The Amadán Mór.') See 'On' in Vocabulary.

There is still another peculiar usage of the English
preposition *for*, which is imitated or translated from
the Irish, the corresponding Irish preposition here
being *mar*.   In this case the prepositional phrase is
added on, not to denote injury, but to express some
sort of mild depreciation :—' Well, how is your new
horse getting on ? ' ' Ah, I'm tired of him *for a horse*:
he is little good.'   A dog keeps up a continuous bark-
ing, and a person says impatiently, 'Ah, choke you *for
a dog* ' (may you be choked).   Lowry Looby, who has
been appointed to a place and is asked how he is
going on with it, replies, ' To lose it I did *for a
place*.' (' Collegians.')   In the Irish story of *Bodach
an Chota Lachtna* ('The Clown with the Grey Coat'),
the Bodach offers Ironbones some bones to pick,
on which Ironbones flies into a passion; and Mangan,
the translator, happily puts into the mouth of the
Bodach :—' Oh, very well, then we will not have
any more words about them, *for bones*.'   Osheen,
talking in a querulous mood about all his companions—the Fena—having left him, says, [were I
in my former condition] *Ní ghoirfinn go bráth orruibh,
mar Fheinn*, 'I would never call on you, *for Fena*.'
This last and its like are the models on which the
Anglo-Irish phrases are formed,

'Of you' (where *of* is not intended for *off*) is very frequently used in the sense of *from you* : 'I'll take the stick *of you* whether you like it or not.' 'Of you' is here simply a translation of the Irish *díot*, which is always used in this connexion in Irish : *bainfead díot é*, 'I will take it of you.' In Irish phrases like this the Irish *uait* ('from you') is not used ; if it were the people would say 'I'll take it *from you*,' not *of you*. (Russell.)

'Oh that news was *on* the paper yesterday.' 'I went *on* the train to Kingstown.' Both these are often heard in Dublin and elsewhere. Correct speakers generally use *in* in such cases. (Father Higgins and Kinahan.)

In some parts of Ulster they use the preposition *on* after *to be married* :—'After Peggy M'Cue had been married *on* Long Micky Diver' (Sheumas MacManus).

'To make a speech *takes a good deal out of me*,' i.e. tires me, exhausts me, an expression heard very often among all classes. The phrase in italics is merely the translation of a very common Irish expression, *baineann sé rud éigin asam*, it takes something out of me.

'I am afraid of her,' 'I am frightened at her,' are both correct English, meaning 'she has frightened me' : and both are expressed in Donegal by 'I am afeard *for* her,' 'I am frightened *for* her,' where in both cases *for* is used in the sense of 'on account of.'

In Irish any sickness, such as fever, is said to be *on* a person, and this idiom is imported into English. If a person wishes to ask 'What ails you?' he often gives it the form of 'What is on you?' (Ulster), which is exactly the English of *Cad é sin ort?*

A visitor stands up to go. 'What hurry is on you?' A mild invitation to stay on (Armagh). In the South, 'What hurry are you in?'

She had *a nose on her*, i.e. looked sour, out of humour ('Knocknagow'). Much used in the South. 'They never asked me had I a mouth on me': universally understood and often used in Ireland, and meaning 'they never offered me anything to eat or drink.'

I find Mark Twain using the same idiom:—[an old horse] 'had a neck *on him* like a bowsprit' ('Innocents Abroad'); but here I think Mark shows a touch of the Gaelic brush, wherever he got it.

'I tried to knock another shilling out of him, but all in vain': i.e. I tried to persuade him to give me another shilling. This is very common with Irish-English speakers, and is a word for word translation of the equally common Irish phrase *bain sgilling eile as.* (Russell.)

'I came against you' (more usually *agin you*) means 'I opposed you and defeated your schemes.' This is merely a translation of an Irish phrase, in which the preposition *le* or *re* is used in the sense of *against* or *in opposition to*: *do tháinic me leat annsin.* (S. H. O'Grady.) 'His sore knee came *against him* during the walk.'

Against is used by us in another sense—that of meeting: 'he went against his father,' i.e. he went to meet his father [who was coming home from town]. This, which is quite common, is, I think, pure Anglo-

Irish.   But 'he laid up a supply of turf against the winter' is correct English as well as Anglo-Irish.

> ' And the cravat of hemp was surely spun
>   *Against* the day when their race was run.'
>
> ('Touchstone' in 'Daily Mail.')

A very common inquiry when you meet a friend is :—' How are all your care ?' Meaning chiefly your family, those persons that are under your care. This is merely a translation of the common Irish inquiry, *Cionnos tá do chúram go léir ?*

A number of idiomatic expressions cluster round the word *head*, all of which are transplanted from Irish in the use of the Irish word *ceann* [cann] ' head. *Head* is used to denote the cause, occasion, or motive of anything. 'Did he really walk that distance in a day ?'   Reply in Irish, *Ní'l contabhairt air bith ann a cheann* : ' there is no doubt at all *on the head of it,*' i.e. about it, in regard to it. 'He is a bad head to me,' i.e. he treats me badly. Merely the Irish *is olc an ceann dom é.   Bhí fearg air da chionn,* he was vexed on the head of it.

A dismissed clerk says :—' I made a mistake in one of the books, and I was sent away *on the head of* that mistake.'

A very common phrase among us is, ' More's the pity ' :—' More's the pity that our friend William should be so afflicted.'

> ' More's the pity one so pretty
>   As I should live alone.'
>
> (Anglo-Irish Folk-Song.)

This is a translation of a very common Irish expression as seen in :—*Budh mhó an sgéile Diarmaid*

do bheith marbh : ' More's the pity Dermot to be dead.'
(Story of 'Dermot and Grania.')

' Who should come up to me in the fair but John.'
Intended not for a question but. for an assertion—an
assertion of something which was hardly expected.
This mode of expression, which is very common, is
a Gaelic construction.   Thus in the song *Fáinne geal
an lae* :—*Cia gheabhainn le m'ais acht cúilfhionn deas* :
' Whom should I find near by me but the pretty fair
haired girl.'   ' Who should walk in only his dead
wife.'   (Gerald Griffin : ' Collegians.')   ' As we were
walking along what should happen but John to
stumble and fall on the road.'

The pronouns *myself, himself,* &c., are very often
used in Ireland in a peculiar way, which will be
understood from the following examples :—' The birds
were singing *for themselves.*'   ' I was looking about
the fair *for myself*' (Gerald Griffin : ' Collegians ') :
' he is pleasant *in himself*' (ibid.) : ' I felt dead [dull]
in myself' (ibid.).   ' Just at that moment I happened
to be walking by myself ' (i.e. alone : Irish, *liom féin*).
Expressions of this kind are all borrowed direct from
Irish.

We have in our Irish-English a curious use of the
personal pronouns which will be understood from
the following examples :—' He interrupted me *and I
writing* my letters ' (as I was writing).   ' I found Phil
there too *and he playing* his fiddle for the company.'
This, although very incorrect English, is˜ a classic
idiom in Irish, from which it has been imported as it
stands into our English.   Thus :—*Do chonnairc mé
Tomás agus é n'a shuidhe cois na teine* : ' I saw Thomas
and he sitting beside the fire.'   ' How could you see

me there *and I to be in bed at the time*?' This latter
part is merely a translation from the correct Irish :--
agus meise do bheith mo luidhe ag an am sin (Irish
Tale). Any number of examples of this usage might
be culled from both English and Irish writings.
Even so classical a writer as Wolfe follows this
usage in 'The Burial of Sir John Moore' :—

> ' We thought . . . .
> That the foe and the stranger would tread o'er his head,
> *And we far away* on the billow.'

(I am reminded of this by Miss Hayden and Prof.
Hartog.)

But there is a variety in our English use of the
pronouns here, namely, that we often use the objective (or accusative) case instead of the nominative.
'How could you expect Davy to do the work *and him
so very sick*?' 'My poor man fell into the fire a
Sunday night *and him hearty*' (*hearty*, half drunk :
Maxwell, 'Wild Sports of the West'). 'Is that
what you lay out for me, mother, *and me after turning
the Voster*' (i.e. after working through the whole of
Voster's Arithmetic : Carleton). 'John and Bill
were both reading and *them eating their dinner*'
(while they were eating their dinner). This is also
from the Irish language. We will first take the third
person plural pronoun. The pronoun 'they' is in
Irish *siad*: and the accusative 'them' is the Irish
iad. But in some Irish constructions this *iad* is
(correctly) used as a nominative ; and in imitation of
this our people often use 'them' as a nominative :—
'*Them* are just the gloves I want.' '*Them* are the
boys' is exactly translated from the correct Irish *is*

iad sin na buachaillidhe. ' Oh she melted the hearts of the swains in *them* parts.' ('The Widow Malone,' by Lever.)

In like manner with the pronouns *sé, si* (he, she), of which the accusatives *é* and *i* are in certain Irish constructions (correctly) used for the nominative forms, which accusative forms are (incorrectly) imported into English. *Do chonnairc mé Seadhán agus é n'a shuidhe,* ' I saw Shaun and *him* sitting down,' i.e. 'as he was sitting down.' So also ' don't ask me to go and *me* having a sore foot.' ' There's the hen and *her* as fat as butter,' i.e. 'she (the hen) being as fat as butter.'

The little phrase ' the way ' is used among us in several senses, all peculiar, and all derived from Irish. Sometimes it is a direct translation from *amhlaidh* (' thus,' ' so,' ' how,' ' in a manner '). An old example of this use of *amhlaidh* in Irish is the following passage from the *Boroma* (*Silva Gadelica*):—
Is amlaid at chonnaic [*Concobar*] *Laigin ocus Uláid mán dabaig ocá hól* : ' It is how (or ' the way ') [Concobar] saw the Lagenians and the Ulstermen [viz. they were] round the vat drinking from it.' *Is amhlaidh do bhí Fergus:* ' It is thus (or the way) Fergus was [conditioned ; that his shout was heard over three cantreds].'

This same sense is also seen in the expression, ' this is the way I made my money,' i.e. ' this is how I made it.'

When this expression, 'the way,' or 'how,' introduces a statement it means ' 'tis how it happened.' ' What do you want, James ? ' ' 'Tis the way ma'am, my mother sent me for the loan of the shovel.' This idiom is very common in Limerick, and is used indeed all through Ireland.

Very often 'the way' is used in the sense of 'in order that':—'Smoking carriages are lined with American cloth *the way* they wouldn't keep the smell'; 'I brought an umbrella *the way* I wouldn't get wet'; 'you want not to let the poor boy do for himself [by marrying] *the way* that you yourself should have all.' (Ir. Pen. Mag.) You constantly hear this in Dublin, even among educated people.

Sometimes the word *way* is a direct translation from the Irish *caoi*, 'a way,' 'a road'; so that the common Irish salutation, *Cad chaoi bh-fuil tu?* is translated with perfect correctness into the equally common Irish-English salute, 'What way are you?' meaning 'How are you?'

'This way' is often used by the people in the sense of 'by this time':—'The horse is ready this way,' i.e. 'ready by this time.' (Gerald Griffin, 'Collegians.')

The word *itself* is used in a curious way in Ireland, which has been something of a puzzle to outsiders. As so used it has no gender, number, or case; it is not in fact a pronoun at all, but a substitute for the word *even*. This has arisen from the fact that in the common colloquial Irish language the usual word to express both *even* and *itself*, is *féin*; and in translating a sentence containing this word *féin*, the people rather avoided *even*, a word not very familiar to them in this sense, and substituted the better known *itself*, in cases where *even* would be the correct word, and *itself* would be incorrect. Thus *da mbeith an meud sin féin agum* is correctly rendered 'if I had

even that much ' : but the people don't like *even*, and
don't well understand it (as applied here), so they
make it ' If I had that much *itself*.' This explains
all such Anglo-Irish sayings as ' if I got it itself it
would be of no use to me,' i.e. ' even if I got it': ' If
she were there itself I wouldn't know her ' ; ' She
wouldn't go to bed till you'd come home, and if she
did itself she couldn't sleep.' (Knocknagow.) A
woman is finding some fault with the arrangements
for a race, and Lowry Looby (Collegians) puts in
' so itself what hurt' i.e. ' even so what harm.'
(Russell and myself.)

The English *when* is expressed by the Irish *an
uair*, which is literally ' the hour ' or ' the time.'
This is often transplanted into English ; as when a
person says ' the time you arrived I was away in
town.'

When you give anything to a poor person the
recipient commonly utters the wish ' God increase
you !' (meaning your substance) : which is an exact
translation of the equally common Irish wish *Go
meádaighe Dia dhuit*. Sometimes the prayer is
' God increase your store,' which expresses exactly
what is meant in the Irish wish.

The very common aspiration ' God help us ' [you,
me, them, &c.] is a translation of the equally common *Go bh-fóireadh Dia orruinn* [*ort*, &c.].

In the north-west instead of ' your father,' ' your
sister,' &c., they often say ' the father of you,'
' the sister of you,' &c.; and correspondingly as to
things :—' I took the hand of her ' (i.e. her hand)
(Seumas Mac Manus).

All through Ireland you will hear *show* used instead of *give* or *hand* (verb), in such phrases as

'Show me that knife,' i.e. hand it to me. 'Show me the cream, please,' says an Irish gentleman at a London restaurant; and he could not see why his English friends were laughing.

'He passed me in the street *by the way* he didn't know me'; 'he refused to give a contribution *by the way* he was so poor.' In both, *by the way* means 'pretending.'

'My own own people' means my immediate relations. This is a translation of *mo mhuinterse féin*. In Irish the repetition of the emphatic pronominal particles is very common, and is imported into English; represented here by 'own own.'

A prayer or a wish in Irish often begins with the particle *go*, meaning 'that' (as a conjunction): *Go raibh maith agut*, '*that* it may be well with you,' i.e. 'May it be well with you.' In imitation or translation of this the corresponding expression in English is often opened by this word *that*: 'that you may soon get well,' i.e., 'may you soon get well.' Instead of 'may I be there to see' (John Gilpin) our people would say 'that I may be there to see.' A person utters some evil wish such as 'may bad luck attend you,' and is answered 'that the prayer may happen the preacher.' A usual ending of a story told orally, when the hero and heroine have been comfortably disposed of is 'And if they don't live happy *that we may*.'

When a person sees anything unusual or unexpected, he says to his companion, 'Oh do you mind that!'

'You want me to give you £10 for that cow : well, I'm not so soft *all out*.' 'He's not so bad as that *all out*.'

A common expression is ' I was talking to him to-day, and I *drew down about* the money,' i.e. I brought on or introduced the subject. This is a translation of the Irish form *do tharrainy me anuas* ' I drew down.'

Quite a common form of expression is ' I had like to be killed,' i.e., I was near being killed : I had a narrow escape of being killed : I escaped being killed *by the black of my nail*.

Where the English say *it rains*, we say ' it is raining ': which is merely a translation of the Irish way of saying it :—*ta se ag fearthainn*.

The usual Gaelic equivalent of ' he gave a roar ' is *do léig sé géim as* (met everywhere in Irish texts), ' he let a roar out of him ' ; which is an expression you will often hear among people who have not well mastered English—who in fact often speak the Irish language with English words.

' I put it before me to do it,' meaning I was resolved to do it, is the literal translation of *chuireas rómhaim é to dheunamh*. Both Irish and Anglo-Irish are very common in the respective languages.

When a narrator has come to the end of some minor episode in his narrative, he often resumes with the opening ' That was well and good ': which is merely a translation of the Gaelic *bhí sin go maith*.

Lowry Looby having related how the mother and daughter raised a terrible *pillilu*, i.e., ' roaring and bawling,' says after a short pause ' that was well and good,' and proceeds with his story. (Gerald Griffin : ' Collegians.')

A common Irish expression interjected into a narrative or discourse, as a sort of stepping stone between what is ended and what is coming is *Ni'l tracht air*, 'there is no talking about it,' corresponding to the English 'in short,' or ' to make a long story short.' These Irish expressions are imported into our English, in which popular phrases like the following are very often heard :—' I went to the fair, and *there's no use in talking*, I found the prices real bad.'

> ' Wisha my bones are exhausted, and *there's no use in talking*,
> My heart is scalded, *a wirrasthru*.'
>
> (Old Song.)

'Where is my use in staying here, so there's no use in talking, go I will.' ('Knocknagow.') Often the expression takes this form:—' Ah 'tis a folly to talk, he'll never get that money.'

Sometimes the original Irish is in question form. *Cid tracht* ('what talking ? ' i.e. ' what need of talking ? ') which is Englished as follows :—' Ah what's the use of talking, your father will never consent.' These expressions are used in conversational Irish-English, not for the purpose of continuing a narrative as in the original Irish, but—as appears from the above examples—merely to add emphasis to an assertion.

' It's a fine day that.' This expression, which is common enough among us, is merely a translation from the common Irish phrase *is breagh an lá é sin*, where the demonstrative *sin* (that) comes last in the proper Irish construction : but when imitated in English it looks queer to an English listener or reader.

' *There is no doubt* that is a splendid animal.' This expression is a direct translation from the Irish *Ni'l contabhairt ann*, and is equivalent to the English ' doubtless.' It occurs often in the Scottish dialect also :—' Ye need na doubt I held my whisht ' (Burns).

You are about to drink from a cup. 'How much shall I put into this cup for you ?' 'Oh you may give me *the full of it.* This is Irish-English : in England they would say—' Give it to me full.' Our expression is a translation from the Irish language. For example, speaking of a drinking-horn, an old writer says, *a lán do'n lionn*, literally, ' the full of it of ale.' In Silva Gadelica we find *lán a ghlaice deise do losaibh*, which an Irishman translating literally would render ' the full of his right hand of herbs,' while an Englishman would express the same idea in this way—' his right hand full of herbs.'

Our Irish-English expression ' to come round a person ' means to induce or *circumvent* him by coaxing cuteness and wheedling : ' He came round me by his *sleudering* to lend him half a crown, fool that I was ' : ' My grandchildren came round me to give them money for sweets.' This expression is borrowed from Irish :—' When the Milesians reached Erin *tanic a ngáes timchioll Tuathi De Danand,* ' their cuteness circumvented (lit. ' came round ') the Dedannans.' (Opening sentence in *Mesca Ulad* in Book of Leinster : Hennessy.)

' Shall I do so and so ?' 'What would prevent you ?' A very usual Hibernian-English reply, meaning ' you may do it of course ; there is nothing to prevent you.' This is borrowed or translated from an Irish phrase. In the very old tale *The Voyage of Maildune*, Maildune's people ask, ' Shall we speak to her [the lady]?' and he replies *Cid gatas uait ce atberaid fria.* ' What [is it] that takes [anything] from you though ye speak to her,' as much as to say, ' what harm will it do you if you speak to her ?'

equivalent to ' of course you may, there's nothing to
prevent you.'

That old horse is *lame of one leg*, one of our very
usual forms of expression, which is merely a translation from *bacach ar aonchois*. (MacCurtin.) 'I'll seem
to be lame, quite useless of one of my hands.' (Old
Song.)

Such constructions as *amadán fir* ' a fool of a
man' are very common in Irish, with the second
noun in the genitive (*fear* ' a man,' gen. *fir*) meaning
' a man who is a fool.'   *Is and is ail ollamhan*, ' it is
then he is a rock of an *ollamh* (doctor), i.e. a doctor
who is a rock [of learning]. (Book of Rights.) So
also ' a thief of a fellow,' ' a steeple of a man,' i.e.
a man who is a steeple—so tall. This form of
expression is however common in England both
among writers and speakers. It is noticed here
because it is far more general among us, for the
obvious reason that it has come to us from two
sources (instead of one)—Irish and English.

' I removed to Dublin this day twelve months, and
this day two years I will go back again to Tralee.' ' I
bought that horse last May was a twelvemonth, and
he will be three years old come Thursday next.'
' I'll not sell my pigs till coming on summer':
a translation of *air theacht an t-samhraidh*. Such
Anglo-Irish expressions are very general, and are all
from the Irish language, of which many examples
might be given, but this one from ' The Courtship of
Emer,' twelve or thirteen centuries old, will be enough.
[It was prophesied] that the boy would come to Erin
that day seven years—*dia secht m-bliadan*. (Kuno
Meyer.)

In our Anglo-Irish dialect the expression *at all* is often duplicated for emphasis : ' I'll grow no corn this year at all at all ' : ' I have no money at all at all.' So prevalent is this among us that in a very good English grammar recently published (written by an Irishman) speakers and writers are warned against it. This is an importation from Irish. One of the Irish words for ' at all ' is *idir* (always used after a negative), old forms *itir* and *etir* :—*nir bo tol do Dubthach recc na cumaile etir*, ' Dubthach did not wish to sell the bondmaid at all.' In the following old passage, and others like it, it is duplicated for emphasis *Cid beac, itir itir, ges do obar* : 'however little it is forbidden to work, at all at all.' (' Prohibitions of beard,' O'Looney.)

When it is a matter of indifference which of two things to choose, we usually say ' It is equal to me ' (or ' all one to me '), which is just a translation of *is cuma liom* (best rendered by ' I don't care '). Both Irish and English expressions are very common in the respective languages. Lowry Looby says :—' It is equal to me whether I walk ten or twenty miles.' (Gerald Griffin.)

> ' I am a bold bachelor, airy and free,
> Both cities and counties are equal to me.'
>
> (Old Song.)

' Do that out of the face,' i.e. begin at the beginning and finish it out and out : a translation of *deun sin as eudan.*

' The day is rising ' means the day is clearing up, —the rain, or snow, or wind is ceasing—the weather is becoming fine : a common saying in Ireland : a translation of the usual Irish expression *tá an lá*

ag éirghidh. During the height of the great wind
storm of 1842 a poor *shooler* or ' travelling man '
from Galway, who knew little English, took refuge
in a house in Westmeath, where the people were
praying in terror that the storm might go down.
He joined in, and unconsciously translating from his
native Irish, he kept repeating ' Musha, that the
Lord may rise it, that the Lord may rise it.' At
which the others were at first indignant, thinking he
was asking God to *raise* the wind higher still.
(Russell.)

Sometimes two prepositions are used where one
would do :—' The dog got *in under* the bed : ' ' Where
is James ? He's *in in* the room—or inside in the
room.'

> ' Old woman, old woman, old woman,' says I,
> ' Where are you going up so high ? '
> ' To sweep the cobwebs *off o*' the sky.'

Whether this duplication *off of* is native Irish or
old English it is not easy to say : but I find this
expression in ' Robinson Crusoe ' :—' For the first
time since the storm *off of* Hull.'

Eva, the witch, says to the children of Lir, when
she had turned them into swans :—*Amach daoibh a
chlann an righ* : ' Out with you [on the water] ye
children of the king.' This idiom which is quite
common in Irish, is constantly heard among English
speakers :—' Away with you now '—' Be off with
yourself.'

' Are you going away now ? ' One of the Irish
forms of answering this is *Ní fós*, which in Kerry the
people translate ' no yet,' considering this nearer to
the original than the usual English ' not yet.'

The usual way in Irish of saying *he died* is *fuair sé bás*, i.e. 'he found (or got) death,' and this is sometimes imitated in Anglo-Irish :—'He was near getting his death from that wetting ' ; 'come out of that draught or you'll get your death.'

The following curious form of expression is very often heard :—' Remember you have gloves to buy for me in town ' ; instead of ' you have to buy me gloves, ' What else have you to do to-day ? ' ' I have a top to bring to Johnny, and when I come home I have the cows to put in the stable '—instead of 'I have to bring a top '—' I have to put the cows.' This is an imitation of Irish, though not, I think, a direct translation.

What may be called the Narrative Infinitive is a very usual construction in Irish. An Irish writer, relating a past event (and using the Irish language) instead of beginning his narrative in this way, ' Donall O'Brien went on an expedition against the English of Athlone,' will begin ' Donall O'Brien *to go* on an expedition,' &c. No Irish examples of this need be given here, as they will be found in every page of the Irish Annals, as well as in other Irish writings. Nothing like this exists in English, but the people constantly imitate it in the Anglo-Irish speech. ' How did you come by all that money ? ' Reply :—' To get into the heart of the fair ' (meaning ' I got into the heart of the fair '), and to cry *old china*, &c. (Gerald Griffin.) ' How was that, Lowry ? ' .asks Mr. Daly : and Lowry answers :—' Some of them Garryowen boys sir to get about Danny Mann.' (Gerald Griffin : ' Collegians.') 'How did the mare get that hurt ? ' ' Oh Tom Cody to leap

her over the garden wall yesterday, and she to fall
on her knees on the stones.'

The Irish language has the word *annso* for *here*,
but it has no corresponding word *derived from annso*,
to signify *hither*, though there are words for this too,
but not from *annso*. A similar observation applies
to the Irish for the words *there* and *thither*, and for
where and *whither*. As a consequence of this our
people do not use *hither*, *thither*, and *whither* at all.
They make *here*, *there*, and *where* do duty for them.
Indeed much the same usage exists in the Irish language too: *Is ann tigdaois eunlaith* (Keating): ' It is
here the birds used to come,' instead of *hither*. In
consequence of all this you will hear everywhere in
Anglo-Irish speech :—' John came here yesterday' :
' come here Patsy' : ' your brother is in Cork and
you ought to go *there* to see him ' : ' *where* did you
go yesterday after you parted from me ? '

' Well Jack how are you these times ? ' ' Oh,
indeed Tom I'm purty well thank you— *all that's
left of me* ' : a mock way of speaking, as if the hard
usage of the world had worn him to a thread. ' Is
Frank Magaveen there ? ' asks the blind fiddler.
' All that's left of me is here,' answers Frank.
(Carleton.) These expressions, which are very usual,
and many others of the kind, are borrowed from the
Irish. In the Irish tale, ' The Battle of Gavra,'
poor old Osheen, the sole survivor of the Fena,
says :—' I know not where to follow them [his lost
friends]; and this makes *the little remnant that is
left of me* wretched. (*D'fúig sin m'iarsma*).

Ned Brophy, introducing his wife to Mr. Lloyd
says, ' this is *herself* sir.' This is an extremely

common form of phrase. 'Is *herself* [i.e. the mistress] at home Jenny?' 'I'm afraid himself [the master of the house] will be very angry when he hears about the accident to the mare.' This is an Irish idiom. The Irish chiefs, when signing their names to any document, always wrote the name in this form, *Misi O'Neill*, i.e. 'Myself O'Neill.'

A usual expression is 'I have no Irish,' i.e. I do not know or speak Irish. This is exactly the way of saying it in Irish, of which the above is a translation :—*Ni'l Gaodhlainn agum.*

To *let on* is to pretend, and in this sense is used everywhere in Ireland. 'Oh your father is very angry': 'Not at all, he's only letting on.' 'If you meet James don't let on you saw me,' is really a positive, not a negative request : equivalent to—'If you meet James, let on (pretend) that you didn't see me.' A Dublin working-man recently writing in a newspaper says, 'they passed me on the bridge (Cork), and never let on to see me' (i.e. 'they let on not to see me').

'He is all *as one as* recovered now'; he is nearly the same as recovered.

At the proper season you will often see auctioneers' posters :—'To be sold by auction 20 acres of splendid meadow *on foot*,' &c. This term *on foot*, which is applied in Ireland to *growing* crops of all kinds—corn, flax, meadow, &c.—is derived from the Irish language, in which it is used in the oldest documents as well as in the everyday spoken modern Irish; the usual word *cos* for 'foot' being used. Thus in the Brehon Laws we are told that a wife's share of the flax is one-ninth if it be on foot (*for a cois,*

' on its foot,' modern form *air a chois*) one-sixth after being dried, &c. In one place a fine is mentioned for appropriating or cutting furze if it be ' on foot.' (Br. Laws.)

This mode of speaking is applied in old documents to animals also. Thus in one of the old Tales is mentioned a present of a swine and an ox *on foot* (*for a coiss*, ' on their foot ') to be given to Mac Con and his people, i.e. to be sent to them alive—not slaughtered. (Silva Gadelica.) But I have not come across this application in our modern Irish-English.

To give a thing ' for God's sake,' i.e. to give it in charity or for mere kindness, is an expression very common at the present day all over Ireland. ' Did you sell your turf-rick to Bill Fennessy?' Oh no, I gave it to him for God's sake : he's very badly off now poor fellow, and I'll never miss it.' Our office attendant Charlie went to the clerk, who was chary of the pens, and got a supply with some difficulty. He came back grumbling :—' A person would think I was asking them for God's sake ' (a thoroughly Hibernian sentence). This expression is common also in Irish, both ancient and modern, from which the English is merely a translation. Thus in the Brehon Laws we find mention of certain young persons being taught a trade ' for God's sake ' (*ar Dia*), i.e. without fee : and in another place a man is spoken of as giving a poor person something ' for God's sake.'

The word '*nough*, shortened from *enough*, is always used in English with the possessive pronouns, in accordance with the Gaelic construction in such phrases as as *gur itheadar a n-doithin diobh*, ' So that they ate their enough of them ' (' Diarmaid and Grainne ') : *d'ith mo shaith* ' I ate my enough.' Accordingly uneducated people use the word '*nough* in this manner, exactly as *fill* is correctly used in ' he ate his fill.' Lowry Looby wouldn't like to be ' a born gentleman' for many reasons—among others that you're expected ' not to ate half your 'nough at dinner.' (Gerald Griffin : ' Collegians.)

The words *world* and *earth* often come into our Anglo-Irish speech in a way that will be understood and recognised from the following examples :— ' Where in the world are you going so early ? ' ' What in the world kept you out so long ? ' ' What on earth is wrong with you ? ' ' That cloud looks for all the world like a man ? ' ' Oh you young thief of the world, why did you do that ? ' (to a child). These expressions are all thrown in for emphasis, and they are mainly or altogether imported from the Irish. They are besides of long standing. In the ' Colloquy '—a very old Irish piece—the king of Leinster says to St. Patrick :— ' I do not know *in the world* how it fares [with my son]. So also in a still older story, ' The Voyage of Maildune ' :—' And they [Maildune and his people] knew not whither *in the world* (*isan bith*) they were going. In modern Irish, *Ni chuirionn sé tábhacht a n-éinidh san domhuin*: ' he minds nothing in the world.' (Mac Curtin.)

But I think some of the above expressions are found in good English too, both old and new. For example in a letter to Queen Elizabeth the Earl of Ormond (an Irishman—one of the Butlers) designates a certain Irish chief ' that most arrogant,

vile, traitor of the world Owney M'Rorye' [O'Moore].
But perhaps he wrote this with an Irish pen.

A person does something to displease me—insults
me, breaks down my hedge—and I say 'I will not
let that go with him': meaning I will bring him to
account for it, I will take satisfaction, I will punish
him.   This, which is very usual, is an Irish idiom.
In the story of The Little Brawl of Allen, Goll
boasts of having slain Finn's father; and Finn
answers *bud maith m'acfainnse ar gan sin do léicen let,*
'I am quite powerful enough not to let that go with
you.' ('Silva Gadelica.')   Sometimes this Anglo-
Irish phrase means to vie with, to rival. 'There's
no doubt that old Tom Long is very rich': 'Yes
indeed, but I think Jack Finnerty *wouldn't let it go
with him.'*   Lory Hanly at the dance, seeing his
three companions sighing and obviously in love
with three of the ladies, feels himself just as bad
for a fourth, and sighing, says to himself that he
'wouldn't let it go with any of them. ('Knocknagow.')

'I give in to you' means 'I yield to you,' 'I
assent to (or believe) what you say,' 'I acknowledge
you are right': 'He doesn't give in that there are
ghosts at all.'   This is an Irish idiom, as will be
seen in the following:—[A lion and three dogs are
struggling for the mastery and] *adnaigit [an triur
eile] do [an leomain]* 'And the three others gave
in to the [lion].'

This mode of expression is however found in
English also:—[Beelzebub] 'proposes a third un-
dertaking which the whole assembly gives in to.'
(Addison in 'Spectator.')

For is constantly used before the infinitive : ' he bought cloth *for to* make a coat.'

> ' And " Oh sailor dear," said she,
> " How came you here by me ? "
> And then she began *for to cry*.'
>> (Old Irish Folk Song.)

> ' King James he pitched his tents between
> His lines *for to retire*.'
>> (Old Irish Folk Song : ' The Boyne Water.')

This idiom is in Irish also : *Deunaidh duthracht le leas bhur n-anma a dheunadh* : ' make an effort *for to accomplish* the amendment of your souls.' (' Dunlevy.') Two Irish prepositions are used in this sense of *for* : *le* (as above) and *chum*. But this use of *for* is also very general in English peasant language, as may be seen everywhere in Dickens.

Is ceangailte do bhidhinn, literally ' It is bound I should be,' i.e. in English ' I should be bound.' This construction (from ' Diarmaid and Grainne '), in which the position of the predicate as it would stand according to the English order is thrown back, is general in the Irish language, and quite as general in our Anglo-Irish, in imitation or translation. I once heard a man say in Irish *is e do chailleamhuin do rinn me* : ' It is to lose it I did ' (I lost it). The following are everyday examples from our dialect of English : ' 'Tis to rob me you want ' : ' Is it at the young woman's house the wedding is to be ?' (' Knocknagow ') : ' Is it reading you are ? ' ' 'Twas to dhrame it I did sir ' (' Knocknagow ') : ' Maybe 'tis turned out I d be ' (' Knocknagow ') : ' To lose it I did ' (Gerald Griffin : ' Collegians ') : ' Well John I am glad to

E 2

see you, and it's right well you look': [Billy thinks
the fairy is mocking him, and says :—] 'Is it after
making a fool of me you'd be?' (Crofton Croker):
'To make for Rosapenna (Donegal) we did:' i.e.,
'We made for Rosapenna': 'I'll tell my father about
your good fortune, and 'tis he that will be delighted.'

In the fine old Irish story the 'Pursuit of Dermot
and Grania,' Grania says to her husband Dermot :—
[Invite guests to a feast to our daughter's house]
agus ni feas nach ann do gheubhaidh fear chéile ; 'and
there is no knowing but that there she may get a
husband.' This is almost identical with what Nelly
Donovan says in our own day—in half joke—when
she is going to Ned Brophy's wedding :—'There'll be
some likely lads there to-night, and who knows what
luck I might have.' ('Knocknagow.') This expression 'there is no knowing but' or 'who knows but,'
borrowed as we see from Gaelic, is very common in
our Anglo-Irish dialect. 'I want the loan of £20
badly to help to stock my farm, but how am I to get
it?' His friend answers :—'Just come to the bank,
and who knows but that they will advance it to you
on my security:' meaning 'it is not unlikely—I
think it rather probable—that they will advance it.'

'He looks like a man *that there would be* no
money in his pocket': 'there's *a man that his wife
leaves him* whenever she pleases.' These phrases and
the like are heard all through the middle of Ireland,
and indeed outside the middle : they are translations
from Irish. Thus the italics of the second phrase
would be in Irish *fear dá d-tréigeann a bhean é* (or
a thréigeas a bhean é). 'Poor brave honest Mat
Donovan that everyone is proud of *him* and fond

of *him* ' ('Knocknagow') : ' He was a descendant of
Sir Thomas More that Henry VIII. cut his head off'
(whose head Henry VIII. cut off).   The phrases
above are incorrect English, as there is redundancy;
but they, and others like them, could generally be
made correct by the use of *whose* or *of whom* :—' He
looks like a man in whose pocket,' &c.—' A man
whose wife leaves him.'   But the people in general
do not make use of *whose*—in fact they do not know
how to use it, except at the beginning of a question :—
' Whose knife is this? ' (Russell.) This is an excellent
example of how a phrase may be good Irish but bad
English.

A man possesses some prominent quality, such as
generosity, for which his father was also distinguished,
and we say ' kind father for him,' i.e. ' He is of the
same *kind* as his father—he took it from his father.'
So also ' 'Tis kind for the cat to drink milk '—' cat
after kind '—' 'Tis kind for John to be good and
honourable [for his father or his people were so before
him].   All this is from Irish, in which various words
are used to express the idea of *kind* in this sense :—
bu cheneulta do—bu dhual do—bu dhuthcha do.

Very anxious to do a thing : ' 'Twas all his trouble
to do so and so ' ('Collegians') : corresponding to
the Irish :—' *Is é mo chúram uile,*' ' He (or it) is all my
care.' (MacCurtin.)

Instead of ' The box will hold all the parcels ' or
' All the parcels will fit into the box,' we in Ireland
commonly say ' All the parcels *will go* into the box.
This is from a very old Gaelic usage, as may be seen
from this quotation from the ' Boroma ' :—*Coire mór
uma i teigtís dá muic déc* : ' A large bronze caldron

into which *would go* (téigtís) twelve [jointed] pigs.'
(' Silva Gadelica.')

Chevilles. What is called in French a *cheville*—I
do not know any Irish or English name for it—is a
phrase interjected into a line of poetry merely to
complete either the measure or the rhyme, with
little or no use besides. The practice of using
chevilles was very common in old Irish poetry, and a
bad practice it was ; for many a good poem is quite
spoiled by the constant and wearisome recurrence of
these *chevilles*. For instance here is a translation of
a couple of verses from ' The Voyage of Maildune '
with their *chevilles* :—

> ' They met with an island after sailing—
> > *wonderful the guidance.*
> ' The third day after, on the end of the rod—
> > *deed of power—*
> The chieftain found—*it was a very great joy—*
> > a cluster of apples.'

In modern *Irish* popular poetry we have *chevilles*
also ; of which I think the commonest is the little
phrase *gan go*, ' without a lie ' ; and this is often
reflected in our Anglo-Irish songs. In ' Handsome
Sally,' published in my ' Old Irish Music and
Songs,' these lines occur :—

> ' Young men and maidens I pray draw near—
> > *The truth to you I will now declare—*
> How a fair young lady's heart was won
> > All by the loving of a farmer's son.'

And in another of our songs :—

> ' Good people all I pray draw near—
> > *No lie I'll tell to ye—*
> About a lovely fair maid,
> > And her name is Polly Lee.'

This practice is met with also in English poetry, both classical and popular; but of course this is quite independent of the Irish custom.

Assonance. In the modern Irish language the verse rhymes are *assonantal*. Assonance is the correspondence of the vowels: the consonants count for nothing. Thus *fair*, *may*, *saint*, *blaze*, *there*, all rhyme assonantally. As it is easy to find words that rhyme in this manner, the rhymes generally occur much oftener in Anglo-Irish verse than in pure English, in which the rhymes are what English grammarians call *perfect*.

Our rustic poets rhyme their English (or Irish-English) verse assonantally in imitation of their native language. For a very good example of this, see the song of Castlehyde in my 'Old Irish Music and Songs'; and it may be seen in very large numbers of our Anglo-Irish Folk-songs. I will give just one example here, a free translation of an elegy, rhyming like its original. To the ear of a person accustomed to assonance—as for instance to mine— the rhymes here are as satisfying as if they were *perfect* English rhymes.

You remember our *neigh*bour Mac*B*rady we buried last YEAR:
His death it a*maz*ed me and *daz*ed me with sorrow and GRIEF;
From *cra*dle to *grave* his *name* was held in ESTEEM:
For at *fairs* and at *wakes* there was no one like him for a SPREE;
And 'tis he knew the *way* how to *make* a good cag of POTTHEEN.
He'd make verses in *Gael*ic quite *ais*y most *plaz*ing to READ;
And he knew how to *plaze* the fair *maids* with his soothering
    SPEECH.
He could clear out a *fair* at his *aise* with his ash clehal*P*EEN;
But ochone he's now *laid* in his *grave* in the churchyard of
    KEEL,

CHAPTER V.

THE DEVIL AND HIS 'TERRITORY.'

BAD as the devil is he has done us some service in Ireland by providing us with a fund of anecdotes and sayings full of drollery and fun. This is all against his own interests; for I remember reading in the works of some good old saint—I think it is St. Liguori—that the devil is always hovering near us watching his opportunity, and that one of the best means of scaring him off is a good honest hearty laugh.

Those who wish to avoid uttering the plain straight name 'devil' often call him 'the Old Boy,' or 'Old Nick.'

In some of the stories relating to the devil he is represented as a great simpleton and easily imposed upon: in others as clever at everything. In many he gets full credit for his badness, and all his attributes and all his actions are just the reverse of the good agencies of the world; so that his attempts at evil often tend for good, while anything he does for good—or pretending to be for good—turns to evil.

When a person suffers punishment or injury of any kind that is well deserved—gets his deserts for misconduct or culpable mismanagement or excessive foolishness of any kind—we say 'the devil's cure to him,' or 'the devil mend him' (as much as to say

in English ' serve him right ') ; for if the devil goes to
cure or to mend he only makes matters ten times
worse.   Dick Millikin of Cork (the poet of ' The
Groves of Blarney') was notoriously a late riser. One
morning as he was going very late to business, one
of his neighbours, a Quaker, met him. ' Ah friend
Dick thou art very late to-day : remember the
early bird picks the worm.' ' The devil mend the
worm for being out so early,' replied Dick.   So also
' the devil bless you ' is a bad wish, because the
devil's blessing is equivalent to the curse of God;
while ' the devil's curse to you ' is considéred a good
wish, for the devil's curse is equal to God's blessing.
(Carleton.)   The devil comes in handy in many
ways. What could be more expressive than this
couplet of an old song describing a ruffian in a
rage:—

> ' He stamped and he cursed and he swore he would fight,
> And I saw the *ould* devil between his two eyes.'

Sometimes the devil is taken as the type of excellence or of great proficiency in anything, or of great
excess, so that you often hear ' That fellow is as old
as the devil,' ' That beefsteak is as tough as the devil,'
' He beats the devil for roguery,' ' My landlord is
civil, but dear as the divil.' (Swift : who wrote this
with a pen dipped in Irish ink.)

A poor wretch or a fellow always in debt and
difficulty, and consequently shabby, is a ' poor devil ' ;
and not very long ago I heard a friend say to
another—who was not sparing of his labour—
' Well, there's no doubt but you're a hard-working
old devil.'

Very bad potatoes :—' Wet and watery, scabby and small, thin in the ground and hard to dig, hard to wash, hard to boil, and *the devil to eat them.*'

' I don't wonder that poor Bill should be always struggling, for he has the devil of an extravagant family.'

> ' Oh confusion to you Dan,' says the T. B. C.,
> ' You're the devil of a man,' says the T. B. C.
>
> (Repeal Song of 1843.)

(But this form of expression occurs in Dickens— ' Our Mutual Friend '—' I have a devil of a temper myself'). An emphatic statement :—' I wouldn't like to trust him, for he's the *devil's own* rogue.'

' There's no use in your trying that race against Johnny Keegan, for Johnny is the very devil at running.' ' Oh your reverence,' says Paddy Galvin, ' don't ax me to fast ; but you may put as much prayers on me as you like : for, your reverence, I'm very bad at fasting, but I'm the divel at the prayers.' According to Mr. A. P. Graves, in 'Father O'Flynn,' the ' Provost and Fellows of Trinity ' [College, Dublin] are ' the divels an' all at Divinity.' This last expression is truly Hibernian, and is very often heard :—A fellow is boasting how he'll leather Jack Fox when next he meets him. ' Oh yes, you'll do the *devil an' all* while Jack is away ; but wait till he comes to the fore.'

In several of the following short stories and sayings the simpleton side of Satan's character is well brought out.

Damer of Shronell, who lived in the eighteenth century, was reputed to be the richest man in Ireland—a sort of Irish Croesus : so that 'as rich as

Damer' has become a proverb in the south of Ireland. An Irish peasant song-writer, philosophising on the vanity of riches, says :—

'There was ould Paddy Murphy had money galore,
And Damer of Shronell had twenty times more—
They are now on their backs under nettles and stones.'

Damer's house in ruins is still to be seen at Shronell, four miles west of Tipperary town. The story goes that he got his money by selling his soul to the devil for as much gold as would fill his boot—a top boot, i.e. one that reaches above the knee. On the appointed day the devil came with his pockets well filled with guineas and sovereigns, as much as he thought was sufficient to fill any boot. But mean-time Damer had removed the heel and fixed the boot in the floor, with a hole in the boards under-neath, opening into the room below. The devil flung in handful after handful till his pockets were empty, but still the boot was not filled. He then sent out a signal, such as they understand in hell—for they had wireless telegraphy there long before Mr. Marconi's Irish mother was born—on which a crowd of little imps arrived all laden with gold coins, which were emptied into the boot, and still no sign of its being filled. He had to send them many times for more, till at last he succeeded in filling *the room beneath* as well as the boot ; on which the transaction was concluded. The legend does not tell what became of Damer in the end ; but such agreements usually wind up (in Ireland) by the sinner tricking Satan out of his bargain.

When a person does an evil deed under cover of some untruthful but plausible justification, or utters a wicked saying under a disguise: that's 'blind-folding the devil in the dark.' The devil is as cute in the dark as in the light: and blindfolding him is useless and foolish : he is only laughing at you.

'You're a very coarse Christian,' as the devil said to the hedgehog.   (Tyrone.)

The name and fame of the great sixteenth-century magician, Dr. Faust or Faustus, found way somehow to our peasantry ; for it was quite common to hear a crooked knavish man spoken of in this way :—' That fellow is a match for the devil and *Dr. Fosther.*' (Munster.)

The magpie has seven drops of the devil's blood in its body: the water-wagtail has three drops. (Munster.)

When a person is unusually cunning, cute, and tricky, we say 'The devil is a poor scholar to you.' (' Poor scholar ' here means a bad shallow scholar.)

'Now since James is after getting all the money, *the devil can't howld him* ' : i.e. he has grown proud and overbearing.

' *Firm and ugly*, as the devil said when he sewed his breeches with gads.'   Here is how it happened. The devil was one day pursuing the soul of a sinner across country, and in leaping over a rough thorn hedge, he tore his breeches badly, so that his tail stuck out ; on which he gave up the chase.   As it was not decent to appear in public in that condition, he sat down and stitched up the rent with next to hand materials—viz. slender tough osier withes or *gads* as we call them in Ireland.   When the job was finished he spread out the garment before him on his knees, and looking admiringly on his handiwork, uttered the above saying—'Firm and ugly!'

The idea of the 'old boy' pursuing a soul appears also in the words of an old Anglo-Irish song about persons who commit great crimes and die unrepentant :—

> 'For committing those crimes unrepented
> The devil shall after them run,
> And slash him for that at a furnace
> Where coal sells for nothing a ton.'

A very wet day—teeming rain—raining cats and dogs—*a fine day for young ducks*:—'The devil wouldn't send out his dog on such a day as this.'

> 'Did you ever see the devil
> With the wooden spade and shovel
> Digging praties for his supper
> And his tail cocked up?'

A person struggling with poverty—constantly in money difficulties—is said to be 'pulling the devil by the tail.'

'Great noise and little wool,' as the devil said when he was shearing a pig.

'What's got over the devil's back goes off under the devil's belly.' This is another form of *ill got ill gone*.

Don't enter on a lawsuit with a person who has in his hands the power of deciding the case. This would be 'going to law against the devil with the courthouse in hell.'

Jack hates that man and all belonging to him 'as the devil hates holy water.'

Yerra or *arrah* is an exclamation very much in use in the South : a phonetic representation of the Irish *airĕ*, meaning *take care, look out, look you* :—'Yerra

Bill why are you in such a hurry?' The old people didn't like our continual use of the word; and in order to deter us we were told that *Yerra* or *Arrah* was the name of the devil's mother! This would point to something like domestic conditions in the lower regions, and it is in a way corroborated by the words of an old song about a woman—a desperate old reprobate of a virago—who kicked up all sorts of ructions the moment she got inside the gate :—

> ' When she saw the *young devils* tied up in their chains
> She up with her crutch and knocked one of their brains.'

'Sufficient for the day is the evil thereof.' The people of Munster do not always put it that way; they have a version of their own :—' Time enough to bid the devil good-morrow when you meet him.' But an intelligent correspondent from Carlow puts a somewhat different interpretation on the last saying, namely, ' Don't go out of your way to seek trouble.'

' When needs must the devil drives ': a man in a great fix is often driven to illegal or criminal acts to extricate himself.

When a man is threatened with a thrashing, another will say to him :—' You'll get Paddy Ryan's supper—*hard knocks and the devil to eat* ': common in Munster.

' When you sup with the devil have a long spoon ': that is to say, if you have any dealings with rogues or criminals, adopt very careful precautions, and don't come into closer contact with them than is absolutely necessary. (Lover: but used generally.)

' Speak the truth and shame the devil' is a very common saying.

' The devil's children have the devil's luck '; or ' the devil is good to his own ' : meaning bad men often prosper. But it is now generally said in joke to a person who has come in for an unexpected piece of good luck.

A holy knave—something like our modern Pecksniff—dies and is sent in the downward direction : and—according to the words of the old folksong—this is his reception :—

> ' When hell's gate was opened the devil jumped with joy,
>   Saying "I have a warm corner for you my holy boy." '

A man is deeply injured by another and threatens reprisal :—' I'll make you smell hell for that ' ; a bitter threat which may be paraphrased : I'll persecute you to death's door; and for you to be near death is to be near hell—I'll put you so near that you'll smell the fumes of the brimstone.

A usual imprecation when a person who has made himself very unpopular is going away: ' the devil go with him.'   One day a fellow was eating his dinner of dry potatoes, and had only one egg half raw for *kitchen*.   He had no spoon, and took the egg in little sips intending to spread it over the dinner. But one time he tilted the shell too much, and down went the whole contents.   After recovering from the gulp, he looked ruefully at the empty shell and blurted out— *the devil go with you down !*

Many people think—and say it too—that it is an article of belief with Catholics that all Protestants when they die go straight to hell—which is a libel. Yet it is often kept up in joke, as in this and other

stories :—The train was skelping away like mad
along the main line to hell—for they have railways
there now—till at last it pulled up at the junction.
Whereupon the porters ran round shouting out,
' Catholics change here for purgatory : Protestants
keep your places ! '

This reminds us of Father O'Leary, a Cork priest
of the end of the eighteenth century, celebrated as
a controversialist and a wit. He was one day
engaged in gentle controversy—or *argufying religion*
as we call it in Ireland—with a Protestant friend,
who plainly had the worst of the encounter. ' Well
now Father O'Leary I want to ask what have you
to say about purgatory ? ' ' Oh nothing,' replied the
priest, ' except that you might go farther and fare
worse.'

The same Father O'Leary once met in the streets a
friend, a witty Protestant clergyman with whom he had
many an encounter of wit and repartee. ' Ah Father
O'Leary, have you heard the bad news ? '   ' No,'
says Father O'Leary. ' Well, the bottom has fallen
out of purgatory, and all the poor Papists have gone
down into hell.' ' Oh the Lord save us,' answered
Father O'Leary, ' what a crushing the poor Protestants must have got ! '

Father O'Leary and Curran—the great orator and
wit—sat side by side once at a dinner party, where
Curran was charmed with his reverend friend. ' Ah
Father O'Leary,' he exclaimed at last, ' I wish you
had the key of heaven.' ' Well Curran it might be
better for you that I had the key of the other place.'

A parish priest only recently dead, a well-known
wit, sat beside a venerable Protestant clergyman at

dinner; and they got on very agreeably. This clergyman rather ostentatiously proclaimed his liberality by saying:—'Well Father —— I have been for *sixty years in this world* and I could never understand that there is any great and essential difference between the Catholic religion and the Protestant.' 'I can tell you,' replied Father ——, 'that when you die you'll not be *sixty minutes in the other world* before you will understand it perfectly.'

The preceding are all in joke: but I once heard the idea enunciated in downright earnest. In my early life, we, the village people, were a mixed community, about half and half Catholics and Protestants, the latter nearly all Palatines, who were Methodists to a man. We got on very well together, and I have very kindly memories of my old playfellows, Palatines as well as Catholics.

One young Palatine, Peter Stuffle, differed in one important respect from the others, as he never attended Church Mass or Meeting. He emigrated to America; and being a level headed fellow and keeping from drink, he got on. At last he came across Nelly Sullivan, a bright eyed colleen all the way from Kerry, a devoted Catholic, and fell head and ears in love with her. She liked him too, but would have nothing to say to him unless he became a Catholic: in the words of the old song, 'Unless that you turn a *Roman* you ne'er shall get me for your bride.' Peter's theology was not proof against Nelly's bright face: he became a Catholic, and a faithful one too: for once he was inside the gate his wife took care to instruct him, and kept him well up to his religious duties.

F

They prospered; so that at the end of some years
he was able to visit his native place. On his arrival
nothing could exceed the consternation and rage of
his former friends to find that instead of denouncing
the Pope, he was now a flaming papist : and they all
disowned and boycotted him. So he visited round
his Catholic neighbours who were very glad to
receive him. I was present at one of the conversa-
tions : when Peter, recounting his successful career,
wound up with :—' So you see, James, that I am now
well off, thanks be to God and to Nelly. I have a large
farm, with ever so many horses, and a fine *baan* of
cows, and you could hardly count the sheep and pigs.
I'd be as happy as the days are long now, James,
only for one thing that's often troubling me ; and
that is, to think that my poor old father and mother
are in hell.'

CHAPTER VI.

SWEARING.

THE general run of our people do not swear much ;
and those that do commonly limit themselves to the
name of the devil either straight out or in some of
its various disguised forms, or to some harmless
imitation of a curse. You do indeed come across
persons who go higher, but they are rare. Yet
while keeping themselves generally within safe
bounds, it must be confessed that many of the
people have a sort of· sneaking admiration—lurking
secretly and seldom expressed in words—for a good
well-balanced curse, so long as it does not shock by
its profanity. I once knew a doctor—not in Dublin

—who, it might be said, was a genius in this line. He could, on the spur of the moment, roll out a magnificent curse that might vie with a passage of the Iliad in the mouth of Homer. ' Oh sir '—as I heard a fellow say—' 'tis grand to listen to him when he's in a rage.' He was known as a skilled physician, and a good fellow in every way, and his splendid swearing crowned his popularity. He had discretion however, and knew when to swear and when not ; but ultimately he swore his way into an extensive and lucrative practice, which lasted during his whole life—a long and honourable one.

Parallel to this is Maxwell's account of the cursing of Major Denis O'Farrell—' the Mad Major,' who appears to have been a dangerous rival to my acquaintance, the doctor. He was once directing the evolutions at a review in presence of Sir Charles, the General, when one important movement was spoiled by the blundering of an incompetent little adjutant. In a towering passion the Mad Major addressed the General :—' Stop, Sir Charles, do stop ; just allow me two minutes to curse that rascally adjutant.' To so reasonable a request (Maxwell goes on to say), Sir Charles readily assented. He heard the whole malediction out, and speaking of it afterwards, he said that ' he never heard a man cursed to his perfect satisfaction until he heard (that adjutant) anathematised in the Phoenix Park.'

The Mad Major was a great favourite ; and when he died, there was not a dry eye in the regiment on the day of the funeral. Two months afterwards when an Irish soldier was questioned on the merits of his successor :—' The man is well enough,' said Pat,

with a heavy sigh, ' but where will we find the equal
of the Major ? By japers, it was a comfort to be
cursed by him !'   (' Wild Sports of the West.')

In my part of the country there is—or was—a
legend—a very circumstantial one too—which however I am not able to verify personally, as the thing
occurred a little before my time—that Father Buckley,
of Glenroe, cured Charley Coscoran, the greatest
swearer in the barony—cured him in a most original
way. He simply directed him to cut out a button
from some part of his dress, no matter where—
to whip it out on the instant—every time he uttered a
serious curse, i.e, one involving the Sacred Name.
Charley made the promise with a light heart,
thinking that by only using a little caution he could
easily avoid snipping off his buttons. But inveterate
habit is strong. Only very shortly after he had left
the priest he saw a cow in one of his cornfields
playing havoc : out came a round curse, and off came
a button on the spot. For Charley was a manly
fellow, with a real sense of religion at bottom : and
he had no notion of shirking his penance. Another
curse after some time and another button. Others
again followed :—coat, waistcoat, trousers, shirt-
collar, were brought under contribution till his clothes
began to fall off him. For a needle and thread were
not always at hand, and at any rate Charley was no
great shakes at the needle. At last things came to
that pass with poor Charley, that life was hardly
worth living ; till he had to put his mind seriously
to work, and by careful watching he gradually cured
himself. But many score buttons passed through
his hands during the process.

Most persons have a sort of craving or instinct to utter a curse of some kind—as a sort of comforting interjection—where there is sufficient provocation ; and in order to satisfy this without incurring the guilt, people have invented ejaculations in the form of curses, but still harmless. Most of them have some resemblance in sound to the forbidden word— they are near enough to satisfy the craving, but still far enough off to avoid the guilt : the process may in fact be designated *dodging a curse*. Hence we have such blank cartridges as *begob, begor,* by my *sowkins,* by *Jove,* by the *laws* [Lord], by *herrings* [heavens], by *this and by that, dang* it, &c. ; all of them ghosts of curses, which are very general among our people. The following additional examples will sufficiently illustrate this part of our subject.

The expression *the dear knows* (or correctly *the deer knows*), which is very common, is a translation from Irish of one of those substitutions. The original expression is *thauss ag Dhee* [given here phonetically], meaning *God knows*; but as this is too solemn and profane for most people, they changed it to *Thauss ag fee,* i.e. *the deer knows* ; and this may be uttered by anyone. *Dia* [Dhee] God : *fiadh* [fee], a deer.

Says Barney Broderick, who is going through his penance after confession at the station, and is interrupted by a woman asking him a question :— ' Salvation seize your soul—God forgive me for cursing—be off out of that and don't set me astray ! ' (' Knocknagow.') Here the substitution has turned a wicked imprecation into a benison : for the first word in the original is not *salvation* but *damnation.*

'By the hole in my coat,' which is often heard,
is regarded as a harmless oath : for if there is no
hole you are swearing by nothing : and if there is a
hole—still the hole is nothing.

'Bad manners to you,' a mild imprecation, to
avoid 'bad luck to you,' which would be considered
wicked : reflecting the people's horror of rude or
offensive manners.

'By all the goats in Kerry,' which I have often
heard, is always said in joke, which takes the venom
out of it. In Leinster they say, 'by all the goats
in Gorey '—which is a big oath. Whether it is a big
oath now or not, I do not know ; but it was so
formerly, for the name *Gorey* (Wexford), like the
Scotch *Gowrie*, means ' swarming with goats.'

'Man,' says the pretty mermaid to Dick Fitzgerald, when he had captured her from the sea,
'man will you eat me ? ' ' *By all the red petticoats
and check aprons between Dingle and Tralee,*' cried
Dick, jumping up in amazement, ' I'd as soon eat
myself, my jewel ! Is it I to eat you, my pet ! '
(Crofton Croker.)

'Where did he get the whiskey ? ' 'Sorrow a
know I know,' said Leary. 'Sorrow fly away with
him.' (Crofton Croker.) In these and such like—
which you often hear—*sorrow* is a substitute for *devil*.

Perhaps the most general exclamations of this
kind among Irish people are *begor, begob, bedad,
begad* (often contracted to *egad*), *faith* and *troth*.
Faith, contracted from *in faith* or *i' faith*, is looked
upon by many people as not quite harmless : it is a
little too serious to be used indiscriminately—' Faith
I feel this day very cold ': ' Is that tea good ? '

'Faith it is no such thing : it is very weak.'　'Did Mick sell his cows to-day at the fair ?'　'Faith I don't know.'　People who shrink from the plain word often soften it to *faix* or *haith* (or *heth* in Ulster).　An intelligent contributor makes the remark that the use of this word *faith* (as above) is a sure mark of an Irishman all over the world.

Even some of the best men will occasionally, in an unguarded moment or in a hasty flash of anger, give way to the swearing instinct.　Father John Burke of Kilfinane—I remember him well—a tall stern-looking man with heavy brows, but really gentle and tender-hearted—held a station at the house of our neighbour Tom Coffey, a truly upright and pious man.　All had gone to confession and Holy Communion, and the station was over.　Tom went out to bring the priest's horse from the paddock, but in leading him through a gap in the hedge the horse stood stock still and refused obstinately to go an inch farther.　Tom pulled and tugged to no purpose, till at last his patience went to pieces, and he flung this, in no gentle voice, at the animal's head :—'Blast your *sowl* will you come on !'　Just then unluckily Father Burke walked up behind : he had witnessed and heard all, and you may well say that Tom's heart dropped down into his shoes ; for he felt thoroughly ashamed.　The crime was not great ; but it looked bad and unbecoming under the circumstances ; and what could the priest do but perform his duty : so the black brows contracted, and on the spot he gave poor Tom *down-the-banks* and no mistake.　I was at that station, though I did not witness the horse scene.

If a person pledges himself to anything, clinching the promise with an adjuration however mild or harmless, he will not by any means break the promise, considering it in a manner as a vow. The old couple are at tea and have just one egg, which causes a mild dispute. At last the father says decisively—'The divel a bit of it I'll eat, so there's an end of it': when the mother instantly and with great solemnity—'FAITH I won't eat it—there now!' The result was that neither would touch it; and they gave it to their little boy who demolished it without the least scruple.

I was one time a witness of a serio-comic scene *on the head of* one of these blank oaths when I was a small boy attending a very small school. The master was a truly good and religious man, but very severe (a *wicked* master, as we used to say), and almost insane in his aversion to swearing in any shape or form. To say *begob* or *begor* or *by Jove* was unpardonably wicked; it was nothing better than blindfolding the devil in the dark.

One day Jack Aimy, then about twelve years of age—*the saint* as we used to call him—for he was always in mischief and always in trouble—said exultingly to the boy sitting next him :—'Oh *by the hokey*, Tom, I have my sum finished all right at last.' In evil hour for him the master happened to be standing just behind his back; and then came the deluge. In an instant the school work was stopped, and poor Jack was called up to stand before the judgment seat. There he got a long lecture— with the usual quotations—as severe and solemn as if he were a man and had perjured himself half a dozen times. As for the rest of us, we sat in the deadly silence shivering in our skins; for we all, to a man, had a guilty consciousness that we were quite as bad as Jack, if the truth were known. Then poor Jack was sent to his seat so wretched and crestfallen after his lecture that a crow wouldn't pick his bones.

'By the hokey' is to this day common all over Ireland.

When we, Irish, go abroad, we of course bring with us our peculiarities and mannerisms—with now and then a little meteoric flash of eccentricity— which on the whole prove rather attractive to foreigners, including Englishmen. One Sunday during the South African war, Mass was celebrated as usual in the temporary chapel, which, after the rough and ready way of the camp, served for both Catholics and Protestants: Mass first; Protestant Service after. On this occasion an Irish officer, a splendid specimen of a man, tall, straight, and athletic—a man born to command, and well known as a strict and devoted Catholic—was serving Mass—aiding and giving the responses to the priest. The congregation was of course of mixed nationalities—English, Irish, and Scotch, and the chapel was filled. Just outside the chapel door a nigger had charge of the big bell to call the congregations. On this day, in blissful ignorance and indifference, he began to ring for the Protestant congregation too soon—while Mass was still going on—so as greatly to disturb the people at their devotions. The officer was observed to show signs of impatience, growing more and more restless as the ringing went on persistently, till at last one concentrated series of bangs burst up his patience utterly. Starting up from his knees during a short interval when his presence was not required—it happened to be after the most solemn part of the Mass—he strode down the middle passage in a mighty rage—to the astonishment of everybody—till he got to the door, and letting fly—in the midst of the perfect silence, —a tremendous volley of *damns*, *blasts*, *scoundrels*, *blackguards*, &c., &c., at the head of the terrified nigger, he shut him up, himself and his bell, while a cat would be licking her ear. He then walked back and resumed his duties, calm and collected, and evidently quite unconscious that there was anything unusual in the proceeding.

The whole thing was so sudden and odd that the congregation were convulsed with suppressed silent laughter ; and I am afraid that some people observed even the priest's sides shaking in spite of all he could do.

This story was obtained from a person who was present at that very Mass ; and it is given here almost in his own words.

CHAPTER VII.

GRAMMAR AND PRONUNCIATION.

Shall and *Will*. It has been pretty clearly shown that the somewhat anomalous and complicated niceties in the English use of *shall* and *will* have been developed within the last 300 years or so. It is of course well known that our Irish popular manner of using these two particles is not in accordance with the present correct English standard ; yet most of our shall-and-will Hibernianisms represent the classical usage of two or three centuries ago : so that this is one of those Irish 'vulgarisms' that are really survivals in Ireland of the correct old English usages, which in England have been superseded by other and often incorrect forms. On this point I received, some years ago, a contribution from an English gentleman who resided long in Ireland, Mr. Marlow Woollett, a man of wide reading, great culture, and sound judgment. He gives several old examples in illustration, of which one is so much to the point—in the use of *will*—that you might imagine the words were spoken by an Irish peasant of the present day. Hamlet says :

'I will win for him an (if) I can ; if not I *will* gain nothing but my shame and the odd hits.' ('Hamlet,' Act v., scene ii.)

This (the second *will*) exactly corresponds with what many of us in Ireland would say now :—'I will win the race if I can ; if not I *will* get some discredit' : 'If I go without my umbrella I am afraid I will get wet.' So also in regard to *shall* ; modern English custom has departed from correct ancient usage and etymology, which in many cases we in Ireland have retained. The old and correct sense of *shall* indicated obligation or duty (as in Chaucer :—'The faith I shal to God ') being derived from A.S. *sceal* 'I owe ' or 'ought' : this has been discarded in England, while we still retain it in our usage in Ireland. You say to an attentive Irish waiter, 'Please have breakfast for me at 8 o'clock to-morrow morning ' ; and he answers, 'I shall sir.' When I was a boy I was present in the chapel of Ardpatrick one Sunday, when Father Dan O'Kennedy, after Mass, called on the two schoolmasters—candidates for a school vacancy—to come forward to him from where they stood at the lower end of the chapel; when one of them, Mat Rea, a good scholar but a terrible pedant, called out magniloquently, 'Yes, doctor, we SHALL go to your reverence,' unconsciously following in the footsteps of Shakespeare.

The language both of the waiter and of Mat Rea is exactly according to the old English usage.

'*Lady Macbeth* (*to Macbeth*):—Be bright and jovial among your
    guests to-night.
'*Macbeth*:—So shall I, love.'   ('Macbeth,' Act iii. scene ii.)

'*Second Murderer* :— We shall, my lord,
        Perform what you command us.'   (*Ibid.*, Act iii. scene i.)

But the Irish waiter's answer would now seem strange to an Englishman. To him, instead of being a dutiful assent, as it is intended to be, and as it would be in England in old times, it would look too emphatic and assertive, something like as if it were an answer to a command *not* to do it.   (Woollett.)

The use of *shall* in such locutions was however not universal in Shakespearian times, as it would be easy to show; but the above quotations—and others that might be brought forward—prove that this usage then prevailed and was correct, which is sufficient for my purpose. Perhaps it might rather be said that *shall* and *will* were used in such cases indifferently :—

    '*Queen* :—Say to the king, I would attend his leisure
    For a few words.
    '*Servant*: Madam, I will.'   ('Macbeth,' Act iii. scene ii.)

Our use of *shall* and *will* prevails also in Scotland, where the English change of custom has not obtained any more than it has in Ireland. The Scotch in fact are quite as bad (or as good) in this respect as we are. Like many another Irish idiom this is also found in American society chiefly through the influence of the Irish. In many parts of Ireland they are shy of using *shall* at all : I know this to be the case in Munster ; and a correspondent informs me that *shall* is hardly ever heard in Derry.

The incorrect use of *will* in questions in the first person singular (' Will I light the fire ma'am ?' ' Will I sing you a song ?'—instead of ' Shall I ?') appears to have been developed in Ireland independently, and not derived from any former correct usage : in other words we have created this incorrect locution—or vulgarism—for ourselves. It is one of our most general and most characteristic speech errors. *Punch* represents an Irish waiter with hand on dish-cover, asking :—' Will I sthrip ma'am ?'

What is called the *regular* formation of the past tense (in *ed*) is commonly known as the weak inflection :—*call, called* : the *irregular* formation (by changing the vowel) is the strong inflection :—*run, ran.* In old English the strong inflection appears to have been almost universal; but for some hundreds of years the English tendency is to replace strong by weak inflection. But our people in Ireland, retaining the old English custom, have a leaning towards the strong inflection, and not only use many of the old-fashioned English strong past tenses, but often form strong ones in their own way :—We use *slep* and *crep*, old English ; and we coin others. ' He *ruz* his hand to me,' 'I *cotch* him stealing the turf,' 'he *gother* sticks for the fire,' 'he *hot* me on the head with his stick,' he *sot* down on the chair' (very common in America). Hyland, the farm manager, is sent with some bullocks to the fair; and returns. 'Well Hyland, are the bullocks sold?'—'Sowld and *ped* for sir.' *Wor* is very usual in the south for *were* : 'tis long since we *wor* on the road so late as this.' (Knocknagow.)

> ' *Wor* you at the fair—did you see the wonder—
> Did you see Moll Roe riding on the gander?'

E'er and *ne'er* are in constant use in Munster :— 'Have you e'er a penny to give me sir? No, I have ne'er a penny for you this time.' Both of these are often met with in Shakespeare.

The Irish schoolmasters knew Irish well, and did their best — generally with success — to master English. This they did partly from their neighbours, but in a large measure from books, including dictionaries. As they were naturally inclined to show forth their learning, they made use, as much as possible, of long and unusual words, mostly taken from dictionaries, but many coined by themselves from Latin. Goldsmith's description of the village master with his 'words of learned length and thundering sound,' applies exactly to a large proportion of the schoolmasters of the eighteenth and first half of the nineteenth century all over Ireland. You heard these words often in conversation, but the schoolmasters most commonly used them in song-writing. Here also they made free use of the classical mythology; but I will not touch on this feature, as I have treated of it, and have given specimens, in my ' Old Irish Folk Music and Songs,' pp. 200–202.

As might be expected, the schoolmasters, as well as others, who used these strange words often made mistakes in applying them ; which will be seen in some of the following examples. Here is one whole verse of a song about a young lady—' The Phoenix of the Hall.'

> ' I being quite captivated and so infatuated
> I then prognosticated my sad forlorn case ;
> But I quickly ruminated—suppose I was *defaited,*
> I would not be implicated or treated with disgrace ;
> So therefore I awaited with my spirits elevated,
> And no more I ponderated let what would me befall ;
> I then to her *repated* how Cupid had me *thrated,*
> And thus expostulated with The Phoenix of the Hall.'

In another verse of this song the poet tells us what he might do for the Phoenix if he had greater command of language :—

> ' Could I indite like Homer that celebrated *pomer.'*

One of these schoolmasters, whom I knew, composed a poem in praise of Queen Victoria just after her accession, of which I remember only two lines :—

> ' In England our queen resides with *alacrity,*
> With civil authority and kind urbanity.'

Another opens his song in this manner :—

> ' One morning serene as I roved in solitude,
> Viewing the magnitude of th' orient ray.

The author of the song in praise of Castlehyde speaks of

> ' The bees *perfuming* the fields with music ' ;

and the same poet winds up by declaring,

> ' In all my ranging and *serenading*
> I met no *aiquel* to Castlehyde.'

Serenading here means wandering about leisurely.

The author of ' The Cottage Maid ' speaks of the danger of Mercury abducting the lady, even

> ' Though an *organising* shepherd be her guardian ' ;

where *organising* is intended to mean playing on an *organ*, i.e. a shepherd's reed.

But endless examples of this kind might be given.

Occasionally you will find the peasantry attempting long or unusual words, of which some examples are scattered through this chapter ; and here also there are often misapplications : ' What had you for dinner to-day ? ' ' Oh I had bacon and goose and several other *combustibles*' (comestibles). I have repeatedly heard this word.

Sometimes the simple past tense is used for one of the subjunctive past forms. ' If they had gone out in their boat that night they were lost men ' ; i.e. ' they would have been lost men.' ' She is now forty, and 'twas well if she was married' (' it would be well ').

> ' Oh Father Murphy, had aid come over, the green flag floated
> from shore to shore '

(i.e. would have floated). See my ' Old Irish Folk Music and Songs,' p. 242.

> ' A summons from William to Limerick, a summons to open their
> gate,
> Their fortress and stores to surrender, else the sword and the gun
> *were* their fate.'
>   (R. D. Joyce : Ballads of Irish Chivalry, p. 15.)

See is very often used for *saw* :—' Did you ever see a cluricaun Molly ?' Oh no sir, I never see one myself.' (Crofton Croker.)   ' Come here Nelly, and point out the bride to us.'   ' I never see her myself Miss [so I don't know her] replied Nelly. (Knocknagow.) This is a survival from old English, in which it was very common.   It is moreover general among the English peasantry at the present day, as may be seen everywhere in Dickens.

The imperative of verbs is often formed by *let* :— instead of ' go to the right ' or ' go you to the right,' our people say ' let you go to the right ' : ' let you look after the cows and I will see to the horses.'   A fellow is arrested for a crime and dares the police with :—' Let ye prove it.'

In Derry porridge or stirabout always takes the plural : ' Have you dished *them* yet ? '

' I didn't go to the fair *'cause why*, the day was too wet.'   This expression *'cause why*, which is very often heard in Ireland, is English at least 500 years old : for we find it in Chaucer.

You often hear *us* for *me* : ' Give us a penny sir to buy sweets ' (i.e. ' Give me ').

In Waterford and South Wexford the people often use such verbal forms as is seen in the following :— ' Does your father grow wheat still ? '   ' He *do*.' ' Has he the old white horse now ? '   ' He *have*.'   As to *has*, Mr. MacCall states that it is unknown in the barony of Forth : there you always hear ' that man *have* plenty of money '—he *have*—she *have*, &c.

The Rev. William Burke tells us that *have* is found as above (a third person singular) all through the old Waterford Bye-Laws ; which would render it

pretty certain that both *have* and *do* in these applications are survivals from the old English colony in
Waterford and Wexford.

In Donegal and thereabout *the yon* is often shortened
to *thon*, which is used as equivalent to *that* or *those* :
' you may take *thon* book.'

In Donegal ' such a thing ' is often made *such an a
thing*.'   I have come across this several times : but
the following quotation is decisive—' No, Dinny
O'Friel, I don't want to make you say any such an
a thing.'   (Seamus MacManus.)

There is a tendency to put *o* at the end of some
words, such as boy-o, lad-o.   A fellow was tried for
sheep-stealing before the late Judge Monahan, and
the jury acquitted him, very much against the
evidence.   ' You may go now,' said the judge, ' as
you are acquitted ; but you stole the sheep all the
same, my buck-o.'

> ' I would hush my lovely laddo
>   In the green arbutus shadow.'
>   (A. P. Graves : ' Irish Songs and Ballads.')

This is found in Irish also, as in ' *a vick-o* ' (' my
boy,' or more exactly ' my son,' where *vick* is *mhic*,
vocative of *mac*, son) heard universally in Munster :
' Well Billy a vick-o, how is your mother this
morning ? '   I suppose the English practice is borrowed from the Irish.

In Irish there is only one article, *an*, which is
equivalent to the English definite article *the*.   This
article (*an*) is much more freely used in Irish than
the is in English, a practice which we are inclined to
imitate in our Anglo-Irish speech.   Our use of *the*

often adds a sort of emphasis to the noun or adjective :—' Ah John was the man,' i.e. the real man, a man pre-eminent for some quality—bravery, generosity, &c. 'Ah that was the trouble in earnest.' The Irish chiefs of long ago 'were the men in the gap' (Thomas Davis) :—i.e. the real men and no mistake. We often use the article in our speech where it would not be used in correct English :— ' I am perished with *the* cold.' ' I don't know much Greek, but I am good at *the* Latin.'

' That was the dear journey to me.' A very common form of expression, signifying that 'I paid dearly for it '—' it cost me dear.' Hugh Reynolds when about to be hanged for attempting the abduction of Catherine McCabe composes (or is supposed to compose) his 'Lamentation,' of which the verses end in 'She's the dear maid to me.' (See my ' Old Irish Folk Music and Songs,' p. 135.) A steamer was in danger of running down a boat rowed by one small boy on the Shannon. ' Get out of the way you young rascal or we'll run over you and drown you!' Little Jacky looks up defiantly and cries out :—' Ye'll drownd me, will ye : if ye do, I'll make it the dear drownding to ye!' In such expressions it is however to be observed that the indefinite article *a* is often used—perhaps as often as *the* :—' That was a dear transaction for me.' ' Oh, green-hilled pleasant Erin you're a dear land to me !' (Robert Dwyer Joyce's 'Ballads of Irish Chivalry,' p. 206.)

In Ulster they say :—' When are you going?' ' Oh I am going *the day*,' i.e. to-day. I am much better *the day* than I was yesterday. In this *the day* is merely a translation of the Irish word for to-day —*andiu*, where *an* is 'the' and *diu* a form of the Irish for 'day.'

The use of the singular of nouns instead of the plural after a numeral is found all through Ireland. Tom Cassidy our office porter—a Westmeath man— once said to me 'I'm in this place now forty-four year' : and we always use such expressions as *nine head of cattle*. A friend of mine, a cultivated and scholarly clergyman, always used phrases like 'that bookcase cost thirteen *pound*.' This is an old English survival. Thus in Macbeth we find 'this three mile.' But I think this phraseology has also come partly under the influence of our Gaelic in which *ten* and numerals that are multiples of *ten* always take the singular of nouns, as *tri-caogad laoch*, 'thrice fifty heroes'—lit. 'thrice fifty *hero*.'

In the south of Ireland *may* is often incorrectly used for *might*, even among educated people :—'Last week when setting out on my long train journey, I brought a book that I *may* read as I travelled along.' I have heard and read, scores of times, expressions of which this is a type—not only among the peasantry, but from newspaper correspondents, professors, &c.—and you can hear and read them from Munstermen to this day in Dublin.

In Ulster *till* is commonly used instead of *to* :— 'I am going *till* Belfast to-morrow' : in like manner *until* is used for *unto*.

There are two tenses in English to which there is nothing corresponding in Irish :—what is sometimes called the perfect—'I *have finished* my work'; and the pluperfect—'I *had finished* my work' [before you

arrived]. The Irish people in general do not use—
or know how to use—these in their English speech ;
but they feel the want of them, and use various
expedients to supply their places. The most common
of these is the use of the word *after* (commonly with
a participle) following the verb *to be.* Thus instead
of the perfect, as expressed above, they will say
' I am after finishing my work,' ' I am after my
supper.' (' Knocknagow.') ' I'm after getting the
lend of an American paper' (*ibid.*) ; and instead
of the pluperfect (as above) they will say ' I was
after finishing my work ' [before you arrived].
Neither of these two expressions would be understood by an Englishman, although they are universal
in Ireland, even among the higher and educated
classes.

This word *after* in such constructions is merely a
translation of the Irish *iar* or *a n-diaigh*—for both
are used in corresponding expressions in Irish.

But this is only one of the expedients for expressing the perfect tense. Sometimes they use the
simple past tense, which is ungrammatical, as our
little newsboy in Kilkee used to do : ' Why haven't
you brought me the paper ?' ' The paper didn't
come from the station yet sir.' Sometimes the
present progressive is used, which also is bad
grammar : ' I am sitting here waiting for you for
the last hour ' (instead of ' I have been sitting ').
Occasionally the *have* or *has* of the perfect (or the
had of the pluperfect) is taken very much in its
primary sense of having or possessing. Instead of
' You have quite distracted me with your talk,' the
people will say ' You have me quite distracted,' &c. :

'I have you found out at last.'   'The children had
me vexed.' (Jane Barlow.)

> 'And she is a comely maid
>   That has my heart betrayed.'
>   (Old Irish Folk-Song.)

> " .   .   .   .   .   .   I fear,
> 'That some cruel goddess *has him captivated*,
>   And has left here in mourning his dear Irish maid.'
>   (See my Old Irish Folk Music and Songs, p. 208.)

Corresponding devices are resorted to for the
pluperfect. Sometimes the simple past is used
where the pluperfect ought to come in :—'An hour
before you came yesterday I finished my work':
where it should be 'I had finished.' Anything to avoid
the pluperfect, which the people cannot manage.

In the Irish language (but not in English) there
is what is called the consuetudinal tense, i.e. denoting habitual action or existence. It is a very
convenient tense, so much so that the Irish, feeling
the want of it in their English, have created one by
the use of the word *do* with *be* : 'I do be at my
lessons every evening from 8 to 9 o'clock.'   'There
does be a meeting of the company every Tuesday.'
' 'Tis humbuggin' me they *do be*.' (' Knocknagow.')

Sometimes this is expressed by *be* alone without
the *do* ; but here the *be* is also often used in the
ordinary sense of *is* without any consuetudinal
meaning. 'My father *bees* always at home in the
morning': 'At night while I *bees* reading my wife
bees knitting.' (Consuetudinal.)   'You had better
not wait till it bees night.' (Indicative.)

> 'I'll seek out my Blackbird wherever he be.' (Indicative.)
>   (Old Folk Song—' The Blackbird.')

This use of *be* for *is* is common in the eastern half of Ireland from Wexford to Antrim.

Such old forms as *anear*, *adown*, *afeard*, *apast*, *afore*, &c., are heard everywhere in Ireland, and are all of old English origin, as it would be easy to show by quotations from English classical writers. 'If my child was standing *anear* that stone.' (Gerald Griffin: 'Collegians.') 'She was never a-shy or ashamed to show' [her respect for me]. ('Knocknagow.') The above words are considered vulgar by our educated people: yet many others remain still in correct English, such as *aboard*, *afoot*, *amidst*, &c.

I think it likely that the Irish language has had some influence in the adoption and retention of those old English words; for we have in Irish a group of words identical with them both in meaning and structure: such as *a-n-aice* (a-near), where *aice* is 'near.' (The *n* comes in for a grammatical reason.)

'I be to do it' in Ulster is used to express 'I have to do it': 'I am bound to do it'; 'it is destined that I shall do it.' 'I be to remain here till he calls,' I am bound to remain. 'The only comfort I have [regarding some loss sure to come on] is that it be to be,' i.e. that 'it is fated to be'—'it is *unavoidable*.' 'What bees to be maun be' (must be).

Father William Burke points out that we use 'every other' in two different senses. He remains at home always on Monday, but goes to town 'every other' day—meaning every day of the week except Monday: which is the most usual application among us. 'My father goes to town every other day,' i.e.

every alternate day. This last is rarely used by our people, who prefer to express it 'My father goes to town *every second day.*' Of two persons it is stated :

> 'You'd like to see them drinking from one cup,
> They took so loving *every second sup.*'
> (Old Irish Folk Song.)

The simple phrase 'the other day' means a few days ago. 'When did you see your brother John ?' 'Oh I saw him the other day.'

> 'The other day he sailed away and parted his dear Nancy.'
> (Old Folk Song.)

The dropping of *thou* was a distinct loss to the English language : for now *you* has to do double duty—for both singular and plural—which some-times leads to obscurity. The Irish try to avoid this obscurity by various devices. They always use *ye* in the plural whenever possible : both as a nominative and as an objective: 'Where are ye going to-day ?' 'I'm afeard that will be a dear journey to ye.' Accepting the *you* as singular, they have created new forms for the plural such as *yous, yez, yiz*, which do not sound pleasant to a correct speaker, but are very clear in sense. In like manner they form a posses-sive case direct on *ye*. Some English soldiers are singing 'Lillibulero'—

> 'And our skeans we'll make good at de Englishman's throat,'

on which Cus Russed (one of the ambush) says— 'That's true for ye at any rate. I'm laughing at the way we'll carry out *yeer* song afore the day is over.' ('The House of Lisbloom,' by Robert D. Joyce.) Similarly '*weer* own' is sometimes used for 'our own.'

The distributive *every* requires to be followed by pronouns in the singular : but this rule is broken even by well-known English writers :—'Every one for themselves' occurs in Robinson Crusoe ; and in Ireland plurals are almost universally used. ' *Let every one mind themselves* as the ass said when he leaped into a flock of chickens.'

Father Burke has shown —a matter that had escaped me—that we often use the verbs *rest* and *perish* in an active sense. The first is seen in the very general Irish prayer 'God rest his soul.' Mangan uses the word in this sense in the Testament of Cathaeir Mór :—

> ' Here is the Will of Cathaeir Mór,
> God rest him.'

And John Keegan in ' Caoch O'Leary ' :—

> ' And there he sleeps his last sweet sleep—
> God rest you, Caoch O'Leary.'

Perish is quoted below in the saying—'That breeze would perish the Danes.'

We have many intensive words, some used locally, some generally :—' This is a *cruel* wet day '; ' that old fellow is *cruel* rich ': that's a *cruel* good man (where *cruel* in all means *very* : Ulster). ' That girl is *fine and fat* : her cheeks are *fine and red*.' ' I was *dead fond* of her ' (very fond) : but *dead certain* occurs in ' Bleak House.' 'That tree has a *mighty* great load of apples.' ' I want a drink badly ; my throat is *powerful* dry.' (' Shanahan's Ould Shebeen,' New York.) 'John Cusack is the finest dancer *at all*.' ' This day is *mortal* cold.' ' I'm *black out* with you.'

'I'm very glad *entirely* to hear it.'   'He is very sick *entirely*.'   This word *entirely* is one of our most general and characteristic intensives.   'He is a very good man *all out*.'   'This day is *guy and* wet': 'that boy is *guy and* fat' (Ulster).   A half fool of a fellow looking at a four-wheeled carriage in motion: 'Aren't the little wheels *damn good* not to let the big wheels overtake them.'   In the early days of cycling a young friend of mine was riding on a five-foot wheel past two countrymen; when one remarked to the other:—'Tim, that's a *gallows* way of travelling.' 'I was up *murdering* late last night.' (Crofton Croker.)

In the Irish language there are many diminutive terminations, all giving the idea of 'little,' which will be found fully enumerated and illustrated in my 'Irish Names of Places,' vol. ii, chap. ii.   Of these it may be said that only one—*in* or *een*—has found its way into Ireland's English speech, carrying with it its full sense of smallness.   There are others— *án* or *aun*, and *óg* or *oge*; but these have in great measure lost their original signification; and although we use them in our Irish-English, they hardly convey any separate meaning.   But *een* is used everywhere: it is even constantly tacked on to Christian names (especially of boys and girls):—*Mickeen* (little Mick), *Noreen, Billeen, Jackeen* (a word applied to the conceited little Dublin citizen).   So also you hear *Birdeen, Robineen*-redbreast, *bonniveen*, &c.   A boy who apes to be a man—puts on airs like a man—is called a *manneen* in contempt (exactly equivalent to the English *mannikin*).   I knew a boy named Tommeen Trassy: and the name stuck to him even when he was a great big whacker of a fellow six feet high. In the south this diminutive is long (*een*) and takes the accent : in the north it is made short (*in*) and is unaccented.

It is well known that three hundred years ago, and even much later, the correct English sound of the diphthong *ea* was the same as long *a* in *fate*: *sea* pronounced *say*, &c. Any number of instances could be brought together from the English poets in illustration of this:—

> ' God moves in a mysterious way,
>   His wonders to perform ;
> He plants His footsteps in the *sea*,
>   And rides upon the storm.'
>   (COWPER (18th century).)

This sound has long since been abandoned in England, but is still preserved among the Irish people. You will hear everywhere in Ireland, 'a pound of *mate*,' 'a cup of *tay*,' 'you're as deep as the *say*,' &c.

' Kind sir be *aisy* and do not *taize* me with your false *praises* most jestingly.'—(Old Irish Folk Song.)

(In this last line *easy* and *teaze* must be sounded so as to rhyme—assonantally—with *praises*).

Many years ago I was travelling on the long car from Macroom to Killarney. On the other side— at my back—sat a young gentleman—a ' superior person,' as anyone could gather from his *dandified* speech. The car stopped where he was to get off : a tall fine-looking old gentleman was waiting for him, and nothing could exceed the dignity and kindness with which he received him. Pointing to his car he said ' Come now and they'll get you a nice refreshing cup of *tay*.' ' Yes,' says the dandy, ' I shall be very glad to get a cup of *tee* '—laying a particular stress on *tee*. I confess I felt a shrinking of shame for our humanity. Now which of these two was the vulgarian ?

The old sound of *ea* is still retained—even in England—in the word *great*; but there was a long contest in the English Parliament over this word. Lord Chesterfield adopted the affected pronunciation (*greet*), saying that only an Irishman would call it *grate*. ' Single-speech Hamilton '—a Dublin man— who was considered, in the English House of Commons, a high authority on such matters, stoutly supported *grate*, and the influence of the Irish orators finally turned the scale. (Woollett.)

A similar statement may be made regarding the diphthong *ei* and long *e*, that is to say, they were both formerly sounded like long *a* in *fate*.

> ' Boast the pure blood of an illustrious race,
> In quiet flow from Lucrece to *Lucrece*.'
>
> (Pope: ' Essay on Man.')

In the same essay Pope rhymes *sphere* with *fair*, showing that he pronounced it *sphaire*. Our *hedge* schoolmaster did the same thing in his song :—

> Of all the maids on this terrestrial *sphaire*
> Young Molly is the fairest of the fair.

> ' The plots are fruitless which my foe
> Unjustly did *conceive* ;
> The pit he digg'd for me has proved
> His own untimely grave.'
>
> (Tate and Brady.)

Our people generally retain the old sounds of long *e* and *ei*; for they say *persaive* for perceive, and *sevare* for *severe*.

> ' The pardon he gave me was hard and *sevare*;
> 'Twas bind him, confine him, he's the rambler from Clare.'

Our Irish way of sounding both *ea* and long *e* is exemplified in what I heard a man say—a man who had some knowledge of Shakespeare—about a girl who was becoming somewhat of an old maid : 'She's now getting into the *sair* and *yellow laif*.'

Observe, the correct old English sound of *ie* and *ee* has not changed : it is the same at present in England as it was formerly; and accordingly the Irish people always sound these correctly. They never say *praste* for priest, *belave* for believe, *indade* for indeed, or *kape* for keep, as some ignorant writers set down.

Ate is pronounced *et* by the educated English. In Munster the educated people pronounce it *ait* : ' Yesterday I *ait* a good dinner'; and when *et* is heard among the uneducated—as it generally is—it is considered very vulgar.

It appears that in correct old English *er* was sounded *ar*—Dryden rhymes *certain* with *parting*— and this is still retained in correct English in a few words, like *sergeant*, *clerk*, &c. Our people retain the old sound in most such words, as *sarvant*, *marchant*, *sartin*. But sometimes in their anxiety to avoid this vulgarity, they overdo the refinement : so that you will hear girls talk mincingly about *derning* a stocking. This is like what happened in the case of one of our servant girls who took it into her head that

mutton was a vulgar way of pronouncing the word,
like *pudden'* for *pudding*; so she set out with her new
grand pronunciation; and one day rather astonished
our butcher by telling him she wanted a small leg of
mutting. I think this vulgarism is heard among the
English peasantry too: though we have the honour
and glory of evolving it independently.

All over Ireland you will hear the words *vault* and
fault sounded *vaut* and *faut*. ' If I don't be able to
shine it will be none of my *faut*.' (Carleton, as cited by
Hume.) We have retained this sound from old
English :

> Let him not dare to vent his dangerous thought :
> A noble fool was never in a *fault* [faut].
> > (POPE, cited by Hume.)

Goldsmith uses this pronunciation more than
once ; but whether he brought it from Ireland or
took it from classical English writers, by whom it
was used (as by Pope) almost down to his time, it is
hard to say. For instance in ' The Deserted Village '
he says of the Village Master :—

> ' Yet he was kind, or if severe in aught
> The love he bore to learning was in *fault* ' [faut].

I remember reading many years ago a criticism of
Goldsmith by a well-known Irish professor of English
literature, in which the professor makes great fun, as
a ' superior person,' of the *Hibernicism* in the above
couplet, evidently ignorant of the fact, which
Dr. Hume has well brought out, that it is classical
English.

In many parts of Munster there is a tendency to give the long *a* the sound of *a* in *car, father* :—

> Were I Paris whose deeds are *vaarious*
> And *arbithraather* on Ida's hill.
> (Old Folk Song—' The Colleen Rue.')*

> The *gladiaathers* both bold and darling,
> Each night and morning to watch the flowers.
> (Old Folk Song—' Castlehyde.')*

So, an intelligent peasant,—a born orator, but illiterate in so far as he could neither read nor write,—told me that he was a *spectaathor* at one of O'Connell's Repeal meetings : and the same man, in reply to a strange gentleman's inquiry as to who planted a certain wood up the hill, replied that the trees were not planted—they grew *spontaan-yus*.

I think this is a remnant of the old classical teaching of Munster : though indeed I ought to mention that the same tendency is found in Monaghan, where on every possible occasion the people give this sound to long *a*.

D before long *u* is generally sounded like *j* ; as in *projuce* for *produce* : the *Juke* of Wellington, &c. Many years ago I knew a fine old gentleman from Galway. He wished to make people believe that in the old fighting times, when he was a young man, he was a desperate *gladiaathor* ; but he really was a gentle creature who never in all his born days hurt man or mortal. Talking one day to some workmen in Kildare, and recounting his exploits, he told them

---

* For both of these songs see my ' Old Irish Folk Music and Songs.'

that he was now *harrished* every night by the ghosts of all the *min* he killed in *juels*.

So *s* before long *u* is sounded *sh*: Dan Kiely, a well-to-do young farmer, told the people of our neighbourhood that he was now looking out for a wife that would *shoot* him. This pronunciation is however still sometimes heard in words of correct English, as in *sure*.

There are some consonants of the Irish language which when they come together do not coalesce in sound, as they would in an English word, so that when they are uttered a very short obscure vowel sound is heard between them : and a native Irish speaker cannot avoid this. By a sort of hereditary custom this peculiarity finds its way into our pronunciation of English. Thus *firm* is sounded in Ireland *ferrum*—two distinct syllables : ' that bird is looking for a *wurrum*.' *Form* (a seat) we call a *furrum*.

> ' His sire he'd seek no more nor descend to Mammon's shore,
>   Nor venture on the tyrant's dire *alaa-rums*,
> But daily place his care on that emblematic fair,
>   Till he'd barter coronations for her *chaa-rums*.'
>
> (Old Folk Song.)*

Herb is sounded *errub* : and we make two syllables of the name Charles [Char-less]. At the time of the Bulgarian massacres, I knew a Dublin doctor, a Tipperary man, who felt very strongly on the subject and was constantly talking about the poor *Bullugarians*.

In the County Monaghan and indeed elsewhere

---

* See my ' Old Irish Folk Music and Songs,' p. 202.

in Ireland, *us* is sounded *huz*, which might seem
a Cockney vulgarism, but I think it is not. In
Roscommon and in the Munster counties a thong
is called a *fong*.

Chaw for *chew*, *oncet* [wonst] for *once*, *twiced* for
twice, and *heighth*, *sighth*, for *height*, *sight*, which are
common in Ireland, are all old English survivals.
Thus in the 'Faerie Queene' (Bk. I., Canto IV.,
XXX.) :—

> ' And next to him malicious Envy rode
> Upon a ravenous wolfe and still did *chaw*
> Between his cankred teeth a venomous tode.'

Chaw is also much used in America. ' *Onst* for
once is in the Chester Plays' (Lowell) ; and *highth* for
height is found all through ' Paradise Lost.' So also
we have *drooth* for *drought* :—

> ' Like other historians I'll stick to the truth
> While I sing of the monarch who died of the *drooth.*'
>   (SAM LOVER.)

Joist is sounded *joice* in Limerick ; and *catch* is
everywhere pronounced *ketch*.

The word *hither* is pronounced in Ireland *hether*,
which is the correct old English usage, but long
since abandoned in England. Thus in a State
Paper of 1598, we read that two captains returned
hether: and in Spenser's ' View,' he mentions a
' colony [sent] *hether* out of Spaine.'

> ' An errant knight or any other wight
> That *hether* turns his steps.'   (' Faerie Queene.')

Hence we have coined the word *comether*, for
come-hether, to denote a sort of spell brought about

H

by coaxing, wheedling, making love, &c.—as in the
phrase ' she put her *comether* on him, so that he
married her up at once.' ' There'll not be six girls in
the fair he'll not be putting the *comether* on.'
(Seumas MacManus.)

The family name ' Bermingham ' is always made
Brimmigem in Ireland, which is a very old English
corruption.   In Friar Clyn's Annals (Latin) written
in the fourteenth century, the death is recorded in
1329 of Johannes de *Brimegham*, i.e., the celebrated
Sir John Bermingham who defeated Edward Bruce
at Faughart.

Leap is pronounced *lep* by our people; and in
racing circles it is still so pronounced by all classes.
The little village of Leap in the County Cork is
always called *Lep*.

There is a curious tendency among us to reverse
the sounds of certain letters, as for instance *sh* and
ch.   ' When you're coming home to-morrow bring
the spade and *chovel*, and a pound of butter fresh
from the *shurn*.'   ' That *shimney* doesn't draw the
smoke well.'   So with the letters *u* and *i*.   ' When I
was crossing the *brudge* I dropped the sweeping *brish*
into the *ruvver*.'   ' I never saw *sich* a sight.'   But
such words are used only by the very uneducated.
Brudge for *bridge* and the like are however of old
English origin.   ' Margaret, mother of Henry VII,
writes *seche* for *such* ' (Lowell).   So in Ireland :—
' *Jestice* is all I ax,' says Mosy in the story (' Ir. Pen.
Mag.) ;   and *churries* for *cherries* (' Knocknagow ').
This tendency corresponds with the vulgar use of *h* in
London and elsewhere in England.   ' The 'en has
just laid a *hegg*' : ' he was singing My 'art's in the

'ighlands or The Brave Old *Hoak.*' (Washington Irving.)

Squeeze is pronounced *squeedge* and *crush scroodge* in Donegal and elsewhere ; but corruptions like these are found among the English peasantry—as may be seen in Dickens.

' You had better *rinsh* that glass ' is heard everywhere in Ireland : an old English survival; for Shakespeare and Lovelace have *renched* for *rinced* (Lowell) : which with the Irish sound of short *e* before *n* gives us our word *rinshed.*

Such words as *old, cold, hold* are pronounced by the Irish people *ould, cowld, hould* (or *howlt*); *gold* is sounded *goold* and *ford foord.* I once heard an old Wicklow woman say of some very rich people ' why these people could *ait goold.*' These are all survivals of the old English way of pronouncing such words. In the State Papers of Elizabeth's time you will constantly meet with such words as *hoult* and *stronghowlt* (hold and stronghold.) In my boyhood days I knew a great large sinewy active woman who lived up in the mountain gap, and who was universally known as ' Thunder the *cowlt* from Poulaflaikeen ' (*cowlt* for *colt*); Poulaflaikeen, the high pass between Glenosheen and Glenanaar, Co. Limerick, for which see Dr. R. D. Joyce's ' Ballads of Irish Chivalry,' pp. 102, 103, 120.

Old Tom Howlett, a Dublin job gardener, speaking to me of the management of fruit trees, recommended the use of butchers' waste. ' Ah sir '—said he, with a luscious roll in his voice as if he had been licking his lips—' Ah sir, there's nothing for the roots of an apple tree like a big tub of fine rotten *ould* guts.'

Final *d* is often omitted after *l* and *n* : you will
see this everywhere in Seumas MacManus's books for
Donegal. Recently we were told by the attendant
boy at one of the Dublin seaside baths that the prices
were—' a shilling for the hot and sixpence for the
cowl.' So we constantly use *an'* for *and* : in a
Waterford folk song we have ' Here's to the swan
that sails on the *pon* ' (the ' swan ' being the poet's
sweetheart) : and I once heard a man say to another
in a fair :—' That horse is sound in win' and
limb.'

Short *e* is always sounded before *n* and *m*, and
sometimes in other positions, like short *i*: ' How
many arrived?' ' *Tin min* and five women ': ' He
always smoked a pipe with a long *stim.*' If you
ask a person for a pin, he will inquire ' Is it a
brass pin or a writing *pin* you want ? '

Again is sounded by the Irish people *agin*, which
is an old English survival. ' Donne rhymes *again*
with *sin*, and Quarles repeatedly with *in.*' (Lowell.)
An Irishman was once landed on the coast of some
unknown country where they spoke English. Some
violent political dispute happened to be going on
there at the time, and the people eagerly asked the
stranger about his political views; on which—
instinctively giving expression to the feelings he
brought with him from the ' ould sod '—he promptly
replied before making any inquiry—' I'm agin the
Government.' This story, which is pretty well
known, is a faked one; but it affords us a good
illustration.

Onion is among our people always pronounced
ingion : constantly heard in Dublin. ' Go out Mike

for the *ingions*,' as I once heard a woman say in
Limerick.

> ' Men are of different opinions,
>   Some like leeks and some like *ingions*.'

This is old English ; ' in one of Dodsley's plays we
have *onions* rhyming with *minions*.' (Lowell.)

The general *English* tendency is to put back the
accent as far from the end of the word as possible.
But among our people there is a contrary tendency—
to throw forward the accent ; as in *ex-cel'lent*, his
Ex-cel'-lency—Nas-sau' Street (Dublin), Ar-bu'-tus,
commit-tee', her-e-dit'tary.

> ' Tele-mach'us though so grand ere the sceptre reached his
>   hand.' (Old Irish Folk Song.)

In Gough's Arithmetic there was a short section
on the laws of radiation and of pendulums. When
I was a boy I once heard one of the old schoolmasters
reading out, in his grandiloquent way, for the
people grouped round Ardpatrick chapel gate after
Mass, his formidable prospectus of the subjects he
could teach, among which were ' the *raddiation* of
light and heat and the vibrations of swinging *pen-
joo'lums*.' The same fine old scholarly pedant once
remarked that our neighbourhood was a very *moun-
taan'-yus* locality. A little later on in my life, when
I had written some pieces in high-flown English—
as young writers will often do—one of these
schoolmasters—a much lower class of man than the
last—said to me by way of compliment : 'Ah ! Mr.
Joyce, you have a fine *voca-bull'ery*.'

Mischievous is in the south accented on the second
syllable—*Mis-chee'-rous* : but I have come across this

in Spenser's Faerie Queene. We accent *character* on the second syllable :—

> ' Said he in a whisper to my benefactor,
> Though good your *charac'ter* has been of that lad.'
> (Song by Mr. Patrick Murray of Kilfinane,
> a schoolmaster of great ability : about 1840).

One of my school companions once wrote an ode in praise of Algebra, of which unfortunately I remember only the opening line : but this fragment shows how we pronounced the word in our old schools in the days of yore :—

> ' Hail sweet *al-jib'era*, you're my heart's delight.'

There is an Irish ballad about the people of Tipperary that I cannot lay my hands on, which speaks of the

> ' Tipperary boys,
> Although we are cross and *contrairy* boys ' ;

and this word ' contrairy ' is universal in Munster.

In Tipperary the vowel *i* is generally sounded *oi*. Mick Hogan a Tipperary boy—he was a man indeed—was a pupil in Mr. Condon's school in Mitchelstown, with the full rich typical accent. One morning as he walked in, a fellow pupil, Tom Burke —a big fellow too—with face down on desk over a book, said, without lifting his head—to make fun of him—'*foine* day, Mick.' ' Yes,' said Mick as he walked past, at the same time laying his hand on Tom's poll and punching his nose down hard against the desk.   Tom let Mick alone after that ' foine day.' Farther south, and in many places all over Ireland, they do the reverse :—' The kettle is *biling*' ;

> ' She smiled on me like the morning sky,
> And she won the heart of the prentice *bye*.'
> (Old Irish Folk Song.)

The old English pronunciation of *oblige* was *obleege* :—

> ' Dreaded by fools, by flatterers besieged,
> And so obliging that he ne'er obliged.'
>
> (POPE.)

Among the old-fashioned and better-educated of our peasantry you will still hear this old pronunciation preserved:—I am very much obleeged to you. It is now generally heard in Kildare among all classes. A similar tendency is in the sound of *whine*, which in Munster is always made *wheen*: ' What's that poor child *wheening* for ?' also everywhere heard :—' All danger [of the fever] is now past : he is over his *creesis*.'

Metathesis, or the changing of the place of a letter or syllable in a word, is very common among the Irish people, as *cruds* for *curds*, *girn* for *grin*, *purty* for *pretty*. I heard a man quoting from Shakespeare about Puck—from hearsay : he said he must have been a wonderful fellow, for he could put a *griddle* round about the earth in forty minutes.' I knew a fellow that could never say *traveller* : it was always *throlliver*.

There is a tendency here as elsewhere to shorten many words : You will hear *garner* for *gardener*, *ornary* for *ordinary*. The late Cardinal Cullen was always spoken of by a friend of mine who revered him, as *The Carnal*.

My and *by* are pronounced *me* and *be* all over Ireland : Now *me* boy I expect you home *be* six o'clock.

The obscure sound of *e* and *i* heard in *her* and *fir* is hardly known in Ireland, at least among the general run of people. *Her* is made either *herr* or *hur*. They sound *sir* either *surr* (to rhyme with cur),

or *serr* ; but in this latter case they always give the
r or *rr* what is called the slender sound in Irish,
which there is no means of indicating by English
letters. *Fir* is also sounded either *fur* or ferr (a *fur*
tree or a *ferr* tree), *Furze* is pronounced rightly;
but they take it to be a plural, and so you will often
hear the people say *a fur bush* instead of *a furze bush*.

In other classes of words *i* before *r* is mis-
pronounced. A young fellow, Johnny Brien,
objected to go by night on a message that would
oblige him to pass by an empty old house that had
the reputation of being haunted, because, as he said,
he was afeard of the *sperrit*.

In like manner, *miracle* is pronounced *merricle*.
Jack Finn—a little busybody noted for perpetually
jibing at sacred things—Jack one day, with innocence
in his face, says to Father Tom, ' Wisha I'd be
terrible thankful entirely to your reverence to tell me
what a merricle is, for I could never understand it.'
' Oh yes Jack,' says the big priest good-naturedly, as
he stood ready equipped for a long ride to a sick call—
poor old Widow Dwan up in the mountain gap: ' Just
tell me exactly how many cows are grazing in that
field there behind you.' Jack, chuckling at the fun
that was coming on, turned round to count, on which
Father Tom dealt him a hearty kick that sent him
sprawling about three yards. He gathered himself
up as best he could ; but before he had time to open
his mouth the priest asked, ' Did you feel that Jack ? '
' Oh Blood-an . . . . Yerra of course I did your
reverence, why the blazes wouldn't I !' ' Well
Jack,' replied Father Tom, benignly, ' If you didn't
feel it—*that* would be a *merricle*.'

CHAPTER VIII.

PROVERBS.

The Irish delighted in sententious maxims and apt illustrations compressed into the fewest possible words. Many of their proverbs were evolved in the Irish language, of which a collection with translations by John O'Donovan may be seen in the ' Dublin Penny Journal,' I. 258; another in the Rev. Ulick Bourke's Irish Grammar; and still another in the Ulster Journ. of Archæology (old series) by Mr. Robert MacAdam, the Editor. The same tendency continued when the people adopted the English language. Those that I give here in collected form were taken from the living lips of the people during the last thirty or forty years.

' Be first in a wood and last in a bog.' If two persons are making their way, one behind the other, through a wood, the hinder man gets slashed in the face by the springy boughs pushed aside by the first : if through a bog, the man behind can always avoid the dangerous holes by seeing the first sink into them. This proverb preserves the memory of a time when there were more woods and bogs than there are now: it is translated from Irish.

In some cases a small amount added on or taken off makes a great difference in the result : ' An inch is a great deal in a man's nose.' In the Crimean war an officer happened to be walking past an Irish soldier on duty, who raised hand to cap to salute.

But the hand was only half way when a stray bullet whizzed by and knocked off the cap without doing any injury. Whereupon Paddy, perfectly unmoved, stooped down, replaced the cap and completed the salute.   The officer, admiring his coolness, said ' That was a narrow shave my man ! ' ' Yes your honour : an inch is as good as a mile.'   This is one of our commonest sayings.

A person is reproved for some trifling harmless liberty, and replies :—' Oh a cat can look at a king.' (A translation from Irish.)

A person who fails to get what he was striving after is often glad to accept something very inferior : ' When all fruit fails welcome haws.'

When a person shows no sign of gratitude for a good turn as if it passed completely from his memory, people say ' Eaten bread is soon forgotten.'

A person is sent upon some dangerous mission, as when the persons he is going to are his deadly enemies :—that is ' Sending the goose on a message to the fox's den.'

If a dishonest avaricious man is put in a position of authority over people from whom he has the power to extort money ; that is ' putting the fox to mind the geese.'

' You have as many kinds of potatoes on the table as if you took them from a beggarman's bag ' : referring to the good old time when beggarmen went about and usually got a *lyre* of potatoes in each house.

' No one can tell what he is able to do till he tries,' as the duck said when she swallowed a dead kitten.

You say to a man who is suffering under some continued hardship:—' This distress is only temporary : have patience and things will come round soon again.'　' O yes indeed; *Live horse till you get grass.*'

A person in your employment is not giving satisfaction ; and yet you are loth to part with him for another: ' Better is the devil you know than the devil you don't know.'

' Least said, soonest mended.'

' You spoke too late,' as the fool said when he swallowed a bad egg, and heard the chicken chirp going down his throat.

' Good soles bad uppers.'　Applied to a person raised from a low to a high station, who did well enough while low, but in his present position is overbearing and offensive.

I have done a person some service : and now he ill-naturedly refuses some reasonable request. I say : ' Oh wait: *apples will grow again.*'　He answers —' Yes *if the trees baint 'cut* '—a defiant and un-grateful answer, as much as to say—you may not have the opportunity to serve me, or I may not want it.

Turf or peat was scarce in Kilmallock (Co. Lime-rick): whence the proverb, ' A Kilmallock fire—two sods and a *kyraun* ' (a bit broken *off of* a sod) .

People are often punished even in this world for their misdeeds: ' God Almighty often pays debts without money.' (Wicklow.)

I advise you not to do so without the master's permission :—' Leave is light.'　A very general saying.

When a person gives much civil talk, makes plausible excuses or fair promises, the remark is made ' Soft words butter no parsnips.' Sometimes also ' Talk is cheap.'

A person who is too complaisant—over anxious to please everyone—is ' like Lanna Mochree's dog—he will go a part of the road with everyone.' (Moran Carlow.) (A witness said this of a policeman in the Celbridge courthouse—Kildare—last year, showing that it is still alive.)

' The first drop of the broth is the hottest' ; the first step in any enterprise is usually the hardest. (Westmeath.)

The light, consisting of a single candle, or the jug of punch from which the company fill their tumblers, ought always to be placed on the middle of the table when people are sitting round it :—' Put the priest in the middle of the parish.'

' After a gathering comes a scattering.' 'A narrow gathering, a broad scattering.' Both allude to the case of a thrifty man who gathers up a fortune during a lifetime, and is succeeded by a spendthrift son who soon *makes ducks and drakes* of the property.

No matter how old a man is he can get a wife if he wants one : ' There never was an old slipper but there was an old stocking to match it.' (Carlow.)

' You might as well go to hell with a load as with a *pahil* ' : ' You might as well hang for a sheep as for a lamb ' : both explain themselves. A *pahil* or *paghil* is a bundle of anything. (Derry.)

If a man treats you badly in any way, you threaten to pay him back in his own coin by saying, ' The cat hasn't eaten the year yet.' (Carlow.)

'A fool and his money are easily parted.'

'A dumb priest never got a parish,' as much as to say if a man wants a thing he must ask and strive for it.

'A slip of the tongue is no fault of the mind.' (Munster.)

You merely hint at something requiring no further explanation :—'A nod is as good as a wink to a blind horse.' (Sam Lover : but heard everywhere.)

A very wise proverb often heard among us is :— 'Let well enough alone.'

'When a man is down, down with him ' : a bitter allusion to the tendency of the world to trample down the unfortunate and helpless.

'The friend that can be bought is not worth buying.' (Moran : Carlow.)

'The life of an old hat is to cock it.' To cock an old hat is to set it jauntingly on the head with the leaf turned up at one side. (S. E. counties.)

'The man that wears the shoe knows where it pinches.' It is only the person holding any position that knows the troubles connected with it.

'Enough and no waste is as good as a *faist*.'

'There are more ways of killing a dog than by choking him with butter.' Applied when some insidious cunning attempt that looks innocent is made to injure another.

'Well James are you quite recovered now ? ' 'Oh yes, I'm *on the baker's list* again ' : i.e., I am well and have recovered my appetite.

'An Irishman before answering a question always asks another ' : he wants to know why he is asked.

Dan O'Loghlin, a working man, drove up to our

house one day on an outside car. It was a sixpenny drive, but rather a long one ; and the carman began to grumble. Whereupon Dan, in the utmost good humour, replied :—' Oh you must take the little potato with the big potato.' A very apt maxim in many of life's affairs, and often heard in and around Dublin.

' Good goods are tied up in small parcels ' : said of a little man or a little woman, in praise or mitigation. (Moran : Carlow.)

' Easy with the hay, there are boys on the ladder.' When a man is on the top of the stack forking down hay, he is warned to look out and be careful if other *boys* are mounting up the ladder, lest he may pitch it on their heads. The proverb is uttered when a person is incautiously giving expression to words likely to offend some one present. (Moran : Carlow.)

Be cautious about believing the words of a man speaking ill of another against whom he has a grudge: ' Spite never spoke well.' (Moran : Carlow.)

Don't encroach too much on a privilege or it may be withdrawn : don't ask too much or you may get nothing at all :—' Covetousness bursts the bag.'

Three things not to be trusted—a cow's horn, a dog's tooth, and a horse's hoof.

Three disagreeable things at home :—a scolding wife ; a squalling child ; and a smoky chimney.

Three good things to have. I heard this given as a toast exactly as I give it here, by a fine old gentleman of the old times :— ' Here's that we may always have a *clane* shirt ; a *clane* conscience ; and a guinea in our pocket.'

Here is another toast. A happy little family party round the farmer's fire with a big jug on the table (a jug of what, do you think ?) The old blind piper is the happiest of all, and holding up his glass says :— ' Here's, if this be war may we never have peace.' (Edw. Walsh.)

Three things no person ever saw :—a highlander's kneebuckle, a dead ass, a tinker's funeral.

' Take care to lay by for the sore foot' : i.e., Provide against accidents, against adversity or want ; against the rainy day.

When you impute another person's actions to evil or unworthy motives : that is ' measuring other people's corn in your own bushel.'

A person has taken some unwise step : another expresses his intention to do a similar thing, and you say :—' One fool is enough in a parish.'

In the middle of last century, the people of Carlow and its neighbourhood prided themselves on being able to give, on the spur of the moment, toasts suitable to the occasion. Here is one such : ' Here's to the herring that never took a bait ' ; a toast reflecting on some person present who had been made a fool of in some transaction. (Moran: Carlow.)

' A man cannot grow rich without his wife's leave ' : as much as to say, a farmer's wife must co-operate to ensure success and prosperity. (Moran : Carlow.)

When something is said that has a meaning under the surface the remark is made ' There's gravel in that.'

' Pity people barefoot in cold frosty weather,
But don't make them boots with other people's leather.'

That is to say : don't be generous at other people's expense. Many years ago this proverb was quoted by the late Serjeant Armstrong in addressing a jury in Wicklow.

' A wet night : a dry morning ' : said to a man who is *craw-sick*—thirsty and sick—after a night's boozing. (Moran : Carlow.)

This last reminds me of an invitation I once got from a country gentleman to go on a visit, holding out as an inducement that he would give me ' a dry bed and a wet bottle.'

' If he's not fishing he's mending his nets ' : said of a man who always makes careful preparations and lays down plans for any enterprise he may have in view.

' If he had a shilling in his pocket it would burn a hole through it ' : said of a man who cannot keep his money together—a spendthrift.

' A bird with one wing can't fly ' : said to a person to make him take a second glass. (Moran : Carlow.)

Protect your rights : ' Don't let your bone go with the dog.'

' An old dog for a hard road ' : said in commendation of a wary person who has overcome some difficulty. *Hard* in this proverb means ' difficult.' (Moran : Carlow.)

' No use sending a boy on a man's errand ' : Don't be satisfied with inadequate steps when undertaking a difficult work : employ a sure person to carry out a hard task.

Oh however he may have acted towards you he has been a good friend to me at any rate ; and I go by the old saying, ' Praise the ford as you find it.' This proverb is a translation from the Irish. It refers to a time when bridges were less general than now; and rivers were commonly crossed by fords—which were sometimes safe, sometimes dangerous, according to the weather.

' Threatened dogs live long.' Abuses often go on for a long time, though people are constantly complaining and threatening to correct them. (Ulster.)

He who expects a legacy when another man dies thinks the time long. ' It is long waiting for a dead man's boots.' (Moran : Carlow.)

A person waiting impatiently for something to come on always thinks the time longer than usual:— 'A watched pot never boils.'

' A poor man must have a poor wedding ': people must live according to their means.

' I could carry my wet finger to him ' : i.e. he is here present, but I won't name him.

' Oh that's all *as I roved out* ' : to express unbelief in what someone says as quite unworthy of credit. In allusion to songs beginning ' As I roved out,' which are generally fictitious.

' Your father was a bad glazier ': said to a person who is standing in one's light.

' As the old cock crows the young cock learns ': generally applied to a son who follows the evil example of his father.

A person remarks that the precautions you are taking in regard to a certain matter are unnecessary or excessive, and you reply ' Better be sure than sorry.'

' She has a good many nicks in her horn ' : said of a girl who is becoming an old maid. A cow is said to have a nick in her horn for every year.

A man of property gets into hopeless debt and difficulty by neglecting his business, and his creditors sell him out. ' Well, how did he get out of it?' asks a neighbour. ' Oh, he got out of it just by a break-up, *as Katty got out of the pot.*' This is how Katty got out of the pot. One day at dinner in the kitchen Katty Murphy the servant girl sat down on a big pot (as I often saw women do)—for seats were scarce; and in the middle of the dinner, through some incautious movement, down she went. She struggled to get up, but failed. Then the others came to help her, and tugged and pulled and tried in every way, but had to give it up; till at last one of them brought a heavy hammer, and with one blow made smithereens of the pot.

' Putting a thing on the long finger' means post-poning it.

On the evil of procrastination:—' *Time enough* lost the ducks.' The ducks should have been secured at once as it was known that a fox was prowling about. But they were not, and——

' *Will you* was never a good fellow.' The bad fellow says ' Will you have some lunch?' (while there is as yet nothing on the table), on the chance that the visitor will say ' No, thank you.' The good hospitable man asks no questions, but has the food brought up and placed before the guest.

' Cut the *gad* next the throat': that is to say, attend to the most urgent need first. You find a man hanging by a *gad* (withe), and you cut him down to save him. Cutting the *gad* next the throat explains itself.

When a work must be done slowly:—' I will do

it by degrees as lawyers go to heaven.'   (Moran : Carlow.)

' That's not a good fit,' as the serpent said when he swallowed a buck goat, horns and all.

Time and patience would bring a snail to America.

' The cold stone leaves the water on St. Patrick's Day.'   About the 17th March (St. Patrick's Day), the winter's cold is nearly gone, and the weather generally takes a milder turn.

' There are more turners than dishmakers ' ; meaning, there may be many members of a profession, but only few of them excel in it : usually pointed at some particular professional man, who is considered not clever.   It is only the most skilful turners that can make wooden dishes.

A person who talks too much cannot escape saying things now and then that would be better left unsaid :—' The mill that is always going grinds coarse and fine.'

' If you lie down with dogs you will get up with fleas ' : if you keep company with bad people you will contract their evil habits.   (Moran : Carlow.)

If you do a kindness don't mar it by any unpleasant drawback : in other words do a kind act graciously :— ' If you give away an old coat don't cut off the buttons.'

Two good things :—A young man courting, an old man smoking : Two bad things :—An old man courting, a young man smoking. (MacCall : Wexford.)

What is the world to a man when his wife is a widow.

Giving help where it is needed is ' helping the lame dog over the stile.'

'Leave him to God': meaning don't you attempt to punish him for the injury he has done you: let God deal with him.   Often carried too far among us.

A hard man at driving a bargain:—'He always wants an egg in the penn'orth.' (Kildare.)

A satirical expression regarding a close-fisted ungenerous man:—'If he had only an egg he'd give you the shell.' (Kildare.)

A man wishes to say to another that they are both of about the same age; and this is how he expresses it:—'When I die of old age you may quake with fear.' (Kildare.)

Speaking of a man with more resources than one:—'It wasn't on one leg St. Patrick came to Ireland.'

When there is a prospect of a good harvest, or any mark of prosperity:—'That's no sign of small potatoes.' (Kildare.)

Your friend is in your pocket. (Kildare.)

[As a safe general principle]:—'If anybody asks you, say you don't know.'

'A good run is better than a bad stand.' When it becomes obvious that you cannot defend your position (whatever it is), better yield than encounter certain defeat by continuing to resist. (Queenstown.)

A man depending for success on a very uncertain contingency:—'God give you better meat than a running hare.' (Tyrone.)

To express the impossibility of doing two inconsistent things at the same time:—'You can't whistle and chaw meal.'

A man who has an excess of smooth plausible talk is 'too sweet to be wholesome.'

'The fox has a good name in his own parish.' They say that a fox does not prey on the fowls in his own neighbourhood. Often said of a rogue whose friends are trying to *whitewash* him.

'A black hen lays white eggs.' A man with rough manners often has a gentle heart and does kindly actions.

Much in the same sense :—'A crabtree has a sweet blossom.'

A person who has smooth words and kind professions for others, but never acts up to them, 'has a hand for everybody but a heart for nobody.' (Munster.)

A person readily finds a lost article when it is missed, and is suspected to have hidden it himself :—'What the Pooka writes he can read.' (Munster.)

A man is making no improvement in his character or circumstances but rather the reverse as he advances in life :—' A year older and a year worse.'

'A shut mouth catches no flies.' Much the same as the English 'Speech is silvern, silence is golden.'

To the same effect is 'Hear and see and say nothing.'

A fool and his money are easily parted.

Oh I see you expect that Jack (a false friend) will stand at your back. Yes, indeed, 'he'll stand at your back while your nose is breaking.'

'You wouldn't do that to your match' as Mick Sheedy said to the fox. Mick Sheedy the game-keeper had a hut in the woods where he often took shelter and rested and smoked. One day when he had arrived at the doorway he saw a fox sitting at the little fire warming himself. Mick instantly spread himself out in the doorway to prevent escape. And so they continued to look at each other. At last Reynard, perceiving that some master-stroke was necessary, took up in his mouth one of a fine pair of shoes that were lying in a corner, brought it over, and deliberately placed it on the top of the fire. We know the rest ! (Limerick.)

'There's a hole in the house'; meant to convey that there is a tell-tale listening. (Meath.)

We are inclined to magnify distant or only half known things : 'Cows far off have long horns.'

'He'll make Dungarvan shake': meaning he will do great things, cut a great figure. Now generally said in ridicule. (Munster.)

A man is told something extraordinary :—'That takes the coal off my pipe'; i.e. it surpasses all I have seen or heard.

A man fails to obtain something he was looking after—a house or a farm to rent—a cow to buy—a girl he wished to marry, &c.—and consoles himself by reflecting or saying :—'There's as good fish in the *say* as ever was caught.'

Well, you were at the dance yesterday—who were there ? Oh 'all the world and Garrett Reilly' were there. (Wicklow and Waterford.)

When a fellow puts on empty airs of great consequence, you say to him, 'Why you're *as grand as Mat Flanagan with the cat*': always said contemptuously. Mat Flanagan went to London one time. After two years he came home on a visit ; but he was now transformed into such a mass of grandeur that he did not recognise any of the old surroundings. He didn't know what the old cat was. 'Hallo, mother,' said he with a lofty air and a killing Cockney accent, 'What's yon long-tailed fellow in yon *cawner*?'

A person reproaching another for something wrong says :—' The back of my hand to you,' as much as to say ' I refuse to shake hands with you.'

To a person hesitating to enter on a doubtful enterprise which looks fairly hopeful, another says :— Go on Jack, try your fortune: 'faint heart never won fair lady.'

A person who is about to make a third and determined attempt at anything exclaims (in assonantal rhyme) :—

> ' First and second go alike :
> The third throw takes the bite.'

I express myself confident of outwitting or circumventing a certain man who is notoriously cautious and wide-awake, and the listener says to me :—' Oh, what a chance you have—*catch a weasel asleep*' (general).

In connexion with this may be given another proverb : of a notoriously wide-awake cautious man, it is said :—' He sleeps a hare's sleep—with one eye open.' For it was said one time that weasels were in the habit of sucking the blood of hares in their sleep ; and as weasels had much increased, the hares took to the plan of sleeping with one eye at a time ; ' and when that's rested and *slep* enough, they open it and shut the other.' (From ' The Building of Mourne,' by Dr. Robert Dwyer Joyce.)

This last perpetuates a legend as old as our literature. In one of the ancient Irish classical tales, the story is told of a young lady so beautiful that all the young chiefs of the territory were in love with her and laying plans to take her off. So her father, to defeat them, slept with only one eye at a time.

CHAPTER IX.

EXAGGERATION AND REDUNDANCY.

I HAVE included both in this Chapter, for they are nearly related; and it is often hard to draw a precise line of distinction.

We in Ireland are rather prone to exaggeration, perhaps more so than the average run of peoples. Very often the expressions are jocose, or the person is fully conscious of the exaggeration; but in numerous cases there is no joke at all: but downright seriousness: all which will be seen in the following examples.

A common saying about a person of persuasive tongue or with a beautiful voice in singing :—'He would coax the birds off the bushes.' This is borrowed from the Irish. In the ' Lament of Richard Cantillon ' (in Irish) he says that at the musical voice of the lady ' the seals would come up from the deep, the stag down from the mist-crag, and the thrush from the tree.' (Petrie : 'Anc. Mus. of Ireland.')

Of a noted liar and perjurer it was said 'He would swear that a coal-porter was a canary.'

A man who is unlucky, with whom everything goes wrong :—'If that man got a hen to hatch duck eggs, the young ducks would be drowned.'   Or again, ' If that man sowed oats in a field, a crop of turnips would come up.'   Or: 'He is always in the field when luck is on the road.'

The following expression is often heard :—' Ah, old James Buckley is a fine piper : *I'd give my eyes* to be listening to him.'

That fellow is so dirty that if you flung him against a wall he'd stick.   (Patterson : Ulster.)

Two young men are about to set off to seek their fortunes, leaving their young brother Roryto stay with their mother.   But Rory, a hard active merry cute little fellow, proposes to go with them :—' I'll follow ye to the world's end.'   On which the eldest says to him—a half playful threat :— ' You presumptious little atomy of a barebones, if I only see the size of a thrush's ankle of you follyin' us on the road, I'll turn back and bate that wiry and freckled little carcase of yours into frog's-jelly!'   (Robert Dwyer Joyce : ' The Building of Mourne.')

' Did Johnny give you any of his sugar-stick ? ' ' Oh not very much indeed: hardly the size of a thrush's ankle.'   This term is often used.

Of a very morose sour person you will hear it said :—' If that man looked at a pail of new milk he'd turn it into curds and whey.'

A very thin man, or one attenuated by sickness : —' You could blow him off your hand.'

A poor fellow complains of the little bit of meat he got for his dinner:—' It was no more than a daisy in a bull's mouth !'   Another says of *his* dinner when it was in his stomach :—' It was no more than a midge in the Glen of the Downs.'

Exhorting a messenger to be quick :—' Don't be there till you're back again.' Another way :—' Now run as quick as you can, and if you fall don't wait to get up.' Warning a person to be expeditious in any work you put him to :—' Now don't let grass grow under your feet.' Barney urging on the ass to go quickly :—' Come Bobby, don't let grass grow under your feet.' (' Knocknagow.')

If a person is secretly very willing to go to a place —as a lover to the house of the girl's parents:—' You could lead him there with a halter of snow.'

' Is this razor sharp ? ' ' Sharp !—why '*twould shave a mouse asleep.*'

A lazy fellow, fond of sitting at the fire, *has the A B C on his shins,* i.e. they are blotched with the heat.

Of an inveterate talker :—That man would talk the teeth out of a saw.

A young fellow gets a great fright :—' It frightened him out of a year's growth.'

When Nancy saw the master so angry she was frightened out of her wits : or frightened out of her seven senses. When I saw the horse ride over him I was frightened out of my life.

A great liar, being suddenly pressed for an answer, told the truth for once. He told the truth because he was *shook* for a lie ; i.e. no lie was ready at hand. *Shook,* to be bad, in a bad way : shook for a thing, to be badly in want of it and not able to get it.

Of a very lazy fellow :—He would not knock a coal off his foot : i.e. when a live coal happens to fall on his foot while sitting by the fire, he wouldn't take the trouble to knock it off.

Says the dragon to Manus :—' If ever I see you here again I'll hang a quarter of you on every tree in the wood.' (Crofton Croker.)

If a person is pretty badly hurt, or suffers hardship, he's *kilt* (killed) : a fellow gets a fall and his friend comes up to inquire :—' Oh let me alone I'm kilt and speechless.'   I heard a Dublin nurse say, ' Oh I'm kilt minding these four children.'   ' The bloody throopers are coming to kill and quarther an' murther every mother's sowl o' ye.' (R. D. Joyce.) The parlour bell rings impatiently for the third time, and Lowry Looby the servant says, ' Oh murther there goes the bell again, I'll be kilt entirely.' (Gerald Griffin.) If a person is really badly hurt he's *murthered entirely*.   A girl telling about a fight in a fair :—' One poor boy was kilt dead for three hours on a car, breathing for all the world like a corpse ! '

If you don't stop your abuse I'll give you a shirt full of sore bones.

Yes, poor Jack was once well off, but now he hasn't as much money as would jingle on a tombstone.

That cloth is very coarse : why you could shoot straws through it.

Strong dislike :—I don't like a bone in his body.

' Do you know Bill Finnerty well ? '   ' Oh indeed I know every bone in his body,' i.e. I know him and all his ways intimately.

A man is low stout and very fat : if you met him in the street you'd rather jump over him than walk round him.

He knew as much Latin as if he swallowed a dictionary. (Gerald Griffin.)

The word *destroy* is very often used to characterize any trifling damage easily remedied :—That car splashed me, and my coat is all destroyed.

' They kept me dancin' for 'em in the kitchen,' says Barney Broderick, ' till I hadn't a leg to put under me.' (' Knocknagow.')

This farm of mine is as bad land as ever a crow flew over.

He's as great a rogue as ever stood in shoe-leather.

When Jack heard the news of the money that was coming to him he was *jumping out of his skin* with delight.

I bought these books at an auction, and I got them for a song : in fact I got them for half nothing.

Very bad slow music is described as *the tune the old cow died of.*

A child is afraid of a dog : ' *Yerra* he won't touch you ' : meaning ' he won't bite you.'

A man having a very bad aim in shooting :— ' He wouldn't hit a hole in a ladder.'

Carleton's blind fiddler says to a young girl : ' You could dance *the Colleen dhas dhown* [a jig] upon a spider's cobweb without breaking it.'

An ill-conducted man :—' That fellow would shame a field of tinkers.' The tinkers of sixty years ago, who were not remarkable for their honesty or good conduct, commonly travelled the country in companies, and camped out in fields or wild places.

I was dying to hear the news ; i.e. excessively anxious.

Where an Englishman will say 'I shall be pleased to accept your invitation,' an Irishman will say ' I will be delighted to accept,' &c.

Mick Fraher is always eating garlick and his breath has a terrible smell—a smell of garlick strong enough to hang your hat on.

A mean thief :—He'd steal a halfpenny out of a blind beggarman's hat.   (P. Reilly : Kild.)

A dexterous thief :—He'd steal the sugar out of your punch.

An inveterate horse thief :—Throw a halter in his grave and he'll start up and steal a horse.

Of an impious and dexterous thief :—' He'd steal the cross off an ass's back,' combining skill and profanation.   According to the religious legend the back of the ass is marked with a cross ever since the day of our Lord's public entry into Jerusalem upon an ass.

A man who makes unreasonably long visits— who outstays his welcome :—' If that man went to a wedding he'd wait for the christening.

I once asked a young Dublin lady friend was she angry at not getting an invitation to the party : ' Oh I was fit to be tied.'   A common expression among us to express great indignation.

A person is expressing confidence that a certain good thing will happen which will bring advantage to everyone, but which after all is very unlikely, and someone replies :—' Oh yes : when the sky falls we'll all catch larks.'

A useless unavailing proceeding, most unlikely to be attended with any result, such as trying to persuade a person who is obstinately bent on having his own way :—' You might as well be whistling jigs to a milestone ' [expecting it to dance].

' Would you know him if you saw him ?' ' Would I know him !—why ' I'd know his skin in a tan-yard' —' I'd know his shadow on a furze-bush !'

A person considered very rich :—That man is *rotten with money.* He doesn't know what to do with his money.

You gave me a great start : you put the heart across in me : my heart jumped into my mouth. The people said that Miss Mary Kearney put the heart across in Mr. Lowe, the young Englishman visitor. (' Knocknagow.')

I heard Mat Halahan the tailor say to a man who had just fitted on a new coat :—That coat fits you just as if you were melted into it.

He is as lazy as the dog that always puts his head against the wall to bark. (Moran : Carlow.)

In running across the field where the young people were congregated Nelly Donovan trips and falls : and Billy Heffernan, running up, says :—' Oh Nelly did you fall : come here till I take you up.' (' Knock-nagow.')

' The road flew under him,' to express the swift-ness of a man galloping or running afoot.

Bessie Morris was such a flirt that Barney Broderick said she'd coort a haggard of sparrows. (' Knoc nagow.')

> I wish I were on yonder hill,
> 'Tis there I'd sit and cry my fill,
> Till ev'ry tear would turn a mill.
>
> (*Shool Aroon* : ' Old Irish Folk Song.')

But after all this is not half so great an exaggeration as what the cultivated English poet wrote :—

> I found her on the floor
> In all the storm of grief, yet beautiful,
> Pouring forth tears at such a lavish rate,
> That were the world on fire it might have drowned
> The wrath of Heaven and quenched the mighty ruin.

A great dandy wears his hat on three hairs of
his head.

He said such funny things that the company were
splitting their sides laughing.

Matt Donovan (in ' Knocknagow ') says of his
potatoes that had fine stalks but little produce—
desavers as he called them—Every stalk of 'em would
make a rafter for a house. But put the best man
in the parish to dig 'em and a duck would swallow
all he'd be able to turn out from morning till
night.

Sometimes distinct numbers come in where they
hardly apply. Not long ago I read in an article in
the ' Daily Mail ' by Mr. Stead, of British ' ships
all over the seven seas.'   So also here at home we
read ' round the four seas of Ireland ' (which is right
enough) : and ' You care for nothing in the world but
your own four bones' (i.e. nothing but yourself).
' Come on then, old beer-swiller, and try yourself
against the four bones of an Irishman ' (R. D. Joyce :
' The House of Lisbloom.')   *Four bones* in this sense
is very common.

A person meeting a friend for the first time after
a long interval says ' Well, it's a cure for sore eyes
to see you.' ' I haven't seen you now for a month of

Sundays,' meaning a long time. *A month of Sundays* is thirty-one Sundays—seven or eight months.

Said jokingly of a person with very big feet:—He wasn't behind the door anyway when the feet were giving out.

When a man has to use the utmost exertion to accomplish anything or to escape a danger he says: 'That business put me to the pin of my collar.' The allusion is to a fellow whose clothes are falling off him for want of buttons and pins. At last to prevent the final catastrophe he has to pull out the brass pin that fastens his collar and pin waistcoat and trousers-band together.

A poor woman who is about to be robbed shrieks out for help; when the villain says to her:—' Not another word or I'll stick you like a pig and give you your guts for garters.' ('Ir. Penny Magazine.')

A man very badly off—all in rags:—'He has forty-five ways of getting into his coat now.' (MacCall: Wexford.)

A great miser—very greedy for money:—He heard the money jingling in his mother's pockets before he was born. (MacCall: Wexford.)

> A drunken man is a terrible curse,
> But a drunken woman is twice as worse;
> For she'd drink Lough Erne dry.
>
> (MacCall.)

To a person who habitually uses unfortunate blundering expressions:—' You never open your mouth but you put your foot in it.'

A girl to express that it is unlikely she will ever be married says: ' I think, miss, my husband's intended mother died an old maid.' ('Penelope in Ireland.')

A young man speaking of his sweetheart says, in the words of the old song :—

'I love the ground she walks upon, *mavourneen gal mochree*' (thou fair love of my heart).

A conceited pompous fellow approaches :—' Here comes *half the town* ! ' A translation from the Irish *leath an bhaile*.

Billy Heffernan played on his fife a succession of jigs and reels that might ' cure a paralytic ' [and set him dancing]. (' Knocknagow.')

In ' Knocknagow ' Billy Heffernan being requested to play on his fife longer than he considered reasonable, asked did they think that he had the bellows of Jack Delany the blacksmith in his stomach ?

Said of a great swearer :—He'd swear a hole in an iron pot.'

Of another :—' He'd curse the bladder out of a goat.'

Of still another :—' He could quench a candle at the other side of the kitchen with a curse.'

A person is much puzzled, or is very much elated, or his mind is disturbed for any reason :—' He doesn't know whether it is on his head or his heels he's standing.

A penurious miserable creature who starves himself to hoard up :—He could live on the smell of an oil-rag. (Moran : Carlow.)

A man complaining that he has been left too long fasting says :—' My stomach will think that my throat is cut.' (MacCall : Wexford.)

' Do you like the new American bacon ? ' ' Oh not at all : I tried it once and that's enough for me : *I wouldn't touch it with a tongs.*' Very common and always used in depreciation as here.

We in Ireland are much inclined to redundancy in our speech. It is quite observable—especially to an outsider—that even in our ordinary conversation and in answering simple questions we use more words than we need. We hardly ever confine ourselves to the simple English *yes* or *no* ; we always answer by a statement. ' Is it raining, Kitty ? ' ' Oh no sir, it isn't raining at all.' ' Are you going to the fair to-day ? ' ' No indeed I am not.' ' Does your father keep on the old business still ? ' ' Oh yes certainly he does : how could he get on without it ? ' ' Did last night's storm injure your house ? ' 'Ah you may well say it did.' A very distinguished Dublin scholar and writer, having no conscious leanings whatever towards the Irish language, mentioned to me once that when he went on a visit to some friends in England they always observed this peculiarity in his conversation, and often laughed at his roundabout expressions. He remarked to me—and an acute remark it was—that he supposed there must be some peculiarity of this kind in the Irish language ; in which conjecture he was quite correct. For this peculiarity of ours—like many others—is borrowed from the Irish language, as anyone may see for himself by looking through an Irish book of question and answer, such as a Catechism. ' Is the Son God ? ' ' Yes certainly He is.' ' Will God reward the good and punish the wicked ? '. ' Certainly : there is no doubt He will.' ' Did God always exist ? ' ' He did ; because He has neither beginning nor end.' And questions and answers like these—from Donlevy's

Irish Catechism for instance—might be given to any length.

But in many other ways we show our tendency to this wordy overflow—still deriving our mannerism from the Irish language—that is to say, from modern and middle Irish.   For in very old Irish—of the tenth, eleventh, and earlier centuries for instance, the tendency is the very reverse.   In the specimens of this very old language that have come down to us, the words and phrases are so closely packed, that it is impossible to translate them either into English or Latin by an equal number of words.*   But this old language is too far off from us to have any influence in our present every-day English speech ; and, as already remarked, we derive this peculiarity from modern Irish, or from middle Irish through modern. Here is a specimen in translation of over-worded modern Irish (Battle of Gavra, p. 141), a type of what was very common :—' Diarmuid himself [fighting] continued in the enjoyment of activity, strength, and vigour, without intermission of action, of weapons, or of power ; until at length he dealt a full stroke of his keen hard-tempered sword on the king's head, by which he clove the skull, and by a second stroke swept his head off his huge body.'   Examples like this, from Irish texts, both modern and middle, might be multiplied to any extent.

---

* See the interesting remarks of O'Donovan in Preface to ' Battle of Magh Rath,' pp. ix–xv.   Sir Samuel Ferguson also has some valuable observations on the close packing of the very old Irish language, but I cannot lay my hands on them. From him I quote (from memory) the remark about translating old Irish into English or Latin.

But let us now have a look at some of our Anglo-Irish redundancies, mixed up as they often are with exaggeration. A man was going to dig by night for a treasure, which of course had a supernatural guardian, like all hidden treasures, and what should he see running towards him but 'a great big red mad bull, with fire flaming out of his eyes, mouth, and nose.' (Ir. Pen. Mag.) Another man sees a leprechaun walking up to him—'a weeny deeny dawny little atomy of an idea of a small taste of a gentleman.' (*Ibid.*) Of a person making noise and uproar you will be told that he was roaring and screeching and bawling and making a terrible hullabulloo all through the house.

Of an emaciated poor creature—'The breath is only just in and out of him, and the grass doesn't know of him walking over it.'

'The gentlemen are not so pleasant *in themselves*' [now as they used to be]. (Gerald Griffin.) Expressions like this are very often heard : 'I was dead in myself,' i.e., I felt dull and lifeless.

[Dermot struck the giant and] 'left him dead without life.' ('Dermot and Grainne.') Further on we find the same expression—*marbh gan anam*, dead without life. This Irish expression is constantly heard in our English dialect : 'he fell from the roof and was *killed dead*.'

> Oh brave King Brian, he knew the way
> To keep the peace and to make the hay :
> For those who were bad he cut off their head ;
> And those who were worse he killed them dead.

Similarly the words 'dead and buried' are used all through Munster :—Oh indeed poor Jack Lacy is dead and buried for the last two years : or ' the whole family are dead and gone these many years.'

A very common Irish expression is ' I invited *every single one* of them.' This is merely a translation from Irish, as we find in ' Gabhra ':—*Do bhéarmaois gach aon bhuadh* : we were wont to win every single victory.

' We do not want any single one of them,' says Mr. Hamilton Fyfe ('Daily Mail'). He puts the saying into the mouth of another ; but the phraseology is probably his own : and at any rate I suppose we may take it as a phrase from Scotch Gaelic, which is all but the same as Irish Gaelic.

Emphatic particles and words, especially the pronouns with *self*, are often used to excess. I heard a highly educated fellow-countryman say, ' I must say myself that I don't believe it ' : and I am afraid I often use such expressions myself. ' His companions remained standing, but he found it more convenient to sit down himself.' A writer or speaker has however to be on his guard or he may be led into a trap. A writer having stated that some young ladies attended a cookery-class, first merely looking on, goes on to say that after a time they took part in the work, and soon learned *to cook themselves.*

I once heard a man say :—' I disown the whole family, *seed breed and generation.*' Very common in Ireland. Goldsmith took the expression from his own country, and has immortalised it in his essay, ' The Distresses of a Common Soldier.'

He was on the tip-top of the steeple—i.e., the very top. This expression is extended in application : that meadow is tip-top, i.e., very excellent : he is a tip-top hurler. 'By no means' is sometimes expanded :—'I asked him to lend me a pound, but he answered that *by no manner of means* would he do any such thing.'

'If you do that you'll be crying down salt tears,' i.e., 'you'll deeply regret it.' *Salt tears* is however in Shakespeare in the same sense. ('Hen. VI.)'

'Down with you now on your two bended knees and give thanks to God.'

If you don't stop, I'll wring the head off o' your neck. (Rev. Maxwell Close.)

The roof of the house fell down on the top of him. (Father Higgins.)

The Irish *air sé* ('says he') is very often repeated in the course of a narrative. It is correct in Irish, but it is often heard echoed in our English where it is incorrect :—And says he to James 'where are you going now?' says he.

In a trial in Dublin a short time ago, the counsel asked of witness :—'Now I ask you in the most solemn manner, had you hand, act, or part in the death of Peter Heffernan?'

A young man died after injuries received in a row, and his friend says :—'It is dreadful about the poor boy : they made at him in the house and killed him there ; then they dragged him out on the road and killed him entirely, so that he lived for only three days after. I wouldn't mind if they shot him at once and put an end to him : but to be murdering him like that—it is terrible.'

The fairy says to Billy :—'I am a thousand years old to-day, and I think it is time for me to get married.' To which Billy replies :—' I think it is quite time without any kind of doubt at all.' (Crofton Croker.)

The squire walks in to Patrick's cabin : and Patrick says :—' Your honour's honour is quite welcome entirely.' (Crofton Croker.)

An expression you will often hear even in Dublin :—' Lend me the loan of your umbrella.'

' She doats down on him ' is often used to express ' She is very fond of him.'

> ' So, my Kathleen, you're going to leave me
> All alone by myself in this place.'
>
> (LADY DUFFERIN.)

He went to America seven years ago, and from that day to this we have never heard any tale or tidings of him.

' Did he treat you hospitably ? ' ' Oh indeed he pretended to forget it entirely, and I never took bit, bite, or sup in his house.' This form of expression is heard everywhere in Ireland.

We have in Ireland an inveterate habit—from the highest to the lowest—educated and uneducated—of constantly interjecting the words ' you know ' into our conversation as a mere expletive, without any particular meaning :—' I had it all the time, you know, in my pocket ' : he had a seat, you know, that he could arrange like a chair : I was walking, you know, into town yesterday, when I met your father.' ' Why in the world did you lend him such a large sum of money ? ' ' Well, you know, the fact is I couldn't avoid it.' This expression is often varied to ' don't you know.'

In Munster a question is often introduced by the

words ' I don't · know,' always shortened to *I'd'no*
(three syllables with the *I* long and the *o* very short—
barely sounded) ' I'd'no is John come home yet ? '
This phrase you will often hear in Dublin from
Munster people, both educated and uneducated.

' The t'other' is often heard in Armagh : it is, of
course, English :—

> ' Sirs,' cried the umpire, cease your pother,
> The creature's neither one nor t'other.

CHAPTER X.

COMPARISONS.

SOME of the items in this chapter would fit very
well in the last ; but this makes no matter ; for ' good
punch drinks well from either dandy or tumbler.'

You attempt in vain to bring a shameless coarse-
minded man to a sense of the evil he has done :—
' Ye might as well put a blister on a hedgehog.'
(Tyrone.)

You're as cross all this day as *a bag of cats.*

If a man is inclined to threaten much but never
acts up to his threats—severe in word but mild in
act :—His bark is worse than his bite.

That turf is as dry as a bone (very common in
Munster.) *Bone-dry* is the term in Ulster.

When a woman has very thick legs, thick almost
down to the feet, she is ' like a Mullingar heifer, beef
to the heels.' The plains of Westmeath round
Mullingar are noted for fattening cattle.

He died roaring like Doran's bull.

A person restless, uneasy, fidgety, and impatient for the time being, is 'like a hen on a hot griddle.'

Of a scapegrace it is said he is past *grace* like a limeburner's brogue (shoe). The point will be caught up when it is remembered that *grease* is pronounced *grace* in Ireland.

You're as blind as a bat.

When a person is boastful—magnifies all his belongings—' all his geese are swans.'

She has a tongue that would *clip a hedge.* The tongue of another would *clip clouts* (cut rags). (Ulster.)

He went *as fast as hops.* When a fellow is hopping along on one leg, he has to go fast, without stopping.

Of a coarse ill-mannered man who uses unmannerly language : — ' What could you expect from a pig but a *grunt.*' (Carlow.)

A person who seems to be getting smaller is growing down like a cow's tail.

Of a wiry muscular active man people say ' he's as hard as nails.'

A person who acts inconsiderately and rudely without any restraint and without respect for others, is 'like a bull in a china shop.'

Of a clever artful schemer : 'If he didn't go to school he met the scholars.'

An active energetic person is ' all alive like a bag of fleas.'

That man knows no more about farming *than a cow knows of a holiday.*

A tall large woman :—' That's a fine doorful of a woman.' (MacCall : Wexford.)

He has a face as yellow as a kite's claw. (Crofton Croker : but heard everywhere.)

Jerry in his new clothes is as proud as a white-washed pig. (MacCall: Wexford.)

That man is as old as a field. (Common in Tipperary.)

'Are you well protected in that coat?' 'Oh yes I'm *as warm as wool*.' (Very common in the south.)

Idle for want of weft *like the Drogheda weavers*. Said of a person who runs short of some neces-sary material in doing any work. (Limerick.)

I watched him as closely as a cat watches a mouse.

He took up the book ; but seeing the owner suddenly appear, he dropped it *like a hot potato*.

'You have a head and so has a pin,' to express contempt for a person's understanding.

How are your new stock of books selling? Oh they are *going like hot cakes*. Hot cakes are a favourite viand, and whenever they are brought to table disappear quickly enough.

He's as poor as a church mouse.

A person expressing love mockingly :—' Come into my heart and pick sugar.'

An extremely thin emaciated person is *like death upon wires* ; alluding to a human skeleton held together by wires.

Oh you need never fear that Mick O'Brien will cheat you : *Mick is as honest as the sun.*

A person who does· not persevere in any one study or pursuit, who is perpetually changing about from one thing to another, is 'like a daddy-long-legs dancing on a window.'

A bitter tongue that utters cutting words is like the keen wind of March that blows at every side of the hedge.

A person praising strong whiskey says :—I felt it like a torchlight procession going down my throat.

A man with a keen sharp look in his face :—' He has an eye like a questing hawk.'   Usually said in an unfavourable sense.

If any commodity is supplied plentifully it is knocked about *like snuff at a wake*. Snuff was supplied free at wakes ; and the people were not sparing of it as they got it for nothing.

A chilly day :—' There's a stepmother's breath in the air.'

Now Biddy clean and polish up those spoons and knives and forks carefully ; don't stop till you make them shine *like a cat's eye under a bed*.   (Limerick.)

It is foolish to threaten unless you have—and show that you have—full power to carry out your threats : —' Don't show your teeth till you're able to bite.'

Greasing the fat sow's lug : i.e. giving money or presents to a rich man who does not need them. (Kildare.)

I went on a visit to Tom and he *fed me like a fighting cock*.

That little chap is as cute as a pet fox.

A useless worthless fellow :—He's fit to mind mice at a cross-roads.   (Kildare.)

How did he look?   Oh he had a weaver's blush— pale cheek and a red nose.   (Wexford.)

When a person clinches an argument, or puts a hard fact in opposition, or a poser of any kind hard to answer :—' Put that in your pipe and smoke it.'

'My stomach is as dry as a lime-burner's wig.' There were professional lime-burners then : alas, we have none now.

I want a drink badly : my throat is as dry as the pipe of Dick the blacksmith's bellows.

Poor Manus was terribly frightened ; he stood shaking *like a dog in a wet sack.* (Crofton Croker : but heard everywhere in Ireland.)

'As happy as the days are long' : that is to say happy while the days last—uninterruptedly happy.

Spending your money before you get it—going in debt till pay day comes round : that's 'eating the calf in the cow's belly.'

He hasn't as much land as would sod a lark ; as much as would make a sod for a lark in a cage.

That fellow is *as crooked as a ram's horn* ; i.e. he is a great schemer. Applied also in general to anything crooked.

'Do you mean to say he is a thief?' 'Yes I do ; last year he stole sheep *as often as he has fingers and toes*' (meaning very often).

You're as welcome as the flowers of May.

'Biddy, are the potatoes boiling?' Biddy takes off the lid to look, and replies 'The *white horses* are on 'em ma'am.' The *white horses* are patches of froth on the top of the pot when the potatoes are coming near boiling.

That's as firm as the Rock of Cashel—as firm as the hob of hell.

That man would tell lies as fast as a horse would trot.

A person who does his business briskly and energetically 'works like a hatter'—'works like a nailer '—referring to the fussy way of these men plying their trade.

A conceited fellow having a dandy way of lifting and placing his legs and feet in moving about ' walks like a hen in stubbles.'

A person who is cool and collected under trying circumstances is ' as cool as a cucumber.' Here the alliteration helps to popularise the saying.

I must put up the horses now and have them ' as clean as a new pin' for the master.

A person who does good either to an individual or to his family or to the community, but afterwards spoils it all by some contrary course of conduct, is like a cow that fills the pail, but kicks it over in the end.

A person quite illiterate ' wouldn't know a **B** from a bull's foot.' The catching point here is partly alliteration, and partly that a bull's foot has some resemblance to a **B**.

Another expression for an illiterate man :—He wouldn't know a **C** from a chest of drawers—where there is a weak alliteration.

He'll tell you a story as long as to-day and to-morrow. Long enough : for you have to wait on indefinitely for ' to-morrow ': or as they say ' to-morrow come never.'

' You'll lose that handkerchief *as sure as a gun.*'

That furrow is *as straight as a die.*

A person who does neither good nor harm—little ill, little good—is ' like a chip in porridge ': almost always said as a reproach.

I was *on pins and needles* till you came home : i.e. I was very uneasy.

The story went round like wildfire: i.e. circulated rapidly.

Of a person very thin :—He's 'as fat as a hen in the forehead.'

A man is staggering along—not with drink :— That poor fellow is 'drunk with hunger like a showman's dog.'

Dick and Bill are 'as great as inkle-weavers :' a saying very common in Limerick and Cork. *Inkle* is a kind of broad linen tape: a Shakespearian word. 'Several pieces of it were formerly woven in the same loom, by as many boys, who sat close together on the same seat-board.' (Dr. A. Hume.)

William is ' the spit out of his father's mouth ' ; i.e. he is strikingly like his father either in person or character or both. Another expression conveying the same sense :—' Your father will never die while you are alive ' : and ' he's a chip off the old block.' Still another, though not quite so strong :—' He's his father's son.' Another saying to the same effect —' kind father for him '—is examined elsewhere.

' I'm a man in myself like Oliver's bull,' a common saying in my native place (in Limerick), and applied to a confident self-helpful person. The Olivers were the local landlords sixty or seventy years ago. (For a tune with this name see my ' Old Irish Music and Songs,' p. 46.)

A person is asked to do any piece of work which ought to be done by his servant :—' Aye indeed, *keep a dog and bark myself.*'

That fellow walks as straight up and stiff as if he took *a breakfast of ramrods.*

A man who passes through many dangers or

meets with many bad accidents and always escapes has ' as many lives as a cat.'   Everyone knows that a cat has nine lives.

Putting on the big pot means empty boasting and big talk. Like a woman who claps a large pot of water on the fire to boil a weeny little bit of meat —which she keeps out of sight—pretending she has *launa-vaula, lashings and leavings*, full and plenty.

If a man is in low spirits—depressed—down in the mouth—' his heart is as low as a *keeroge's* kidney' (*keeroge*, a beetle or clock). This last now usually said in jest.

James O'Brien is a good scholar, but he's not *in it* with Tom Long : meaning that he is not at all to be compared with Tom Long.

If a person is indifferent about any occurrence — doesn't care one way or the other—he is ' neither glad nor sorry like a dog at his father's wake.' (South.)

CHAPTER XI.

THE MEMORY OF HISTORY AND OF OLD CUSTOMS.

Church, Chapel, Scallan.   All through Ireland it is customary to call a Protestant place of worship a ' church,' and that belonging to Roman Catholics a ' chapel : and this usage not only prevails among the people, but has found its way into official documents. For instance, take the Ordnance maps. In almost every village and town on the map you will

see in one place the word ' Church,' while near by is
printed ' R.C. Chapel.' This custom has its roots far
back in the time when it was attempted to extend
the doctrines of the Reformation to Ireland. Then
wherever the authority of the government prevailed, the church belonging to the Catholics was
taken from them ; the priest was expelled; and a
Protestant minister was installed. But the law went
much farther, and forbade under fearful penalties
the celebration of Mass—penalties for both priest and
congregation. As the people had now no churches,
the custom began of celebrating Mass in the open
air, always in remote lonely places where there was
little fear of discovery. Many of these places retain
to this day names formed from the Irish word *Affrionn*
[affrin], the Mass ; such as the mountain called
Knockanaffrinn in Waterford (the hill of the Mass),
Ardanaffrinn, Lissanaffrinn, and many others, While
Mass was going on, a watcher was always placed
on an adjacent height to have a look-out for the
approach of a party of military, or of a spy with the
offered reward in view.

After a long interval however, when the sharp fangs
of the Penal Laws began to be blunted or drawn, the
Catholics commenced to build for themselves little
places of worship : very timidly at first, and always
in some out-of-the-way place. But they had many
difficulties to contend with. Poverty was one of them ;
for the great body of the congregations were labourers
or tradesmen, as the Catholic people had been almost
crushed out of existence, soul and body, for five or
six generations, by the terrible Penal Laws, which,
with careful attention to details, omitted nothing

that could impoverish and degrade them. But even poverty, bad as it was, never stood decidedly in the way ; for the buildings were not expensive, and the poor people gladly contributed shillings coppers and labour for the luxury of a chapel. A more serious obstacle was the refusal of landlords in some districts to lease a plot of land for the building. In Donegal and elsewhere they had a movable little wooden shed that just sheltered the priest and the sacred appliances while he celebrated Mass, and which was wheeled about from place to place in the parish wherever required. A shed of this kind was called a *scallan* (Irish : a shield, a protecting shelter). Some of these *scallans* are preserved with reverence to this day, as for instance one in Carrigaholt in Clare, where a large district was for many years without any Catholic place of worship, as the local landlord obstinately refused to let a bit of land. You may now see that very *scallan*—not much larger than a sentry-box—beside the new chapel in Carrigaholt.

And so those humble little buildings gradually rose up all over the country. Then many of the small towns and villages through the country presented this spectacle. In one place was the ‘ decent church ’ that had formerly belonged to the Catholics, now in possession of a Protestant congregation of perhaps half a dozen—church, minister, and clerk maintained by contributions of tithes forced from the Catholic people ; and not far off a poor little thatched building with clay floor and rough walls for a Roman Catholic congregation of 500, 1000, or more, all except the few that found room within kneeling on the ground outside, only too glad to be able to be present at Mass under any conditions.

These little buildings were always called 'chapels,' to distinguish them from what were now the Protestant churches. Many of these primitive places of worship remained in use to a period within living memory—perhaps some remain still. When I was a boy I generally heard Mass in one of them, in Ballyorgan, Co. Limerick: clay floor, no seats, walls of rough stone unplastered, thatch not far above our heads. Just over the altar was suspended a level canopy of thin boards, to hide the thatch from the sacred spot: and on its under surface was roughly painted by some rustic artist a figure of a dove—emblematic of the Holy Ghost—which to my childish fancy was a work of art equal at least to anything ever executed by Michael Angelo. Many and many a time I heard exhortations from that poor altar, sometimes in English, sometimes in Irish, by the Rev. Darby Buckley, the parish priest of Glenroe (of which Ballyorgan formed a part), delivered with such earnestness and power as to produce extraordinary effects on the congregation. You saw men and women in tears everywhere around you, and at the few words of unstudied peroration they flung themselves on their knees in a passionate burst of piety and sorrow. Ah, God be with Father Darby Buckley: a small man, full of fire and energy: somewhat overbearing, and rather severe in judging of small transgressions; but all the same, a great and saintly parish priest.

That little chapel has long been superseded by a solid structure, suitable to the neighbourhood and its people.

What has happened in the neighbouring town of Kilfinane is still more typical of the advance of the Catholics. There also stood a large thatched chapel with a clay floor: and the Catholics were just beginning to emerge from their state of servility when the Rev. Father Sheehy was appointed parish priest about the beginning of the last century. He was a tall man of splendid physique: when I was a boy I knew him in his old age, and even then you could not help admiring his imposing figure. At that time the lord of the soil was Captain Oliver, one of that Cromwellian family to whom was granted all the district belonging to their Catholic predecessors, Sir John Ponsonby and Sir Edward Fitzharris, both of whom were impeached and disinherited,

On the Monday morning following the new priest's first Mass he strolled down to have a good view of the chapel and grounds, and was much astonished to find in the chapel yard a cartload of oats in sheaf, in charge of a man whom he recognized as having been at Mass on the day before. He called him over and questioned him, on which the man told him that the captain had sent him with the oats to have it threshed on the chapel floor, as he always did. The priest was amazed and indignant, and instantly ordered the man off the grounds, threatening him with personal chastisement, which—considering the priest's brawny figure and determined look—he perhaps feared more than bell book and candle. The exact words Father Sheehy used were, ' If ever I find you here again with a load of oats or a load of anything else, *I'll break your back for you*: and then I'll go up and break your master's back too!' The fellow went off hot foot with his load, and told his master, expecting all sorts of ructions. But the captain took it in good part, and had his oats threshed elsewhere : and as a matter of fact he and the priest soon after met and became acquainted.

In sending his corn to be threshed on the chapel floor, it is right to remark that the captain intended no offence and no undue exercise of power ; and besides he was always careful to send a couple of men on Saturday evening to sweep the floor and clean up the chapel for the service of next day. But it was a custom of some years' standing, and Father Sheehy's predecessor never considered it necessary to expostulate. It is likely enough indeed that he himself got a few scratches in his day from the Penal Laws, and thought it as well to let matters go on quietly.

After a little time Father Sheehy had a new church built, a solid slate-roofed structure suitable for the time, which, having stood for nearly a century, was succeeded by the present church. This, which was erected after almost incredible labour and perseverance in collecting the funds by the late parish priest, the Very Rev. Patrick Lee, V.F., is one of the most beautiful parish churches in all Ireland. What has happened in Ballyorgan and Kilfinane may be considered a type of what has taken place all over the country. Within the short space of a century the poor thatched clay-floor chapels have been everywhere replaced by solid or beautiful or stately churches, which have sprung up all through Ireland as if by magic, through the exertions of the pastors, and the contributions of the people.

This popular application of the terms 'chapel' and 'church' found—and still finds—expression in many ways. Thus a man who neglects religion: 'he never goes to Church, Mass, or Meeting' (this last word meaning Non-conformist Service). A man says, 'I didn't see Jack Delany at Mass to-day': 'Oh, didn't you hear about him—sure he's going to *church* now' (i.e. he has turned Protestant). And do they never talk of those [young people] who go to church' [i.e. Protestants]. (Knocknagow.)

The term 'chapel' has so ingrained itself in my mind that to this hour the word instinctively springs to my lips when I am about to mention a Catholic place of worship; and I always feel some sort of hesitation or reluctance in substituting the word 'church.' I positively could not bring myself to say, 'Come, it is time now to set out for church': it must be either 'Mass' or 'the chapel.'

I see no reason against our retaining these two words, with their distinction; for they tell in brief a vivid chapter in our history.

Hedge-Schools. Evil memories of the bad old penal days come down to us clustering round this word. At the end of the seventeenth century, among many other penal enactments,* a law was passed that Catholics were not to be educated. Catholic schoolmasters were forbidden to teach, either in schools or in private houses; and Catholic parents were forbidden to send their children to any foreign country to be educated—all under heavy penalties; from which it will be seen that care was taken to

---

* For the Penal Laws, see my 'Child's Hist. of Ireland,' chaps. lv, lvi.

deprive Catholics—as such—altogether of the means of education.

But priests and schoolmasters and people combined all through the country—and not without some measure of success—to evade this unnatural law. Schools were kept secretly, though at great risk, in remote places—up in the mountain glens or in the middle of bogs. Half a dozen young men with spades and shovels built up a rude cabin in a few hours, which served the purpose of a schoolhouse: and from the common plan of erecting these in the shelter of hedges, walls, and groves, the schools came to be known as 'Hedge Schools.' These hedge schools held on for generations, and kept alive the lamp of learning, which burned on—but in a flickering ineffective sort of way—' burned through long ages of darkness and storm '—till at last the restrictions were removed, and Catholics were permitted to have schools of their own openly and without let or hindrance. Then the ancient hereditary love of learning was free to manifest itself once more ; and schools sprang up all over the country, each conducted by a private teacher who lived on the fees paid by his pupils. Moreover, the old designation was retained; for these schools, no longer held in wild places, were called—as they are sometimes called to this day—' hedge schools.'

The schools that arose in this manner, which were of different classes, were spread all over the country during the eighteenth century and the first half of the nineteenth. The most numerous were little elementary schools, which will be described farther on. The higher class of schools, which answered to what we now call Intermediate schools, were found all over the southern half of Ireland, especially in Munster. Some were for classics, some for science, and not a few for both; nearly all conducted by men of learning and ability; and they were everywhere eagerly attended. 'Many of the students had professions in view, some intended for the priesthood, for which the classical schools afforded an admirable preparation; some seeking to become medical doctors, teachers, surveyors, &c. But a large proportion were the sons of farmers, tradesmen, shopkeepers, or others, who had no particular end in view, but, with the instincts of the days of old, studied classics or mathematics for the pure love of learning. I knew many of that class.

'These schools continued to exist down to our own time, till they were finally broken up by the famine of 1847. In my own immediate neighbourhood were some of them, in which I received a part of my early education; and I remember with pleasure several of my old teachers; rough and unpolished men many of them, but excellent solid scholars and full of enthusiasm for learning—which enthusiasm they communicated to their pupils. All the students were adults or grown boys; and there was no instruction in the elementary subjects—reading, writing, and arithmetic—as no scholar attended who had not sufficiently mastered these. Among the students were always half a dozen or more " poor scholars " from distant parts of Ireland, who lived free in the hospitable farmers' houses all round : just as the scholars from Britain and elsewhere were supported in the time of Bede—twelve centuries before.'*

In every town all over Munster there was—down to a period well within my memory—one of those schools, for either classics or science—and in most indeed there were two, one for each branch, besides one or more smaller schools for the elementary branches, taught by less distinguished men.

There was extraordinary intellectual activity among the schoolmasters of those times: some of them indeed thought and dreamed and talked of nothing else but learning; and if you met one of them and fell into conversation, he was sure to give you a strong dose as long as you listened, heedless as to whether you understood him or not. In their eyes learning was the main interest of the world. They often met on Saturdays; and on these occasions certain subjects were threshed out in discussion by the principal men. There were often formal disputations when two of the chief men of a district met, each attended by a number of his senior pupils, to discuss some knotty point in dispute, of classics, science, or grammar.

There was one subject that long divided the teachers of Limerick and Tipperary into two hostile camps of learning—the verb *To be*. There is a well-known rule of grammar that ' the verb *to be* takes the same case after it as goes before it.' One party headed by the two Dannahys, father and son, very scholarly men, of north Limerick, held that the verb

* For ' Poor Scholars,' see O'Curry, ' Man. & Cust.,' i. 79, 80 : Dr. Healy, ' Ireland's Anc. Sch.,' 475 : and, for a modern instance, Carleton's story, ' The Poor Scholar.' The above passage is quoted from my ' Social Hist. of Anc. Ireland.'

to be governed the case following ; while the other, at
the head of whom was Mr. Patrick Murray of
Kilfinane in south Limerick, maintained that the
correspondence of the two cases, after and before,
was mere *agreement*, not *government*. And they
argued with as much earnestness as the Continental
Nominalists and Realists of an older time.

Sometimes the discussions on various points
found their way into print, either in newspapers or
in special broadsheets coarsely printed ; and in these
the mutual criticisms were by no means gentle.

There were poets too, who called in the aid of the
muses to help their cause. One of these, who was
only a schoolmaster in embryo—one of Dannahy's
pupils—wrote a sort of pedagogic Dunciad, in which
he impaled most of the prominent teachers of south
Limerick who were followers of Murray. Here is
how he deals with Mr. Murray himself :—

> Lo, forward he comes, in oblivion long lain,
> Great Murray, the soul of the light-headed train ;
> A punster, a mimic, a jibe, and a quiz,
> His acumen stamped on his all-knowing phiz :
> He declares that the subsequent noun should *agree*
> With the noun or the pronoun preceding *To be*.

Another teacher, from Mountrussell, was great in
astronomy, and was continually holding forth on
his favourite subject and his own knowledge of it.
The poet makes him say :—

> The course of a comet with ease I can trail,
> And with my ferula I measure his tail ;
> On the wings of pure Science without a balloon
> Like Baron Munchausen I visit the moon ;
> Along the ecliptic and great milky way,
> In mighty excursions I soaringly stray ;
> With legs wide extended on the poles I can stand,
> And like marbles the planets I toss in my hand.

The poet then, returning to his own words, goes on to say

> The gods being amused at his logical blab,
> They built him a castle near Cancer the Crab.

But this same astronomer, though having as we see a free residence, never went to live there: he emigrated to Australia where he entered the priesthood and ultimately became a bishop.

One of the ablest of all the Munster teachers of that period was Mr. Patrick Murray, already mentioned, who kept his school in the upper story of the market house of Kilfinane in south Limerick. He was particularly eminent in English Grammar and Literature. I went to his school for one year when I was very young, and I am afraid I was looked upon as very slow, especially in his pet subject Grammar. I never could be got to parse correctly such complications as 'I might, could, would, or should have been loving.' Mr. Murray was a poet too. I will give here a humorous specimen of one of his parodies. It was on the occasion of his coming home one night very late, and not as sober as he should be, when he got ' Ballyhooly ' and no mistake from his wife. It was after Moore's ' The valley lay smiling before me '; and the following are two verses of the original with the corresponding two of the parody, of which the opening line is ' The candle was lighting before me.' But I have the whole parody in my memory.

> MOORE: I flew to her chamber—'twas lonely
>   As if the lov'd tenant lay dead ;
>   Ah would it were death and death only,
>   But no, the young false one had fled.

And *there* hung the lute that could soften
  My very worst pains into bliss,
And the hand that had waked it so often
  Now throbb'd to my proud rival's kiss.

Already the curse is upon her
  And strangers her valleys profane ;
They come to divide—to dishonour—
  And tyrants there long will remain :
But onward—the green banner rearing,
  Go flesh ev'ry brand to the hilt :
On *our* side is Virtue and Erin,
  And *theirs* is the Saxon and Guilt.

         .   .   .   .   .   .

MURRAY :   I flew to the room—'twas *not* lonely :
  My wife and her *grawls* were in bed ;
You'd think it was then and then only
  The tongue had been placed in her head.
For there raged the voice that could soften
  My very worst pains into bliss,
And those lips that embraced me so often
  I dared not approach with a kiss.

A change has come surely upon her :—
  The child which she yet did not *wane*
She flung me—then rolled the clothes on her,
  And naked we both now remain.
But had I been a man less forbearing
  Your blood would be certainly spilt,
For on *my* side there's plunging and tearing
  And on *yours* both the blankets and quilt.

I was a pupil in four of the higher class of schools, in which was finished my school education such as it was. The best conducted was that of Mr. John Condon which was held in the upper story of the market house in Mitchelstown, Co. Cork, a large apartment fully and properly furnished, forming an admirable schoolroom. This was one of the best schools in Munster. It was truly an excellent Intermediate school, and was attended by all the school-going students of the town, Protestant as well as Catholic — with many from the surrounding country. Mr. Condon was a cultured and scholarly man, and he taught science, including mathematics, surveying, and the use of the globes, and also geography and English grammar. He had an assistant who taught Greek and Latin. I was one of the very few who attempted the double work of learning both science and classics. To learn surveying we went once a week—on Saturdays—to Mr. Condon's farm near the town, with theodolite and chain, in the use of which we all—i.e. those of us learning the subject—had to take part in turn. Mr. Condon was thorough master of the science of the Use of the Globes, a very beautiful branch of education which gave the learners a knowledge of the earth, of the solar system, and of astronomy in general. But the use of the globes no longer forms a part of our school teaching :—more's the pity.

The year before going to Mitchelstown I attended a science school of a very different character kept by Mr. Simon Cox in Galbally, a little village in Limerick under the shadow of the Galty Mountains. This was a very rough sort of school, but mathematics and the use of the globes were well taught. There were about forty students. Half a dozen were grown boys, of whom I was one ; the rest were men, mostly young, but a few in middle life—schoolmasters bent on improving their knowledge of science in preparation for opening schools in their own parts of the country.

In that school, and indeed in all schools like it through the country, there were 'poor scholars,' a class already spoken of, who paid for nothing—they were taught for nothing and freely entertained, with bed, supper, and breakfast in the farmers' houses of the neighbourhood. We had four or five of these, not one of whom knew in the morning where he was to sleep at night. When school was over they all set out in different directions, and called at the farmers' houses to ask for lodging ; and although there might be a few refusals, all were sure to be put up for the night. They were expected however to help the children at their lessons for the elementary school before the family retired.

In some cases if a farmer was favourably impressed with a poor scholar's manner and character he kept him—lodging and feeding him in his house—during the whole time of his schooling—the young fellow paying nothing of course, but always helping the little ones at their lessons. As might be expected many of these poor scholars were made of the best stuff ; and I have now in my eye one who was entertained for a couple of years in my grandmother's house, and who subsequently became one of the ablest and most respected teachers in Munster.

Let us remark here that this entertainment of poor scholars was not looked upon in the light of a charity : it was regarded as a duty ; for the instinct ran in the people's blood derived from ancient times when Ireland was the ' Island of Saints and Scholars.'* It was a custom of long standing ; for

---

* See my ' Smaller Social Hist. of Anc. Ireland,' chap. vii.

the popular feeling in favour of learning was always maintained, even through the long dark night of the Penal Laws.

'Tis marvellous how I escaped smoking: I had many opportunities in early life, of which surely the best of all was this Galbally school. For every one I think smoked except the half dozen boys, and even of these one or two were learning industriously. And each scholar took his smoke without ceremony in the schoolroom whenever he pleased, so that the room was never quite clear of the fragrant blue haze. I remember well on one occasion, a class of ten, of whom I was one, sitting round the master, whose chair stood on a slightly elevated platform, and all, both master and scholars, were smoking, except myself. The lesson was on some of the hard problems in Luby's Euclid, which we had been unable to solve, and of which Mr. Cox was now showing us the solutions. He made his diagram for each problem on a large slate turned towards us ; and as we knew the meaning of almost every turn and twist of his pencil as he developed the solution, he spoke very little ; and we followed him over the diagram, *twigging* readily the function of every point, line, angle, and circle. And when at last someone had to ask a brief question, Mr. Cox removed his pipe with his left hand and uttered a few monosyllabic words, which enabled us to pick up the lost thread ; then replacing the pipe, he went on in silence as before.

I was the delight and joy of that school; for I generally carried in my pocket a little fife from which I could roll off jigs, reels, hornpipes, hop-jigs, song tunes, &c., without limit. The school was held in a good-sized room in the second story of a house, of which the landlady and her family lived in the kitchen and bedrooms beneath—on the ground-floor. Some dozen or more of the scholars were always in attendance in the mornings half an hour or so before the arrival of the master, of whom I was sure to be one—what could they do without me?—and then out came the fife, and they cleared the floor for a dance. It was simply magnificent to see and hear these athletic fellows dancing on the bare boards with their thick-soled well-nailed heavy shoes—so as to shake the whole house. And not one in the lot was more joyous than I was; for they were mostly good dancers and did full justice to my spirited strains. At last in came the master: there was no cessation; and he took his seat, looking on complacently till that bout was finished, when I put up my fife, and the serious business of the day was commenced.

We must now have a look at the elementary schools —for teaching Reading, Writing, and Arithmetic to children. They were by far the most numerous, for there was one in every village and hamlet, and two or three or more in every town. These schools were very primitive and rude. The parish priests appointed the teachers, and kept an eye over the schools, which were generally mixed—boys and girls. There was no attempt at classification, and little or no class teaching; the children were taught individually. Each bought whatever Reading Book he or his parents pleased. So there was an odd mixture. A very usual book was a 'Spelling and

Reading book,' which was pretty sure to have the story of Tommy and Harry. In this there were almost always a series of lessons headed ' Principles of Politeness,' which were in fact selected from the writings of Chesterfield. In these there were elaborate instructions how we were to comport ourselves in a drawing room ; and we were to be particularly careful when entering not to let our sword get between our legs and trip us up. We were to bear offences or insults from our companions as long as possible, but if a fellow went too far we were to ' call him out.' It must be confessed there was some of the ' calling out ' business—though not in Chesterfield's sense ; and if the fellows didn't fight with pistols and swords, they gave and got some black eyes and bloody noses. But this was at their peril ; for if the master came to hear of it, they were sure to get further punishment, though not exactly on the face.

Then some scholars had ' The Seven Champions of Christendom,' others ' St. George and the Dragon,' or ' Don Bellianis of Greece,' ' The Seven Wonders of the World,' or ' The History of Reynard the Fox,' a great favourite, translated from an old German mock heroic. And sometimes I have seen girls learning to read from a Catholic Prayerbook. Each had his lesson for next day marked in pencil by the master, which he was to prepare. The pupils were called up one by one each to read his own lesson—whole or part—for the master, and woe betide him if he stumbled at too many words.

The schools were nearly always held in the small ordinary dwelling-houses of the people, or perhaps a barn was utilised: at any rate there was only one room. Not unfrequently the family that owned the house lived in that same room—the kitchen—and went on with their simple household work while the school was buzzing about their ears, neither in any way interfering with the other. There was hardly ever any *school* furniture—no desks of any kind. There were seats enough, of a motley kind—one or two ordinary forms placed at the walls: some chairs with *sugaun* seats; several little stools, and perhaps a few big stones. In fine weather the scholars spent much of their time in the front yard in the open air, where they worked their sums or wrote their copies with the copybooks resting on their knees.

When the priest visited one of these schools, which he did whenever in the neighbourhood, it was a great event for both master and scholars. Conor Leahy was one of those masters—a very rough diamond indeed, though a good teacher and not over severe—whose school was in Fanningstown near my home. One day Billy Moroney ran in breathless, with eyes starting out of his head, to say—as well as he could get it out—that Father Bourke was coming up the road. Now we were all—master and scholars—mortally afraid of Father Bourke and his heavy brows—though never was fear more misplaced (p. 71). The master instantly bounced up and warned us to be of good behaviour—not to stir hand or foot—while the priest was present. He happened to be standing at the fireplace; and he finished up the brief and vigorous exhortation by thumping his fist down on the hob :—' By this stone, if one of ye opens your mouth while the priest is here, I'll knock your

M

brains out after he's gone away!' That visit passed off in great style.

These elementary teachers, or 'hedge teachers,' as they were commonly called, were a respectable body of men, and were well liked by the people. Many of them were rough and uncultivated in speech, but all had sufficient scholarship for their purpose, and many indeed very much more. They were poor, for they had to live on the small fees of their pupils; but they loved learning—so far as their attainments went—and inspired their pupils with the same love. These private elementary schools gradually diminished in numbers as the National Schools spread, and finally disappeared about the year 1850.

These were the schools of the small villages and hamlets, which were to be found everywhere—all over the country : and such were the schools that the Catholic people were only too glad to have after the chains had been struck off—the very schools in which many men that afterwards made a figure in the world received their early education.

The elementary schools of the towns were of a higher class. The attendance was larger ; there were generally desks and seats of the ordinary kind ; and the higher classes were commonly taught something beyond Reading, Writing, and Arithmetic; such as Grammar, or Book-keeping, with occasionally a spice of Euclid, Mensuration, Surveying, or Algebra.

It very often happened that the school took its prevailing tone from the taste of the master; so that the higher classes in one were great at Grammar, those of another at Penmanship, some at Higher

Arithmetic, some at ' Short Accounts ' (i.e. short methods of Mental Arithmetic), others at Book-keeping. For there were then no fixed Programmes and no Inspectors, and each master (in addition to the ordinary elementary subjects) taught just whatever he liked best, and lit up his own special tastes among his pupils.

So far have these words, *church, chapel, scallan, hedge-school,* led us through the bye-ways of History ; and perhaps the reader will not be sorry to turn to something else.

Rattle the hasp: Tent pot. During Fair-days—all over the country—there were half a dozen or more booths or tents on the fair field, put up by publicans, in which was always uproarious fun ; for they were full of people—young and old—eating and drinking, dancing and singing and match-making. There was sure to be a piper or a fiddler for the young people ; and usually a barn door, lifted off its hinges—hasp and all—was laid flat, or perhaps two or three doors were laid side by side, for the dancers ; a custom adopted elsewhere as well as in fairs--

> ' But they couldn't keep time on the cold earthen floor,
> So to humour the music they danced on the door.'
>
> (CROFTON CROKER: *Old Song.*)

There was one particular tune—a jig—which, from the custom of dancing on a door, got the name of ' Rattle the hasp.'

Just at the mouth of the tent it was common to have a great pot hung on hooks over a fire sunk in the ground underneath, and full of pigs cheeks, flitches of bacon, pigs' legs and *croobeens* galore, kept

M 2

perpetually boiling like the chiefs' caldrons of old, so that no one need be hungry or thirsty so long as he had a penny in his pocket.   These pots were so large that they came to be spoken of as a symbol of plenty: 'Why you have as much bacon and cabbage there as would fill a tent-pot.'

One day—long long ago—at the fair of Ardpatrick in Limerick—I was then a little boy, but old enough to laugh at the story when I heard it in the fair—a fellow with a wattle in his hand having a sharp iron spike on the end, walked up to one of these tent-pots during the momentary absence of the owner, and thrusting the spike into a pig's cheek, calmly stood there holding the stick in his hand till the man came up.   'What are you doing there?'—When the other looking sheepish and frightened:—'Wisha sir I have a little bit of a pig's cheek here that isn't done well enough all out, and I was thinking that may be you wouldn't mind if I gave it a couple of *biles* in your pot.' 'Be off out of that you impudent blaa-guard, yourself and your pig's cheek, or I'll break every bone in your body.'   The poor innocent boy said nothing, but lifted the stick out of the pot with the pig's cheek on the end of it, and putting it on his shoulder, walked off through the fair with meek resignation.

More than a thousand years ago it was usual in Ireland for ladies who went to banquets with their husbands or other near relations to wear a mask. This lady's mask was called *fethal*, which is the old form of the word, modern form *fidil*. The memory of this old custom is preserved in the name now given to a mask by both English and Irish speakers— *i fiddle*, *eye-fiddle*, *hi-fiddle*, or *hy-fiddle* (the first two being the most correct). The full Irish name is *aghaidh-fidil*, of which the first part *agaidh*, pronounced *i* or *eye*, means the face :—*agaidh-fidil*, 'face-mask.' This word was quite common in Munster sixty or seventy years ago, when we, boys, made our own *i-fiddles*, commonly of brown paper, daubed in colour—hideous-looking things when worn —enough to frighten a horse from his oats.

Among those who fought against the insurgents in Ireland during the Rebellion of 1798 were some German cavalry called Hessians. They wore a sort of long boots so remarkable that boots of the same pattern are to this day called *Hessian boots*. One day in a skirmish one of the rebels shot down a Hessian, and brought away his fine boots as his lawful prize. One of his comrades asked him for the boots : and he answered ' Kill a Hessian for yourself,' which has passed into a proverb. When by labour and trouble you obtain anything which another seeks to get from you on easy terms, you answer *Kill a Hessian for yourself.*

During the War of the Confederation in Ireland in the seventeenth century Murrogh O'Brien earl of Inchiquin took the side of the Government against his own countrymen, and committed such merciless ravages among the people that he is known to this day as ' Murrogh the Burner' ; and his name has passed into a proverb for outrage and cruelty. When a person persists in doing anything likely to bring on heavy punishment of some kind, the people say ' If you go on in that way *you'll see Murrogh*,' meaning ' you will suffer for it.' Or when a person seems scared or frightened :—' He saw Murrogh or

the bush next to him.' The original sayings are in
Irish, of which these are translations, which however
are now heard oftener than the Irish.

In Armagh where Murrogh is not known they say
in a similar sense, ' You'll catch Lanty,' Lanty no
doubt being some former local bully.

When one desires to give another a particularly
evil wish he says, ' The curse of Cromwell on you !'
So that Cromwell's atrocities are stored up in the
people's memories to this day, in the form of a
proverb.

In Ulster they say ' The curse of *Crummie*.'

' Were you talking to Tim in town to-day ?' ' No,
but I saw him *from me* as the soldier saw Bunratty.'
Bunratty a strong castle in Co. Clare, so strong that
besiegers often had to content themselves with view-
ing it from a distance. ' Seeing a person from me'
means seeing him at a distance. ' Did you meet
your cousin James in the fair to-day ?' ' Oh I just
caught sight of him *from me* for a second, but I
wasn't speaking to him.

Sweating-House.—We know that the Turkish bath
is of recent introduction in these countries. But the
hot-air or vapour bath, which is much the same
thing, was well known in Ireland from very early
times, and was used as a cure for rheumatism down
to a few years ago. The structures in which these
baths were given are known by the name of *tigh 'n
alluis* [teenollish], or in English, ' sweating-house '
(*allus*, ' sweat '). They are still well known in the
northern parts of Ireland—small houses entirely
of stone, from five to seven feet long inside, with a
low little door through which one must creep:

always placed remote from habitations : and near by was commonly a pool or tank of water four or five feet deep. They were used in this way. A great fire of turf was kindled inside till the house became heated like an oven ; after which the embers and ashes were swept out, and water was splashed on the stones, which produced a thick warm vapour. Then the person, wrapping himself in a blanket, crept in and sat down on a bench of sods, after which the door was closed up. He remained there an hour or so till he was in a profuse perspiration : and then creeping out, plunged right into the cold water ; after emerging from which he was well rubbed till he became warm. After several baths at intervals of some days he commonly got cured. Persons are still living who used these baths or saw them used. (See the chapter on 'Ancient Irish Medicine' in 'Smaller Soc. Hist. of Anc. Ireland,' from which the above passage is taken.)

The lurking conviction that times long ago were better than at present—a belief in 'the good old times' —is indicated in the common opening to a story :— 'Long and merry ago, there lived a king,' &c.

'That poor man is as thin as a *whipping* post': a very general saying in Ireland. Preserving the memory of the old custom of tying culprits to a firm post in order to be whipped. A whipping post received many of the slashes, and got gradually worn down.

The hardiness of the northern rovers—the Danes— who made a great figure in Ireland, as in England and elsewhere, is still remembered, after nine or ten centuries, in the sayings of our people. Scores of

times I heard such expressions as the following:—
'Ah shut that door: there's a breeze in through it
that *would perish the Danes.*'

The cardinal points are designated on the supposition that the face is turned to the east: a custom
which has descended in Ireland from the earliest times
of history and tradition, and which also prevailed
among other ancient nations.   Hence in Irish 'east'
is 'front'; 'west' is 'behind' or 'back'; north is
'left hand'; and south is 'right hand.'   The people
sometimes import these terms into English. 'Where
is the tooth?' says the dentist.   'Just here sir, in
the *west* of my jaw,' replies the patient—meaning at
the back of the jaw.

Tailors were made the butt of much good-natured
harmless raillery, often founded on the well-known
fact that a tailor is the ninth part of a man.   If a
person leaves little after a meal, or little material
after any work—that is 'tailor's leavings'; alluding to
an alleged custom of the craft.   According to this
calumny your tailor, when sending home your finished
suit, sends with it a few little scraps as what was
left of the cloth you gave him, though he had really
much left, which he has cribbed.

When you delay the performance of any work,
or business with some secret object in view, you 'put
the pot in the tailor's link.'   Formerly tailors
commonly worked in the houses of the families who
bought their own material and employed them to
make the clothes.   The custom was to work till
supper time, when their day ended.   Accordingly the
good housewife often hung the pot-hangers on the
highest hook or link of the pot-hooks so as to raise

the supper-pot well up from the fire and delay the boiling. (Ulster.)

The following two old rhymes are very common :—

> Four and twenty tailors went out to kill a snail,
> The biggest of them all put his foot upon his tail—
> The snail put out his horns just like a cow :
> ' O Lord says the tailor we're all killed now ! '

> As I was going to Dub-l-in
> I met a pack of tailors,
> I put them in my pocket,
> In fear the ducks might *ait* them.

In the Co. Down the Roman Catholics are called ' back-o'-the-hill folk': an echo of the Plantations of James I—three centuries ago—when the Catholics, driven from their rich lowland farms, which were given to the Scottish Presbyterian planters, had to eke out a living among the glens and mountains.

When a person does anything out of the common—which is not expected of him—especially anything with a look of unusual prosperity :—' It is not every day that Manus kills a bullock.' (Derry.) This saying, which is always understood to refer to Roman Catholics, is a memorial, in one flash, of the plantation of the northern districts. Manus is a common Christian name among the Catholics round Derry, who are nearly all very poor : how could they be otherwise ? That Manus—i.e. a Catholic—should kill a bullock is consequently taken as a type of things very unusual, unexpected and exceptional. Maxwell, in ' Wild Sports of the West,' quotes this saying as he heard it in Mayo ; but naturally enough the saying alone had reached the west without its background of history, which is not known there as it is in Derry.

Even in the everyday language of the people the memory of those Plantations is sometimes preserved, as in the following sayings and their like, which are often heard. 'The very day after Jack Ryan was evicted, he *planted himself* on the bit of land between his farm and the river.' 'Bill came and *planted* himself on my chair, right in front of the fire.'

'He that calls the tune should pay the piper' is a saying that commemorates one of our dancing customs. A couple are up for a dance : the young man asks the girl in a low voice what tune she'd like, and on hearing her reply he calls to the piper (or fiddler) for the tune. When the dance is ended and they have made their bow, he slips a coin into her hand, which she brings over and places in the hand of the piper. That was the invariable formula in Munster sixty years ago.

The old Irish name of May-day—the 1st May—was *Belltaine* or *Beltene* [Beltina], and this name is still used by those speaking Irish ; while in Scotland and Ulster they retain it as a common English word—Beltane :—

> 'Ours is no sapling, chance sown by the fountain,
>   Blooming at Beltane, in winter to fade.'
>   ('Lady of the Lake.')

Before St. Patrick's time there was a great pagan festival in Ireland on 1st May in honour of the god *Bél* [Bail], in which fire played a prominent part : a custom evidently derived in some way from the Phœnician fire festival in honour of the Phœnician god *Baal*. For we know that the Phœnicians were well acquainted with Ireland, and that wherever they went they introduced the worship of Baal with his festivals.

Among other usages the Irish drove cattle through or between big fires to preserve them from the diseases of the year; and this custom was practised in Limerick and Clare down a period within my own memory: I saw it done. But it was necessary that the fires should be kindled from *tenaigin* [*g* sounded as in *pagan*]—'forced fire'—i.e., fire produced by the friction of two pieces of dry wood rubbed together till they burst into a flame: Irish *teine-éigin* from *teinĕ*, fire, and *éigean*, force. This word is still known in the South; so that the memory of the old pagan May-day festival and its fire customs is preserved in these two words *Beltane* and *tenaigin*.

Mummers were companies of itinerant play-actors, who acted at popular gatherings, such as fairs, *patterns*, weddings, wakes, &c. Formerly they were all masked, and then young *squireens*, and the young sons of strong farmers, often joined them for the mere fun of the thing; but in later times masking became illegal, after which the breed greatly degenerated. On the whole they were not unwelcome to the people, as they were generally the source of much amusement; but their antics at weddings and wakes were sometimes very objectionable, as well as very offensive to the families. This was especially the case at wakes, if the dead person had been unpopular or ridiculous, and at weddings if an old woman married a boy, or a girl an old man for the sake of his money. Sometimes they came bent on mischievous tricks as well as on a *shindy*; and if wind of this got out, the faction of the family gathered to protect them; and then there was sure to be a fight. (Kinahan.)

Mummers were well known in England, from which the custom was evidently imported to Ireland. The mummers are all gone, but the name remains.

We know that in former times in Ireland the professions ran in families; so that members of the same household devoted themselves to one particular Science or Art—Poetry, History, Medicine, Building, Law, as the case might be—for generations (of this custom a full account may be seen in my 'Smaller Social History of Ancient Ireland,' chap. vii., especially page 184). A curious example of how the memory of this is preserved occurs in Armagh. There is a little worm called *dirab* found in bog-water. If this be swallowed by any accident it causes a swelling, which can be cured only by a person of the name of Cassidy, who puts his arms round the patient, and the worm dies. The O'Cassidys were hereditary physicians to the Maguires, chiefs of Fermanagh. Several eminent physicians of the name are commemorated in the Irish Annals: and it is interesting to find that they are still remembered in tradition—though quite unconsciously —for their skill in leechcraft.

'I'll make you dance Jack Lattin'—a threat of chastisement, often heard in Kildare. John Lattin of Morristown House county Kildare (near Naas) wagered that he'd dance home to Morristown from Dublin—more than twenty miles—changing his dancing-steps every furlong: and won the wager. 'I'll make you dance' is a common threat heard everywhere : but ' I'll make you dance Jack Lattin' is ten times worse—'I'll make you dance excessively.'

Morristown, Jack Lattin's residence, is near Lyons the seat of Lord Cloncurry, where Jack was often a guest, in the first half of the last century. Lady Morgan has an entry in her Memoirs (1830):—
'Returned from Lyons—Lord Cloncurry's, a large party—the first day good—Sheil, Curran, Jack Lattin.'

It is worthy of remark that there is a well-known Irish tune called 'Jack Lattin,' which some of our Scotch friends have quietly appropriated; and not only that, but have turned Jack himself into a Scotchman by calling the tune 'Jockey Latin'! They have done precisely the same with our 'Eileen Aroon' which they call 'Robin Adair.' The same Robin Adair—or to call him by his proper name Robert Adair—was a well-known county Wicklow man and a member of the Irish Parliament.

The word *sculloge* or *scolloge* is applied to a small farmer, especially one that does his own farm work: it is often used in a somewhat depreciatory sense to denote a mere rustic: and in both senses it is well known all over the South. This word has a long history. It was originally applied—a thousand years ago or more—to the younger monks of a monastery, who did most of the farm work on the land belonging to the religious community. These young men were of course students indoors, as well as tillers outside, and hence the name, from *scol*, a school:— *scológ*, a young scholar. But as farm work constituted a large part of their employment the name gradually came to mean a working farmer; and in this sense it has come down to our time.

To a rich man whose forefathers made their

money by smuggling *pottheen* (illicit whiskey) from
Innishowen in Donegal (formerly celebrated for its
pottheen manufacture), they say in Derry ' your
granny was a Dogherty who wore a tin pocket.'
(Doherty a prevalent name in the neighbourhood.)
For this was a favourite way of smuggling from the
highlands—bringing the stuff in a tin pocket.   Tom
Boyle had a more ambitious plan :—he got a tinker
to make a hollow figure of tin, something like the
figure of his wife, who was a little woman, which
Tom dressed up in his wife's clothes and placed on
the pillion behind him on the horse—filled with
pottheen : for in those times it was a common custom
for the wife to ride behind her husband.   At last a
sharp-eyed policeman, seeing the man's affectionate
attention so often repeated, kept on the watch, and
satisfied himself at last that Tom had a tin wife.
So one day, coming behind the animal he gave the
poor little woman a whack of a stick which brought
forth, not a screech, but a hard metallic sound, to
the astonishment of everybody : and then it was all
up with poor Tom and his wife.

There are current in Ireland many stories of gaugers
and pottheen distillers which hardly belong to my
subject, except this one, which I may claim, because it
has *left its name on* a well-known Irish tune :—' Paddy
outwitted the gauger,' also called by three other
names, ' The Irishman's heart for the ladies,' ' Drops
of brandy,' and *Cummilum* (Moore's : ' Fairest put on
Awhile '). Paddy Fogarty kept a little public-house at
the cross-roads in which he sold ' parliament,' i.e.
legal whiskey on whichthe duty had been paid ; but
it was well known that friends could get a little drop

of pottheen too, on the sly. One hot July day he was returning home from Thurles with a ten-gallon cag on his back, slung by a strong *soogaun* (hay rope). He had still two good miles before him, and he sat down to rest, when who should walk up but the new gauger. ' Well my good fellow, what have you got in that cask ? ' Paddy dropped his jaw, looking the picture of terror, and mumbled out some tomfoolery like an excuse. ' Ah, my man, you needn't think of coming over me : I see how it is : I seize this cask in the name of the king.' Poor Paddy begged and prayed, and talked about Biddy and the childher at home—all to no use : the gauger slung up the cag on his back (about a hundredweight) and walked on, with Paddy, heart-broken, walking behind—for the gauger's road lay towards Paddy's house. At last when they were near the cross-roads the gauger sat down to rest, and laying down the big load began to wipe his face with his handkerchief. ' Sorry I am,' says Paddy, ' to see your honour so dead *bet* up : sure you're sweating like a bull : maybe I could relieve you.' And with that he pulled his legal *permit* out of his pocket and laid it on the cag. The gauger was astounded : ' Why the d—— didn't you show me that before?' 'Why then 'tis the way your honour,' says Paddy, looking as innocent as a lamb, ' I didn't like to make so bould as I wasn't axed to show it ? ' So the gauger, after a volley of something that needn't be particularised here, walked off *with himself without an inch of the tail.* ' Faix,' says Paddy, ' 'tis easy to know 'twasn't our last gauger, ould Warnock, that was here : 'twouldn't be so easy to come round him ; for he had a nose that would *smell a needle in a forge,*'

In Sligo if a person is sick in a house, and one of
the cattle dies, they say ‘ a life for a life,’ and the
patient will recover. Mr. Kinahan says, ‘ This is so
universal in the wilds of Sligo that Protestants and
Catholics believe it alike.’

As an expression of welcome, a person says, ‘ We’ll
spread green rushes under your feet ’; a memory of
the time when there were neither boards nor carpets
on the floors—nothing but the naked clay—in Ireland
as well as in England ; and in both countries, it was
the custom to strew the floors of the better class of
houses with rushes, which were renewed for any
distinguished visitor. This was always done by the
women-servants : and the custom was so general and
so well understood that there was a knife of special
shape for cutting the rushes. (See my ‘ Smaller
Social Hist. of Ancient Ireland,’ p. 305.)

A common exclamation of drivers for urging on a
horse, heard everywhere in Ireland, is *hupp, hupp!*
It has found its way even into our nursery rhymes ;
as when a mother is dancing her baby up and down
on her knee, she sings :—

> ‘ How many miles to Dub-l-in ?
>   Three score and ten,
>   Will we be there by candle light ?
>   Yes and back again :
>   *Hupp, hupp* my little horse,
>   *Hupp, hupp* again.’

This Irish word, insignificant as it seems, has come
down from a period thirteen or fourteen hundred years
ago, or probably much farther back. In the library
of St. Gall in Switzerland there is a manuscript
written in the eighth century by some scholarly Irish

monk—who he was we cannot tell : and in this the old writer *glosses* or explains many Latin words by corresponding Irish words. Among others the Latin interjection *ei* or *hei* (meaning ho! quick! come on) is explained by *upp* or *hupp* (Zeuss).

Before Christianity had widely spread in Ireland, the pagans had a numerous pantheon of gods and goddesses, one of which was *Badb* [bibe], a terrible war-fury. Her name is pronounced *Bibe* or *Bybe*, and in this form it is still preserved all over Cork and round about, not indeed for a war-fury, but for what—in the opinion of some people—is nearly as bad, a *scolding woman*. (For *Badb* and all the other pagan Irish gods and goddesses, see my 'Smaller Social History of Ancient Ireland,' chap. v.)

From the earliest times in Ireland animals were classified with regard to grazing ; and the classification is recognised and fully laid down in the Brehon Law. The legal classification was this :—two geese are equivalent to a sheep ; two sheep to a *dairt* or one-year-old heifer ; two *dairts* to one *colpach* or *collop* (as it is now called) or two-year-old heifer ; two *collops* to one cow. Suppose a man had a right to graze a certain number of cows on a common (i.e. pasture land not belonging to individuals but common to all the people of the place collectively) ; he might turn out the exact number of cows or the equivalent of any other animals he pleased, so long as the total did not exceed the total amount of his privilege.

In many parts of Ireland this system almost exactly as described above is kept up to this day, the collop being taken as the unit : it was universal in my native place sixty years ago ; and in a way it exists

N

there still. The custom is recognised in the present-
day land courts, with some modifications in the
classification—as Mr. Maurice Healy informs me in
an interesting and valuable communication—the
collop being still the unit—and constantly referred to
by the lawyers in the conduct of cases. So the old
Brehon Law process has existed continuously from
old times, and is repeated by the lawyers of our own
day ; and its memory is preserved in the word *collop*.
(See my ' Smaller Soc. Hist. of Anc. Ireland,' p. 431.)

In pagan times the religion of Ireland was
Druidism, which was taught by the druids : and far
off as the time is the name of these druids still exists
in our popular speech. The Irish name for a druid
is *drui* [dree] ; and in the South any crabbed cunning
old-fashioned-looking little boy is called—even by
speakers of English—a *shoundree*, which exactly
represents in sound the Irish *sean-drui*, old druid ;
from *sean* [shoun or shan], old. See ' Irish Names
of Places,' I. 98.)

There are two words much in use in Munster,
of which the phonetic representations are *thoothach*
or *thoohagh* and *hóchan* (ó long), which tell a tale of
remote times. A *thoothach* or *thoohagh* is an ignorant
unmannerly clownish fellow: and *hóchan* means much
the same thing, except that it is rather lower in the
sense of ignorance or uncouthness. Passing through
the Liberties of Dublin I once heard a woman—
evidently from Limerick—call a man a dirty *hóchan*.
Both words are derived from *tuath* [thooa], a layman,
as distinguished from a cleric or a man of learning.
The Irish form of the first is *tuathtach* : of the second
thuathcháin (vocative). Both are a memory of the

time when illiterate people were looked down upon as boorish and ill-mannered as compared with clerics or with men of learning in general.

The people had great respect and veneration for the old families of landed gentry—*the real old stock* as they were called. If a man of a lower class became rich so as to vie with or exceed in possessions many of the old families, he was never recognised as on their level or as a gentleman. Such a man was called by the people a *half-sir*, which bears its meaning on its face.

Sixty years ago people very generally used home-made and home-grown produce — frieze — linen — butter—bacon—potatoes and vegetables in general. A good custom, for 'a cow never burst herself by chewing her cud.' (MacCall : Wexford.)

To see one magpie or more is a sign of bad or good luck, viz. :—'One for sorrow ; two for mirth ; three for a wedding ; four for a birth.' (MacCall : Wexford.)

The war-cry of the great family of O'Neill of Tyrone was *Lauv-derg-aboo* (the Red Hand to Victory : the Red Hand being the cognisance of the O'Neills) : and this cry the clansmen shouted when advancing to battle. It is many a generation since this same cry was heard in battle ; and yet it is remembered in popular sayings to this day. In Tyrone when a fight is expected one man will say to another 'there will be *Dergaboos* to-day' : not that the cry will be actually raised ; but *Dergaboo* has come to be a sort of symbolic name for a fight.

In and around Ballina in Mayo, a great strong fellow is called an *allay-foozee*, which represents the sound of the French *Allez-fusil* (musket or musketry forward), preserving the memory of the landing of the French at Killala (near Ballina) in 1798.

When a person looks as if he were likely to die soon :—' He's in the raven's book.' Because when a person is about to die, the raven croaks over the house. (MacCall : Wexford.)

A ' cross ' was a small old Irish coin so called from a figure of St. Patrick stamped on it with a conspicuous cross. Hence a person who has no money says ' I haven't a cross.' In Wexford they have the same saying with a little touch of drollery added on :—' There isn't as much as a cross in my pocket to keep the devil from dancing in it.' (MacCall.) For of course the devil dare not come near a cross of any shape or form.

A *keenoge* (which exactly represents the pronunciation of the Irish *cianóg*) is a very small coin, a farthing or half a farthing. It was originally applied to a small foreign coin, probably Spanish, for the Irish *cian* is ' far off,' ' foreign ': *óg* is the diminutive termination. It is often used like ' cross': ' I haven't as much as a keenoge in my pocket.' ' Are you not going to lend me any money at all ? ' ' Not a keenoge.'

A person not succeeding in approaching the house or spot he wants to reach ; hitting wide of the mark in shooting ; not coming to the point in argument or explanation :—' Oh you didn't come within the bray of an ass of it.' This is the echo of a very old custom. More than a thousand years ago distance was often vaguely measured in Ireland by sound. A man felling a tree was ' bound by the Brehon Law to give warning as far as his voice could reach,' so as to obviate danger to cattle or people. We find a like measure used in Donegal to this day :—[The Dublin house where you'll get the book to buy is on the Quays] ' about a mountain man's call below the Four Courts.' (Seumas MacManus.) The crow of a cock and the sound of a bell (i.e. the small hand-bell then used) as measures of distances are very often met with in ancient Irish writings. An old commentator on the Brehon Laws defines a certain distance to be ' as far as the sound of the bell or the crow of a barn-door cock could be heard. This custom also prevailed among other ancient nations. (See my ' Smaller Soc. Hist. of Anc. Ireland,' p. 473.)

The 'Duty.' Formerly all through Ireland the tenants were obliged to work for their landlords on a certain number of days free, except that they generally got food. Such work was commonly called in English the ' duty.' In Wicklow for example—until very recently—or possibly still— those who had horses had to draw home the land-lord's turf on certain days. In Wexford they had in a similar way to draw stones for the embankments on the Barrow. The tenants commonly collected in numbers on the same day and worked all together. The Irish word used to designate such gatherings was *bal*—still so called in Connaught. It was usual to hear such English expressions as—' Are you going to the duty?' or ' Are you going to the bal?' (Kinahan.)

(N.B. I do not know the Irish word *bal* in this sense, and cannot find it in the Dictionaries.)

'Duty' is used in a religious sense by Roman

Catholics all through Ireland to designate the
obligation on all Catholics to go to Confession and
Holy Communion at Easter time. 'I am going to
my duty, please God, next week.'

'I'll return you this book on next Saturday *as
sure as the hearth-money*': a very common expression
in Ireland. The old English oppressive impost
called *hearth-money*—a tax on hearths—which every
householder had to pay, was imported into Ireland
by the English settlers. Like all other taxes it was
certain to be called for and gathered at the proper
time, so that our saying is an apt one; but while the
bad old impost is gone, its memory is preserved in
the everyday language of the people.

A king, whether of a small or large territory, had
in his service a champion or chief fighting man
whose duty it was to avenge all insults or offences
offered to the families of the king and tribe,
particularly murder; like the 'Avenger of blood' of
the Jews and other ancient nations. In any expected
danger from without he had to keep watch—with a
sufficient force—at the most dangerous ford or
pass—called *bearna baoghaill* [barna beel] or gap of
danger—on that part of the border where invasion
was expected, and prevent the entrance of any
enemy. This custom, which is as old as our race in
Ireland, is remembered in our present-day speech,
whether Irish or Anglo-Irish; for the man who
courageously and successfully defends any cause or
any position, either by actual fighting or by speeches
or written articles, is 'the man in the gap.' Of the
old Irish chiefs Thomas Davis writes:—

'Their hearts were as soft as the child in the lap,
    Yet they were the men in the gap.'

In the old heroic semi-historic times in Ireland, a champion often gave a challenge by standing in front of the hostile camp or fort and striking a few resounding blows with the handle of his spear either on his own shield or on a shield hung up for the purpose at the entrance gate outside.*

The memory of this very old custom lives in a word still very common in the South of Ireland —*boolimskee*, Irish *buailim-sciath*, 'I strike the shield,' applied to a man much given to fighting, a quarrelsome fellow, a swaggering bully—a swash-buckler.

Paying on the nail, paying down on the nail; paying on the spot—ready cash. This expression had its origin in a custom formerly prevailing in Limerick city. In a broad thoroughfare under the Exchange stood a pillar about four feet high, on the top of which was a circular plate of copper about three feet in diameter. This pillar was called 'The Nail.' The purchaser of anything laid down the stipulated price or the earnest *on the nail*, i.e. on the brass plate, which the seller took up: when this was done before witnesses the transaction was as binding as if entered on parchment. (O'Keeffe's Recollections.) 'The Nail' is still to the fore, and may now be seen in the Museum of the Carnegie Library building, to which it was transferred a short time ago.

The change in the Calendar from the old style to the new style, a century and a half ago, is noted in the names for Christmas. All through the South,

---

* See for an example Dr. Hyde's 'Children of the King of Norway,' 153. (Irish Texts Soc.)

and in other parts of Ireland, the 6th January ('Twelfth Day') is called 'Old Christmas' and 'Little Christmas' (for before the change of style it was *the* Christmas): and in many parts of the north our present Christmas is called New Christmas. So in Donegal the 12th of May is called by the people 'Old May day.' (Seumas MacManus.)

Palm, Palm-Sunday. The usual name in Ireland for the yew-tree is 'palm,' from the custom of using yew branches instead of the real palm, to celebrate Palm Sunday — the Sunday before Easter — commemorating the palm branches that were strewed before our Lord on His public entry into Jerusalem. I was quite a grown boy before I knew the yew-tree by its proper name—it was always *palm-tree.*

Oliver's Summons.—When a lazy fellow was driven to work either by hunger or by any unavoidable circumstance he was said to have got *Oliver's Summons,* a common household word in parts of the county Limerick in my younger days, originating in the following circumstance. When a good plentiful harvest came round, many of the men of our neighbourhood at this time—about the beginning of last century—the good old easy-going times— worked very little—as little as ever they could. What was the use of working when they had plenty of beautiful floury potatoes for half nothing, with salt or *dip*, or perhaps a piggin of fine thick milk to crown the luxury. Captain Oliver, the local landlord, and absolute monarch so far as ordinary life was concerned, often—in those seasons—found it hard or impossible to get men to come to do the necessary work about his grounds—though paying the usual wages—till at last he hit on an original plan. He sent round, the evening before, to the houses of the men he wanted, a couple of fellows with a horse and cart, who seized some necessary article in each house—a spinning-wheel, a bed, the pot, the single table, &c.—and brought them all away body and bones, and kept them impounded. Next morning he was sure to have half a dozen or more strapping fellows, who fell to work; and when it was finished and wages paid, the captain sent home the articles. I had this story from old men who saw the carts going round with their loads.

CHAPTER XII.

A VARIETY OF PHRASES.

AMONG fireside amusements propounding riddles was very general sixty or seventy years ago. This is a custom that has existed in Ireland from very early times, as the reader may see by looking at my 'Old Celtic Romances,' pp. 69, 186, 187, where he will find some characteristic ancient Irish ones. And we know that it was common among other ancient nations. I have a number of our modern Irish riddles, many in my memory, and some supplied to me from Wexford by Mr. Patrick J. MacCall of Dublin, who knows Wexford well. Some are easy enough: but there are others that might defy the Witch of Endor to answer them. They hardly come within my scope, but I will give a few examples.

A steel grey with a flaxen tail and a brass boy driving.   Answer: needle and thread; thimble.

Little Jennie Whiteface has a red nose,
The longer she lives the shorter she grows.
Answer: a lighted candle.

> A man without eyes
> Went out to view the skies,
>   He saw a tree with apples on:
> He took no apples,
> He ate no apples,
>   And still he left no apples on.

Answer: a one-eyed man: the tree had two apples: he took one.

Long legs, crooked thighs, little head, no eyes. Answer: a tongs.

Ink-ank under a bank ten drawing four.   Answer: a girl milking a cow.

> Four-and-twenty white bulls tied in a stall:
> In comes a red bull and over licks them all.

Answer: teeth and tongue.

These are perhaps not very hard, though not quite so easy as the Sphinx's riddle to the Thebans, which Œdipus answered to his immortal renown. But I should like to see Œdipus try his hand at the following. Samson's riddle about the bees is hard enough, but ours beats it hollow. Though Solomon solved all the puzzles propounded to him by the Queen of Sheba, I think this would put him to the pin of his collar. I learned it in Limerick two generations ago; and I have got a Wexford version from Mr. MacCall. Observe the delightful inconsequence of riddle and answer.

Riddle me, riddle me right :
What did I see last night ?
　　The wind blew,
　　The cock crew,
　　The bells of heaven
　　Struck eleven.
'Tis time for my poor *sowl* to go to heaven.

Answer : the fox burying his mother under a holly tree.

To a person who begins his dinner without saying grace : ' You begin your meal like a fox ' : for a fox never says grace. A fox once ran off with a cock—neck in mouth—to make a meal of him. Just as he was about to fall to, the cock said—' Won't you thank God ? ' So the fox opened his mouth to say grace, and the cock escaped and flew up into a tree. On which the fox swore he'd never more say grace or any other prayer. (From Clare : Healy.)

In depreciation of a person's honour : ' Your honour and goat's wool would make good stockings ' : i.e. your honour is as far from true honour as goat's hair is from wool.

' For the life of me ' I can't see why you vex yourself for so small a matter.

Of a pair of well-matched bad men :—' They might lick thumbs.' Also ' A pity to spoil two houses with them.' (Moran : Carlow.)

A person is said to be ' belled through the parish ' when some discreditable report concerning him has gone about in the neighbourhood. The allusion is to a bellman announcing something to the public. (Moran : Carlow.)

A person addresses some abusive and offensive words to another, who replies 'Talk away: *your tongue is no scandal.*'   The meaning is, 'You are so well known for the foulness of your tongue that no one will pay any attention to you when you are speaking evil of another.'   (Moran: Carlow.)

'Come and have a drink,' said the dragoon.   'I don't take anything; *thank you all the same,*' replied Billy Heffernan.   (Knocknagow.)   Very general everywhere in Ireland.

Regarding a person in consumption :—

> March will *sarch* [search],
> April will try,
> May will see
> Whether you'll live or die.
>
> (MacCall : Wexford.)

When a man inherits some failing from his parents, 'He didn't catch it in the wind'—'It wasn't off the wind he took it.'   (Moran: Carlow.)

When a man declines to talk with or discuss matters with another, he says 'I owe you no discourse' —used in a more or less offensive sense—and heard all through Ireland.

When a person shows himself very cute and clever another says to him 'Who let you out?'—an ironical expression of fun : as much as to say that he must have been confined in an asylum as a confirmed fool. (Moran: Carlow.)

When a person for any reason feels elated, he says 'I wouldn't call the king my uncle.' ('Knocknagow'; but heard everywhere in Ireland.)

When a person who is kind enough while he is with

you grows careless about you once he goes away:—
'Out of sight out of mind.'

To go *with your finger in your mouth* is to go on a
fool's errand, to go without exactly knowing why you
are going—without knowing particulars.

When a person singing a song has to stop up
because he forgets the next verse, he says (mostly
in joke) 'there's a hole in the ballad'—throwing the
blame on the old ballad sheet on which the words
were imperfect on account of a big hole.

Searching for some small article where it is hard
to find it among a lot of other things is 'looking for
a needle in a bundle of straw.'

When a mistake or any circumstance that entails
loss or trouble is irreparable—'there's no help for
spilt milk.'

Seventy or eighty years ago the accomplishments
of an Irishman should be:

> To smoke his dudheen,
> To drink his cruiskeen,
> To flourish his alpeen,
> To wallop a spalpeen.
>
> (MacCall : Wexford.)

It is reported about that Tom Fox stole Dick Finn's
sheep : but he didn't. Driven to desperation by the
false report, Tom now really steals one, and says :—
'As I have the name of it, I may as well have the
gain of it.'

A person is told of some extraordinary occurrence
and exclaims :—' Well such a thing as that was never
before heard of *since Adam was a boy.*' This last
expression is very general.

The Chairman of the Banbridge Board of Guardians

lately asked a tramp what was his occupation : to which the fellow—cancelling his impudence by his drollery—replied :—'I'm a hailstone maker out of work owing to the want of snow.'

My partner in any business has acted against my advice and has persisted, notwithstanding my repeated friendly remonstrances, till at last he brings failure and discredit. Yet when the trial comes I *stand black for him* ; i.e. I act loyally towards him—I defend him : I take my share of the blame, and never give the least hint that the failure is all his doing. *Standing black* often heard.

' He's not all there,' i.e. he is a little daft, a little *cracked*, weak-minded, foolish, has a slight touch of insanity : ' there's a slate off,' ' he has a bee in his bonnet' (Scotch): ' he wants a square ' (this last Old English).

A man gets into an angry fit and you take no trouble to pacify him :—' Let him cool in the skin he heated in.' (Moran : Carlow.)

A person asks me for money : I give him all I have, which is less than he asked for :—' That is all [the corn] there's threshed.' (Moran : Carlow.)

A man with a very thin face ' could kiss a goat between the horns.' (Moran : Carlow.)

' Never put a tooth on it': an invitation to speak out plainly, whatever the consequences.

A woman giving evidence at Drumcondra Petty Sessions last year says ' I was born and reared in Finglas, and there isn't one—man or woman—that dare say *black was the white of my eye* ': that is, no one could allege any wrong-doing against her. Heard everywhere in Ireland.

A man who is going backwards or down the hill in circumstances is said to be 'going after his back.' The sense is obvious. (Moran : Wexford.)

'Come day go day God send Sunday,' applied to an easy-going idle good-for-nothing person, who never looks to the future.

When a person is asked about something of which for some reason he does not wish to speak, he says 'Ask me no questions and I'll tell you no lies.' (General.)

A man who is of opinion that his friend has bought a cow too dear says 'You bought every hair in her tail.'

To a person everlastingly talking :—' Give your tongue a holiday.'

He always visits us *of a Saturday*. Halliwell says this is common in several English dialects. (Rev. Wm. Burke.)

Johnny Dunn, a job gardener of Dublin, being asked about his young wife, who was living apart from him :—' Oh she's just doing nothing, but walking about town with a *mug of cónsequence* on her.'

'I'm blue-moulded for want of a beating,' says a fellow who pretends to be anxious for a fight, but can find no one to fight with him.

A whistling woman and a crowing hen
Will make a man wealthy but deer knows when.

(Moran : Carlow.)
The people have an almost superstitious dislike for both : they are considered unlucky.

'I'll make him scratch where he doesn't itch': meaning I'll punish him sorely in some way. (Moran : Carlow.)

When flinging an abusive epithet at a person, 'you' is often put in twice, first as an opening tip, and last as a finishing home blow:—'What else could I expect from your like, *you unnatural vagabone, you*!'

'I'm afraid he turns up his little finger too often'; i.e.—he is given to drink: alluding to the position of the hand when a person is taking a glass.

> My neighbour Jack Donovan asked me one day,
> How many strawberries grew in the *say*;
> I made him an answer as well as I could,
> As many red herrings as grew in the wood.

When a person is obliged to utter anything bordering on coarseness, he always adds, by way of a sort of apology, 'saving your presence': or 'with respect to you.'

Small trifling things are expressed by a variety of words :—'Those sausages are not worth a *mallamadee*': 'I don't care a *traneen* what he says': 'I don't care two rows of pins.'

To be rid of a person or thing is expressed by 'I got shut of him,' or 'I am done of it.'   (Limerick.)

'How did you travel to town?'   'Oh I went *on shanks' mare*:' i.e. I walked.

'His bread is baked'; i.e. he is doomed to die soon. (See p. 109 bottom.)

Banagher is a village in King's Co. on the Shannon : Ballinasloe is a town in Galway at the other side of the river. When anything very unusual or unexpected occurs, the people say, 'Well that bangs Banagher!' or 'that bangs Banagher and Ballinasloe!'

'Have you got a shilling to spare for a friend?' 'Indeed I have not.'   'Ah you must give it to me; it is for your cousin Tom.' 'Oh, *that's a horse of another colour.*' (So he gives it.)

' *Well done mother !* ' says the blacksmith when the tooth was out. This is how it was pulled. He tied one end of a strong string round the tooth, and the other end to the horn of the anvil, and made the old woman keep back her head so as to tighten the string. ' *Asy* now mother,' says he. Then taking the flaming horseshoe from the fire with the tongs he suddenly thrust it towards her face. Anyone can finish the story.

If she catches you she'll *comb your hair with the creepy stool* : i.e. she'll whack and beat you with it. (Ulster.)

They say pigs can see the wind, and that it is red. In very old times the Irish believed that there were twelve different winds with twelve colours. (For these see my ' Smaller Soc. Hist. of Anc. Ireland,' p. 527.) The people also will tell you that a pig will swim till the water cuts its throat.

Ah, I see you want *to walk up my sleeve* : i.e. you want to deceive me — *to take me in.* (Kerry.)

An expression often heard in the South :—Such and such a thing will happen now and then *if you were to put your eyes on sticks* ; i.e. however watchful you may be. 'Well, if I was to put my eyes upon sticks, Misther Mann, I never would know your sister again.' (Gerald Griffin.)

He *is down in the mouth,* i.e. he is in low spirits. I suppose this is from the dropping down of the corners of the mouth.

To scold a person—to reprimand him—to give him a good ' setting down '—to give him 'all sorts ' —to give him ' the rough side of your tongue.'

o

Anything that cheers you up 'takes the cockles off your heart': 'Here drink this [glass of punch, wine, &c.] and 'twill take the cockles off your heart.' 'It raises the very cockles o' my heart to see you.' ('Collegians.')   ''Twould rise the cockles av your heart to hear her singing the Coolin.' ('Knocknagow.') Probably the origin is this:—Cares and troubles clog the heart as cockles clog a ship.

Instead of 'No blame to you' or 'Small blame to you,' the people often say, ''Tis a stepmother would blame you.'

'Cut your stick, now,' 'cut away'; both mean *go away* : the idea being that you want a walking stick and that it is time for you to cut it.

'I hear William is out of his situation.' 'Yes indeed, that is true.' 'And how is he living?' 'I don't know; I suppose he's living *on the fat of his guts*': meaning he is living on whatever he has saved.   But it is sometimes used in the direct sense. Poor old Hill, while his shop prospered, had an immense paunch, but he became poor and had to live on poor food and little of it, so that the belly got flat; and the people used to say—he's living now on the fat of his guts, poor old fellow.

Tom Hogan is managing his farm in a way likely to bring him to poverty, and Phil Lahy says to him— 'Tom, you'll scratch a beggarman's back yet': meaning that Tom will himself be the beggarman. ('Knocknagow.')   Common all over Munster.

The people have a gentle laudable habit of mixing up sacred names and pious phrases with their ordinary conversation, in a purely reverential spirit.   This is one of the many peculiarities of Anglo-Irish

speech derived from the Irish language : for pious
expressions pervaded Irish to its very heart, of
which the people lost a large part when they ceased
to speak the language.   Yet it continues very
prevalent among our English-speaking people ; and
nearly all the expressions they use are direct translations from Irish.

' I hear there is a mad dog running about the
town.'   ' Oh do you tell me so—the Lord between
us and harm !' or ' the Lord preserve us !' both
very common exclamations in case of danger.

Sudden news is brought about something serious
happening to a neighbour, and the people say:—
' Oh, God bless the hearers,' or ' God bless the mark.'
This last is however generally used in derision.
John Cox, a notorious schemer and miser, ' has put
down his name for £20 for a charity—God bless the
mark !' an intimation that the £20 will never be
heard of again.

When a person goes away for ever or dies, the
friends and people say ' God be with him,' a very
beautiful expression, as it is the concentration of
human affection and regret, and also a prayer. It
is merely the translation of the Irish *Dia leis*, which
has forms for all the three persons and two genders :
—' with her,' ' with you,' ' with them,' &c.

Under any discouraging or distressing circumstances, the expressions ' God help me ' and ' God
help us ' are continually in the mouths of the people.
They are merely translations of *go bh-fóireadh
Dia orruinn*, &c.   Similarly, expressions of pity for
another such as ' That poor woman is in great trouble,
God help her,' are translations.

In Dublin, Roman Catholics when passing a Catholic church (or ' chapel ') remove the hat or cap for a moment as a mark of respect, and usually utter a short aspiration or prayer under breath. This custom is I think spreading.

When one expresses his intention to do anything even moderately important, he always adds ' please God.' Even in our English speech this is of old standing. During the Irish wars of Elizabeth, it was told to an Irish chief that one of the English captains had stated he would take such and such a castle, when the chief retorted, ' Oh yes, but did he say *please God*': as much as to say, ' yes if God pleases, but not otherwise.'

' This sickness kept me from Mass for a long time ; but *with the help of God*, I'll venture next Sunday.' ' Yes, poor Kitty is in great danger, but *with the help of God* she will pull through.'

' I am afraid that poor Nellie will die after that accident.' ' Oh, God forbid,' is the response.

People have a pleasing habit of applying the word *blessèd* [2-syll.] to many natural objects, to days, nights, &c. ' Well, you have teased me terribly the whole of this blessèd day—you young vagabone.'

' Were it not that full of sorrow from my people forth I go,
By the blessèd sun 'tis royally I'd sing thy praise Mayo.'
　　　　Translation of Irish Song on ' The County Mayo.'

A mother says to her mischievous child, ' Oh blessèd hour, what am I to do with you at all at all!'

' Oh we're in a precious plight
By your means this blessèd night.'
　　　　(Repeal Song of 1843.)

'God help me this blessèd night.' ('Mun Carberry and the Pooka' by Robert Dwyer Joyce.)

A man is on the verge of ruin, or in some other great trouble, and the neighbours will say, 'the Lord will open a gap for him': meaning God will find some means of extricating him.   Father Higgins, who sent me this, truly remarks:—'This is a fine expressive phrase showing the poetical temperament of our people, and their religious spirit too.'

When anything happens very much out of the common:—'Glory be to God, isn't that wonderful.'

At the mention of the name of a person that is dead, the Roman Catholic people invariably utter the little prayer 'God rest his soul' or 'the Lord have mercy on him.'

The people thank God for everything, whatever it may be His will to send, good or bad.   'Isn't this a beautiful day, Mike.'   ''Tis indeed, thank God.' 'This is a terrible wet day, William, and very bad for the crops.'   'It is indeed Tom, thanks be to God for all : He knows best.'

As might be expected where expressions of this kind are so constantly in the people's mouths, it happens occasionally that they come in rather awkwardly.   Little Kitty, running in from the dairy with the eyes starting out of her head, says to her mother who is talking to a neighbour in the kitchen : 'Oh, mother, mother, I saw a terrible thing in the cream.'   'Ah, never mind, child,' says the mother, suspecting the truth and anxious to hush it up, 'it's nothing but the grace of God.'   'Oh but mother, sure the grace of God hasn't a long tail.'

The following story was current when I was a

child, long before Charles Kickham wrote 'Knocknagow,' in which he tells the story too : but I will
give it in his words. A station is held at Maurice
Kearney's, where the family and servants and the
neighbours go to Confession and receive Holy
Communion : among the rest Barney Broderick the
stable boy. After all was over, Father MacMahon's
driver provokes and insults Barney, who is kept back,
and keeps himself back with difficulty from falling
on him and 'knocking his two eyes into one' and
afterwards 'breaking every tooth in his head.'
'Damn well the *blagard* knows,' exclaims Barney,
'that I'm in a state of grace to-day. But '—he
continued, shaking his fist at the fellow—' but, please
God I won't be in a state of grace always.'

When a person is smooth-tongued, meek-looking,
over civil, and deceitful, he is *plauzy* [plausible],
'as mild as ever on stirabout smiled.' 'Oh she is
sly enough ; she looks as if *butter wouldn't melt in her
mouth.*' (Charles Macklin—an Irish writer—in *The
Man of the World.*) This last expression of Macklin's
is heard everywhere here.

A person is in some sore fix, or there is trouble
before him : 'I wouldn't like to be *in his shoes* just
now.'

A person falls in for some piece of good fortune:—
'Oh you're *made up*, John : you're a *med* man ;
you're *on the pig's back* now.'

In a house where the wife is master—the husband
henpecked :—' the grey mare is the better horse.'
(General.)

He got the father of a beating ; i.e. a great
beating.

'How did poor Jack get .that mark on his face?'
'Oh he fell over his shadow': meaning he fell while
he was drunk.

A good dancer 'handles his feet well.' (MacCall:
Wexford.)

A pensioner, a loafer, or anyone that has nothing
to do but walk about, is *an inspector of public
buildings.*

Those who leave Ireland commonly become all
the more attached to it: they get to love *the old sod*
all the more intensely. A poor old woman was
dying in Liverpool, and Father O'Neill came and
administered the last sacraments. He noticed that
she still hesitated as if she wished to say something
more; and after some encouragement she at length
said :— 'Well, father, I only wanted to ask you,
will my soul pass through Ireland on its journey ?'
('Knocknagow.') According to a religious legend in
'The Second Vision of Adamnan' the soul, on
parting from the body, visits four places before
setting out for its final destination :—the place of
birth, the place of death, the place of baptism, and
the place of burial. So this poor old woman got her
wish.

'Well, I don't like to say anything bad about you;
and as for the other side, *the less I praise you the less
I lie.'* (North.)

There is a touch of heredity in this :—'You're
nothing but a schemer like your seven generations
before you.' (Kildare.)

'Oh you need not be afraid: I'll call only very
seldom henceforward.' Reply :—'The seldomer the
welcomer.'

'Never dread the winter till the snow is on the blanket': i.e. as long as you have a roof over your head. An allusion to the misery of those poor people—numerous enough in the evil days of past times—who were evicted from house and home. (P. Reilly: Kildare.)

Of a lucky man:—'That man's ducks are laying.'

When a baby is born, the previous baby's 'nose is out of joint.' Said also of a young man who is supplanted by another in courtship.

A man who supplants another in any pursuit or design is said to 'come inside him.'

A person is speaking bitterly or uncharitably of one who is dead; and another says reprovingly— 'let the dead rest.'

When it is proposed to give a person something he doesn't need or something much too good for him, you oppose or refuse it by saying:—*Cock him up with it*—how much he wants it!—I'll do no such thing.' Two gentlemen staying for a night in a small hotel in a remote country town ordered toast for breakfast, which it seems was very unusual there. They sat down to breakfast, but there was no sign of the toast. 'What about the toast?' asks one. Whereupon the impudent waiter replies— 'Ah, then cock yez up with toast: how bad yez are for it.'

A very general form of expression to point to a person's identity in a very vague way is seen in the following example:—'From whom did you buy that horse, James?' Reply:—'From *a man of the Burkes* living over there in Ballinvreena': i.e. a man named Burke. Mr. Seumas MacManus has adopted this idiom in the name of one of his books :—' A Lad of the O'Friels.'

'I never saw the froth of your pot or the bead of your naggin' : i.e. you have never entertained me. *Bead*, the string of little bubbles that rise when you shake whiskey in a bottle. (Kildare.)

Of a man likely to die : ' he'll soon be a load for four' : i.e. the four coffin-bearers. (Reilly : Kildare.)

When a person attempts to correct you when you are not in error :—' Don't take me up till I fall.'

When you make a good attempt :—' If I didn't knock it down, I staggered it.'

'Love daddy, love mammy, love yourself best.' Said of a very selfish person.

An odd expression :—' You are making such noise that *I can't hear my ears.*' (Derry ; and also Limerick.)

Plato to a young man who asked his advice about getting married :—' If you don't get married you'll be sorry : and if you do you'll be sorry.'

Our Irish cynic is more bitter :—

> If a man doesn't marry he'll rue it sore :
> And if he gets married he'll rue it more.

The children were great pets with their grandmother : ' She wouldn't let anyone *look crooked* at them ' : i.e. she wouldn't permit the least unkindness.

' Can he read a Latin book ? ' ' Read one ! why, he can write Latin books, *let alone* reading them.' *Let alone* in this sense very common all over Ireland.

A person offers to do you some kindness, and you accept it jokingly with ' Sweet is your hand in a pitcher of honey.' (Crofton Croker.)

When a man falls into error, not very serious or criminal—gets drunk accidentally for instance—the people will say, by way of extenuation :—' 'Tis a good man's case.'

You may be sure Tim will be at the fair to-morrow, *dead or alive or a-horseback.*

'You never spoke but you said something': said to a person who makes a silly remark or gives foolish advice. (Kinahan).

'He will never comb a grey hair': said of a young person who looks unhealthy and is likely to die early.

Two persons had an angry dispute; and *one word borrowed another* till at last they came to blows. Heard everywhere in Ireland.

The robin and the wren are God's cock and hen.

'I'll take the book *and no thanks to you,*' i.e. I'll take it in spite of you, whether you like or no, against your will—' I'll take it in spite of your teeth '—' in spite of your nose ' : all very common.

A person arrives barely in time for his purpose or to fulfil his engagement :—' You have just saved your distance.'

To *put a person off the walk* means to kill him, to remove him in some way. (Meath.)

A man has had a long fit of illness, and the wife, telling about it, says :—' For six weeks coal nor candle never went out.' (Antrim.)

' To cure a person's hiccup ' means to make him submit, to bring him to his senses, to make him acknowledge his error, by some decided course of action. A shopkeeper goes to a customer for pay-ment of a debt, and gets no satisfaction, but, on the

contrary, impudence. ' Oh well, I'll send you an
attorney's letter to-morrow, and may be that will
cure your hiccup.' The origin of this expression is
the general belief through Ireland that a troublesome
fit of hiccup may be cured by suddenly making some
very startling and alarming announcement to the
person—an announcement in which he is deeply
concerned : such as that the stacks in the haggard
are on fire—that three of his cows have just been
drowned, &c. Fiachra MacBrady, a schoolmaster
and poet, of Stradone in Cavan (1712), wrote a
humorous description of his travels through Ireland
of whic the translation has this verse :—

> ' I drank till quite mellow, then like a brave fellow,
>   Began for to bellow and shouted for more ;
> But my host held his stick up, which soon *cured my hiccup*,
>   As no cash I could pick up to pay off the score.'

The host was the publican, and the stick that he
held up was the tally stick on which were marked in
nicks all the drinks poor MacBrady had taken—a
usual way of keeping accounts in old times. The
sight of the *score* brought him to his senses at once—
cured his hiccup.

A verse of which the following is a type is very
often found in our Anglo-Irish songs :—

> ' The flowers in those valleys no more shall spring,
>   The blackbirds and thrushes no more shall sing,
>   The sea shall dry up and no water shall be,
>   At the hour I'll prove false to sweet graw-mochree.'

So in Scotland :—' I will luve thee still, my dear, till
a' the seas gang dry.' (Burns.)

A warning sometimes given to a messenger :—
' Now don't forget it like Billy and the pepper': This

is the story of Billy and the pepper. A gander got killed accidentally; and as the family hardly ever tasted meat, there was to be a great treat that day. To top the grandeur they sent little Billy to town for a pennyworth of pepper. But Billy forgot the name, and only remembered that it was something hot; so he asked the shopman for a penn'orth of *hot-thing*. The man couldn't make head or tail of the *hot-thing*, so he questioned Billy. Is it mustard? No. Is it ginger? No. Is it pepper? Oh that's just it—*gandher's pepper*.

A man has done me some intentional injury, and I say to him, using a very common phrase:—'Oh, well, wait; *I'll pay you off* for that': meaning 'I'll punish you for it—I'll have satisfaction.'

Dry for *thirsty* is an old English usage; for in Middleton's Plays it is found used in this sense. (Lowell.) It is almost universal in Ireland, where of course it survives from old English. There is an old Irish air and song called 'I think it no treason to drink when I'm *dry*': and in another old Folk Song we find this couplet:

> 'There was an old soldier riding by,
> He called for a quart because he was *dry*.'

Instances of the odd perversion of sense by misplacing some little clause are common in all countries: and I will give here just one that came under my own observation. A young friend, a boy, had remained away an unusually long time without visiting us; and on being asked the reason he replied:— 'I could not come, sir; I got a bite in the leg of dog'—an example which I think is unique.

On the first appearance of the new moon, a number of children linked hands and danced, keeping time to the following verse—

> I see the moon, the moon sees me,
> God bless the moon and God bless me :
> There's grace in the cottage and grace in the hall;
> And the grace of God is over us all.

For the air to which this was sung see my 'Old Irish Folk Music and Songs,' p. 60.

'Do you really mean to drive that horse of William's to pound?' 'Certainly I will.' 'Oh very well; let ye take what you'll get.' Meaning you are likely to pay dear for it—you may take the consequences. (Ulster.)

'If he tries to remove that stone without any help *it will take him all his time*' : it will require his utmost exertions. (Ulster: very common.)

When rain is badly wanted and often threatens but still doesn't come they say :—' It has great *hould* [hold of the rain.' On the other hand when there is long continued wet weather :—' It is very fond of the rain.'

When flakes of snow begin to fall :—' They are plucking the geese in Connaught.' 'Formerly in all the congested districts of Ireland [which are more common in Connaught than elsewhere] goose and duck feathers formed one of the largest industries.' (Kinahan.)

Now James you should put down your name for more than 5*s*. : there's Tom Gallagher, not half so well off as you, *put the shame on you* by subscribing £1. (Kinahan : pretty general.)

In stories ' a day ' is often added on to a period of time, especially to a year. A person is banished out of Ireland for a year and a day.

The battle of Ventry Harbour lasted for a year and a day, when at last the foreigners were defeated.

> There's a colleen fair as May,
> For a year and for a day
> I have sought by ev'ry way
> Her heart to gain.
>
> (PETRIE.)

' Billy MacDaniel,' said the fairy, ' you shall be my servant for seven years and a day.' (Crofton Croker.) Borrowed from the Irish.

The word *all* is often used by our rustic poets exactly as it is found in English folk-songs. Gay has happily imitated this popular usage in ' Black-eyed Susan ':—

> ' All in the Downs the fleet was moored '—

and Scott in ' The Lay of the Last Minstrel ':—

> ' All as they left the listed plain.'

Any number of examples might be given from our peasant songs, but these two will be sufficient:—

> 'As I roved out one evening two miles below Pomeroy
> I met a farmer's daughter *all on* the mountains high.'

> ' How a young lady's heart was won
> *All by* the loving of a farmer's son.'

(The two lovely airs of these will be found in two of my books: for the first, see ' The Mountains high' in 'Ancient Irish Music'; and for the second see 'Handsome Sally' in 'Old Irish Folk Music and Songs.')

'He saw her on that day, and *never laid eyes on her* alive afterwards.' (Speech of Irish counsel in murder case: 1909.) A common expression.

A wish for success either in life or in some particular undertaking—purely figurative of course :— 'That the road may rise under you.' As the road continually rises under foot there is always an easy down hill in front. (Kerry.)

Regarding some proposal or offer :—' I never said against it ' ; i.e. I never disapproved of it—declined it —refused it.

Be said by me : i.e. take my advice. (General.)

When a cart-wheel screeches because the axletree has not been greased, it is *cursing for grease.* (Munster.)

When a person wishes to keep out from another— to avoid argument or conflict, he says :—' The child's bargain—let me alone and I'll let you alone.'

When a person goes to law expenses trying to recover a debt which it is very unlikely he will recover, that is ' throwing good money after bad.'

' I'm the second tallest man in Mitchelstown '—or ' I'm the next tallest.' Both mean ' there is just one other man in Mitchelstown taller than me, and I come next to him.'

' Your honour.' Old English : very common as a term of courtesy in the time of Elizabeth, and to be met with everywhere in the State papers and correspondence of that period. Used now all through Ireland by the peasantry when addressing persons very much above them.

The cabman's answer. I am indebted to this cabman for giving me an opportunity of saying something here about myself. It is quite a common thing for people to write to me for information that they could easily find in my books: and this is especially the case in connexion with Irish place-names. I have always made it a point to reply to these communications. But of late they have become embarrassingly numerous, while my time is getting more circumscribed with every year of my long life. Now, this is to give notice to *all the world and Garrett Reilly* that henceforward I will give these good people the reply that the Dublin cabman gave the lady. ' Please, sir,' said she, ' will you kindly tell me the shortest way to St. Patrick's Cathedral.' He opened the door of his cab with his left hand, and pointing in with the forefinger of his right, answered—' In there ma'am.'

CHAPTER XIII.

VOCABULARY AND INDEX.

[In this Vocabulary, as well indeed as through the whole book, *gh* and *ch* are to be sounded guttural, as in *lough* and *loch*, unless otherwise stated or implied.   Those who cannot sound the guttural may take the sound of *k* instead, and they will not be far wrong.]

Able; strong, muscular, and vigorous:—' Nagle was a strong able man.'

Able dealer ; a schemer.   (Limerick.)

Acushla ; see Cushlamochree.

Adam's ale ; plain drinking-water.

Affirming, assenting, and saluting, 9.

Agra or Agraw : a term of endearment ; my love : vocative of Irish *grádh*, love.

Ahaygar ; a pet term ; my friend, my love : vocative of Irish *téagur*, love, a dear person.

Aims-ace ; a small amount, quantity, or distance. Applied in the following way very generally in Munster :—' He was within an aim's-ace of being drowned ' (very near).   A survival in Ireland of the old Shakesperian word *ambs-ace*, meaning two aces or two single points in throwing dice, the smallest possible throw.

Air : a visitor comes in :—' Won't you sit down Joe and take an *air* of the fire.'   (Very usual.)

Airt used in Ulster and Scotland for a single point of the compass :—

' Of a' the airts the wind can blaw I dearly like the west.'
                                          (Burns.)
It is the Irish *áird*, a point of the compass.

P

Airy ; ghostly, fearsome : an *airy* place, a haunted place. Same as Scotch *eerie*. From Gaelic *áedha-raigh*, same sound and meaning. A survival of the old Irish pagan belief that air-demons were the most malignant of all supernatural beings : see Joyce's ' Old Celtic Romances,' p. 15.

Alanna ; my child : vocative case of Irish *leanbh* [lannav], a child.

Allow ; admit. ' I allow that you lent me a pound ' : ' if you allow that you cannot deny so and so.' This is an old English usage. (Ducange.) To advise or recommend : ' I would not allow you to go by that road ' (' I would not recommend '). ' I'd allow you to sow that field with oats ' (advise).

All to ; means except :—' I've sold my sheep all to six,' i.e. except six. This is merely a translation from the Irish as in *Do marbhadh na daoine uile go haon triúr* : ' The people were slain all to a single three.' (Keating.)

Along of ; on account of. Why did you keep me waiting [at night] so long at the door, Pat ? ' ' Why then 'twas all along of Judy there being so much afraid of the fairies.' (Crofton Croker.)

Alpeen, a stick or hand-wattle with a knob at the lower end : diminutive of Irish *alp*, a knob. Sometimes called a *clehalpeen* : where *cleh* is the Irish *cleath* a stick. *Clehalpeen*, a knobbed cudgel.

Amadaun, a fool (man or boy), a half-fool, a foolish person. Irish *amadán*, a fool : a form of *onmitán* ; from *ón*, a fool : see *Oanshagh*.

American wake ; a meeting of friends on the evening before the departure of some young people for

America, as a farewell celebration. (See my 'Old Irish Folk-Music and Songs,' p. 191.)

Amplush, a fix, a difficulty : he was in a great amplush. (North and South.) (Edw. Walsh in Dub. Pen. Journal.)

Amshagh ; a sudden hurt, an accident. (Derry.)

Ang-ishore ; a poor miserable creature—man or woman. It is merely the Irish word *aindeiseóir*. (Chiefly South.)

Any is used for *no* (in *no more*) in parts of West and North-west. 'James, you left the gate open this morning and the calves got out.' 'Oh I'm sorry sir ; I will do it any more.' This is merely a mistranslation of *nios mo*, from some confused idea of the sense of two (Irish) negatives (*nios* being one, with another preceding) leading to the omission of an English negative from the correct construction—'' I will *not* do it any more:' *Nios mo* meaning in English ' no more ' or ' any more ' according to the omission or insertion of an English negative.

Aree often used after *ochone* (alas) in Donegal and elsewhere. *Aree* gives the exact pronunciation of *a Righ*, and *neimhe* (heaven) is understood. The full Irish exclamation is *ochón a Righ neimhe*, ' alas, O King of heaven.'

Arnaun or arnaul, to sit up working at night later than usual. Irish *airneán* or *airneál*, same meaning.

Aroon, a term of endearment, my love, my dear : *Eileen Aroon*, the name of a celebrated Irish air : vocative of Irish *rún* [roon], a secret, a secret treasure. In Limerick commonly shortened to *aroo*. 'Where are you going now *aroo* ? '

Art-loochra or arc-loochra, a harmless lizard five or
six inches long : Irish *art* or *arc* is a lizard :
luachra, rushes ; the 'lizard of the rushes.'

Ask, a water-newt, a small water-lizard : from *esc* or
easc ⌊ask⌋, an old Irish word for water. From
the same root comes the next word, the diminutive form—

Askeen ; land made by cutting away bog. which
generally remains more or less watery. (Reilly :
Kildare.)

Asthore, a term of endearment, 'my treasure.' The
vocative case of Irish *stór* [store], treasure.

Athurt ; to confront :—' Oh well I will athurt him
with that lie he told about me.' (Cork.) Possibly
a mispronunciation of *athwart*.

Avourneen, my love : the vocative case of Irish
muirnín , a sweetheart, a loved person.

Baan : a field covered with short grass :—' A baan
field': 'a *baan* of cows': i.e. a grass farm with
its proper number of cows. Irish *bán*, whitish.

Back ; a faction : ' I have a good back in the country,
so I defy my enemies.'

Back of God-speed ; a place very remote, out of the
way: so far off that the virtue of your wish of
God-speed to a person will not go with him so
far.

Bacon : to ' save one's bacon'; to succeed in escaping
some serious personal injury—death, a beating,
&c. ' They fled from the fight to save their
bacon': 'Here a lodging I'd taken, but loth to
awaken, for fear of my bacon, either man, wife, or
babe.' (Old Anglo-Irish poem.)

Bad member; a doer of evil; a bad character; a treacherous fellow : ' I'm ruined,' says he, ' for some bad member has wrote to the bishop about me.' (' Wild Sports of the West.')

Baffity, unbleached or blay calico. (Munster.)

Bails or bales, frames made of perpendicular wooden bars in which cows are fastened for the night in the stable. (Munster.)

Baithershin ; may be so, perhaps. Irish *b'féidir-sin*, same sound and meaning.

Ballowr (Bal-yore in Ulster); to bellow, roar, bawl, talk loudly and coarsely.

Ballyhooly, a village near Fermoy in Cork, formerly notorious for its faction fights, so that it has passed into a proverb. A man is late coming home and expects *Ballyhooly* from his wife, i.e. ' the length and breadth of her tongue.' Father Carroll has neglected to visit his relatives, the Kearneys, for a long time, so that he knows he's *in the black books* with Mrs. Kearney, and expects Ballyhooly from her the first time he meets her. (' Knocknagow.')

Ballyorgan in Co. Limerick, 146.

Banagher and Ballinasloe, 192.

Bannalanna : a woman who sells ale over the counter. Irish *bean-na-leanna*, ' woman of the ale,' ' ale-woman ' (*leann*, ale).

Ballyrag ; to give loud abuse in torrents. (General.)

Bandle ; a 2-foot measure for home-made flannel. (Munster.)

Bang-up ; a frieze overcoat with high collar and long cape.

Banshee'; a female fairy : Irish *bean-sidhe* [banshee], a ' woman from the *shee* or fairy-dwelling.' This was the original meaning; but in modern times, and among English speakers, the word *banshee* has become narrowed in its application, and signifies a female spirit that attends certain families, and is heard *keening* or crying aloud at night round the house when some member of the family is about to die.

Barcelona ; a silk kerchief for the neck :—

> ' His clothes spick and span new without e'er a speck ;
> A neat Barcelona tied round his white neck.'
>
> (EDWARD LYSAGHT, in ' The Sprig of Shillelah.')

So called because imported from Barcelona, preserving a memory of the old days of smuggling.

Barsa, barsaun ; a scold. (Kild. and Ulst.)

Barth ; a back-load of rushes, straw, heath, &c. Irish *beart*.

Baury, baura, baur-yă, bairy ; the goal in football, hurling, &c. Irish *báire* [2-syll.], a game, a goal.

Bawn ; an enclosure near a farmhouse for cattle, sheep, &c. ; in some districts, simply a farmyard. Irish *badhun* [bawn], a cow-keep, from *ba*, cows, and *dún*, a keep or fortress. Now generally applied to the green field near the homestead where the cows are brought to be milked.

Bawneen ; a loose whitish jacket of home-made undyed flannel worn by men at out-door work. Very general : *banyan* in Derry. From Irish *bán* [bawn], whitish, with the diminutive termination.

Bawnoge ; a dancing-green. (MacCall : Leinster.)

From *bán* [baan], a field covered with short grass; and the dim. *óg* (p. 90).

Bawshill, a *fetch* or double. (See Fetch.) (MacCall: S. Wexford.) I think this is a derivative of *Bow*, which see.

Beestings ; new milk from a cow that has just calved.

Be-knownst ; known : unbe-knownst ; unknown. (Antrim.)

Better than ; more than :—' It is better than a year since I saw him last' ; ' better than a mile,' &c. (Leinster and Munster.)

Bian' [by-ann'] ; one of Bianconi's long cars. (See Jingle.)

Binnen ; the rope tying a cow to a stake in a field. (Knowles : Ulster.)

Birragh ; a muzzle-band with spikes on a calf's or a foal's muzzle to prevent it sucking its mother. From Irish *bir*, a sharp spit : *birragh*, full of sharp points or spits. (Munster : see Gubbaun.)

Blackfast : among Roman Catholics, there is a ' black fast' on Ash Wednesday, Spy Wednesday, and Good Friday, i.e. no flesh meat or *whitemeat* is allowed—no flesh, butter, eggs, cheese, or milk.

Blackfeet. The members of one of the secret societies of a century ago were called ' Ribbonmen.' Some of them acknowledged the priests : those were ' whitefeet' : others did not—' blackfeet.'

Black man, black fellow ; a surly vindictive implacable irreconcilable fellow.

Black man ; the man who accompanies a suitor to the house of the intended father-in-law, to help to make the match.

Black of one's nail. 'You just escaped by the black of your nail': 'there's no cloth left—not the size of the black of my nail.' (North and South.)

Black swop. When two fellows have two wretched articles—such as two old penknives—each thinking his own to be the worst in the universe, they sometimes agree for the pure humour of the thing to make a *black swóp*, i.e. to swop without first looking at the articles. When they are looked at after the swop, there is always great fun. (See Hool.)

Blarney ; smooth, plausible, cajoling talk. From Blarney Castle near Cork, in which there is a certain stone hard to reach, with this virtue, that if a person kisses it, he will be endowed with the gift of *blarney*.

Blast ; when a child suddenly fades in health and pines away, he has got a blast,—i.e. a puff of evil wind sent by some baleful sprite has struck him. *Blast* when applied to fruit or crops means a blight in the ordinary sense—nothing supernatural.

Blather, bladdher ; a person who utters vulgarly foolish boastful talk : used also as a verb—to blather. Hence *blatherumskite*, applied to a person or to his talk in much the same sense ; 'I never heard such a blatherumskite.' Ulster and Scotch form *blether*, *blethering* : Burns speaks of stringing 'blethers up in rhyme.' ('The Vision.')

Blaze, blazes, blazing : favourite words everywhere in Ireland. Why are you in such a blazing hurry ? Jack ran away like blazes : now work at that job like blazes : he is blazing drunk. Used also by the English peasantry :—'That's a blazing strange

answer,' says Jerry Cruncher in 'A Tale of Two
Cities.' There's a touch of slang in some of these :
yet the word has been in a way made classical
by Lord Morley's expression that Lord Salisbury
never made a speech without uttering 'some
blazing indiscretion.'

Blind Billy. In coming to an agreement take care
you don't make ' Blind Billy's Bargain,' by either
overreaching yourself or allowing the other party
to overreach you. Blind Billy was the hangman
in Limerick, and on one particular occasion he
flatly refused to do his work unless he got £50
down on the nail : so the high sheriff had to agree
and the hangman put the money in his pocket.
When all was over the sheriff refused point-blank
to send the usual escort without a fee of £50 down.
So Blind Billy had to hand over the £50—for if he
went without an escort he would be torn in pieces
—and had nothing in the end for his job.

Blind lane ; a lane stopped up at one end.

Blind window ; an old window stopped up, but still
plain to be seen.

Blink ; to exercise an evil influence by a glance of
the ' evil eye'; to ' overlook '; hence ' blinked,'
blighted by the eye. When the butter does not
come in churning, the milk has been *blinked* by
some one.

Blirt ; to weep : as a noun, a rainy wind. (Ulster.)

Blob (*blab* often in Ulster), a raised blister : a drop
of honey, or of anything liquid.

Blue look-out ; a bad look-out, bad prospect.

Boal or bole ; a shelved recess in a room. (North.)

Boarhaun ; dried cowdung used for fuel like turf.
Irish *boithreán* [boarhaun], from bo, a cow.

Boccach [accented on 2nd syll. in Munster, but elsewhere on 1st]; a lame person. From the fact that so many beggars are lame or pretend to be lame, *boccach* has come to mean a beggar. Irish *bacach*, a lame person : from *bac*, to halt. *Bockady*, another form of *boccach* in Munster. *Bockeen* (the diminutive added on to *bac*), another form heard in Mayo.

Boddagh [accented on 2nd syll. in Munster; in Ulster on 1st], a rich churlish clownish fellow. Tom Cuddihy wouldn't bear insult from any purse-proud old *boddagh*. (' Knocknagow.')

Body-coat ; a coat like the present dress-coat, cut away in front so as to leave a narrow pointed tail-skirt behind : usually made of frieze and worn with the knee-breeches.

Body-glass ; a large mirror in which the whole body can be seen. (Limerick.)

Body-lilty ; heels over head. (Derry.)

Bog ; what is called in England a ' peat moss.' Merely the Irish *bog*, soft. Bog (verb), to be bogged ; to sink in a bog or any soft soil or swampy place.

Bog-butter ; butter found deep in bogs, where it had been buried in old times for a purpose, and forgotten : a good deal changed now by the action of the bog. (See Joyce's ' Smaller Soc. Hist. of Anc. Ireland,' p. 260.)

Bog-Latin ; bad incorrect Latin ; Latin that had been learned in the hedge schools among the bogs. This derisive and reproachful epithet was given in bad old times by pupils and others of the favoured, legal, and endowed schools, sometimes with reason, but oftener very unjustly. For those *bog* or hedge schools sent out numbers of scholarly men, who afterwards entered the church or lay professions. (See p. 151.)

Boghaleen ; the same as Crusheen, which see.

Bohaun ; a cabin or hut. Irish *both* [boh], a hut, with the diminutive *án*.

Bold ; applied to girls and boys in the sense of ' forward,' ' impudent.'

Boliaun, also called *booghalaun bwee* and *geōsadaun* ; the common yellow ragwort : all these are Irish word s

Bolting-hole ; the second or backward entrance made by rats, mice, rabbits, &c., from their burrows, so that if attacked at the ordinary entrance, they can escape by this, which is always left unused except in case of attack. (Kinahan.)

Bones. If a person magnifies the importance of any matter and talks as if it were some great affair, the other will reply :—' Oh, you're *making great bones* about it.'

Bonnive, a sucking-pig. Irish *banbh*, same sound and meaning. Often used with the diminutive —bonniveen, bonneen. ' Oh look at the *baby pigs*,' says an Irish lady one day in the hearing of others and myself, ashamed to use the Irish word. After that she always bore the nickname ' Baby pig':—' Oh, there's the Baby pig.'

Bonnyclabber ; thick milk. Irish *bainne* [bonny] milk ; and *clabar*, anything thick or half liquid. ' In use all over America.' (Russell.)

Boochalawn bwee ; ragweed : same as boliaun, which see.

Boolanthroor; three men threshing together, instead of the usual two : striking always in time. Irish *buail-an-triúr*, ' the striking of three.'

Booley as a noun ; a temporary settlement in the grassy uplands where the people of the adjacent lowland village lived during the summer with their cattle, and milked them and made butter, returning in autumn—cattle and all—to their lowland farms to take up the crops. Used as a verb also : *to booley*. See my ' Smaller Soc. Hist. of Anc. Ireland,' p. 431 ; or ' Irish Names of Places,' I. 239.

Boolthaun, boulhaun, booltheen, boolshin : the striking part of a flail : from Irish *buail* [bool], to strike, with the diminutive.

Boon in Ulster, same as *Mihul* elsewhere ; which see.

Boreen or bohereen, a narrow road. Irish *bóthar* [boher], a road, with the diminutive.

Borick ; a small wooden ball used by boys in hurling or goaling, when the proper leather-covered ball is not to hand. Called in Ulster a *nag* and also a *golley*. (Knowles.)

Borreen-brack, ' speckled cake,' speckled with currants and raisins, from Irish *bairghin* [borreen], a cake, and *breac* [brack], speckled : specially baked for Hallow-eve. Sometimes corruptly called *barm-brack* or *barn-brack*.

Bosthoon : a flexible rod or whip made of a number of green rushes laid together and bound up with single rushes wound round and round. Made by boys in play—as I often made them. Hence ' *bosthoon* is applied contemptuously to a soft worthless spiritless fellow, in much the same sense as *poltroon*.

Bother; merely the Irish word *bodhar*, deaf, used both as a noun and a verb in English (in the sense of deafening, annoying, troubling, perplexing, teasing) : a person deaf or partially deaf is said to be *bothered* :—' Who should come in but *bothered* Nancy Fay.   Now be it known that *bothered* signifies deaf; and Nancy was a little old cranky *bothered* woman.' (Ir. Pen. Mag.)   You ' turn the *bothered* ear' to a person when you do not wish to hear what he says or grant his request.   In these applications *bother* is universal in Ireland among all classes—educated as well as uneducated : accordingly, as Murray notes, it was first brought into use by Irishmen, such as Sheridan, Swift, and Sterne ; just as Irishmen of to-day are bringing into currency *galore*, *smithereens*, and many other Irish words.   In its primary sense of deaf or to deafen, *bother* is used in the oldest Irish documents : thus in the Book of Leinster we have :— *Ro bodrais sind oc imradud do maic*, ' You have made us deaf (you have *bothered* us) talking about your son' (Kuno Meyer) : and a similar expression is in use at the present day in the very common phrase ' don't *bother* me ' (don't deafen me, don't annoy me), which is an exact translation of the equally common Irish phrase *ná bi am' bhodradh.* Those who derive *bother* from the English *pother* make a guess, and not a good one.   See Bowraun.

Bottheen, a short thick stick or cudgel: the Irish *bata* with the diminutive :—*baitin.*

Bottom ; a clue or ball of thread.   One of the tricks

of girls on Hallow-eve to find out the destined husband is to go out to the limekiln at night with a ball of yarn ; throw in the ball still holding the thread ; re-wind the thread, till it is suddenly stopped ; call out 'who *howlds* my bottom of yarn ?' when she expects to hear ˛the name of the young man she is to marry.

Bouchal or boochal, a boy : the Irish *buachaill*, same meaning.

Bouilly-bawn, white home-made bread of wheaten flour; often called *bully-bread*. (MacCall: Wexford.) From Irish *bul* or *búilidhe*, a loaf, and *bán*, white.

Boundhalaun, a plant with thick hollow stem with joints, of which boys make rude syringes. From Irish *banndal* or *bannlamh*, a *bandle* (which see), with the dim. termination *án*. I never saw true boundhalauns outside Munster.

Bourke, the Rev. Father, 71, 161.

Bownloch, a sore on the sole of the foot always at the edge : from *bonn* the foot-sole [pron. bown in the South], and *loch* a mere termination. Also called a *Bine-lock*.

Bowraun, a sieve-shaped vessel for holding or measuring out corn, with the flat bottom made of dried sheepskin stretched tight ; sometimes used as a rude tambourine, from which it gets the name *bowraun* ; Irish *bodhur* [pron. bower here], deaf, from the *bothered* or indistinct sound. (South.)

Bow [to rhyme with *cow*]; a *banshee*, a *fetch* (both which see. MacCall : South Leinster). This word has come down to us from very old times, for it preserves the memory of *Bugh* [Boo], a *banshee* or fairy queen once very celebrated, the daughter of

Bove Derg king of the Dedannans or faery-race,
of whom information will be obtained in the
classical Irish story, ' The Fate of the Children of
Lir,' the first in my ' Old Celtic Romances.'
She has given her name to many hills all
through Ireland. (See my ' Irish Names of
Places,' I. 182, 183.   See Bawshill.)

Box and dice; used to denote the whole lot : I'll
send you all the books and manuscripts, box and
dice.

Boxty ; same as the Limerick *muddly*, which see.

Boy.   Every Irishman is a ' boy ' till he is married,
and indeed often long after.   (Crofton Croker : ' Ir.
Fairy Legends.')

Brablins : a crowd of children : a rabble. (Monaghan.)

Bracket ;   speckled :   a ' bracket cow.'   Ir. *breac*,
speckled.

Braddach ; given to mischief ; roguish.   Ir. *bradach*,
a thief : in the same sense as when a mother says
to her child, ' You young thief, stop that mischief.'
Often applied to cows inclined to break down and
cross fences.   (Meath and Monaghan.)

Brander ; a gridiron. (North.)   From Eng. *brand*.

Brash ; a turn of sickness (North.)   Water-brash
(Munster), severe acidity of the stomach with a
flow of watery saliva from the mouth.   Brash
(North), a short turn at churning, or at anything ;
a stroke of the churndash : ' Give the churn a few
brashes.'   In Donegal you will hear ' that's a
good brash of hail.'

Brave ; often used as an intensive :—' This is a
brave fine day '; ' that's a brave big dog ': (Ulster.)
Also fine or admirable ' a brave stack of hay ':

tall, strong, hearty (not necessarily brave in fighting):—' I have as brave a set of sons as you'd find in a day's walk.' 'How is your sick boy doing?' 'Oh bravely, thank you.'

Braw ; fine, handsome : Ir. *breagh*, same sound and meanings. (Ulster.)

Break. You *break* a grass field when you plough or dig it up for tillage. ' I'm going to break the kiln field.' (' Knocknagow.') Used all over Ireland : almost in the same sense as in Gray's Elegy :— ' Their furrow oft the stubborn glebe *has bróke*.'

Break ; to dismiss from employment : ' Poor William O'Donnell was *broke* last week.' This usage is derived from the Irish language ; and a very old usage it is ; for we read in the Brehon Laws :—' *Cid nod m-bris in fer-so a bo-airechus?* ' ' What is it that breaks (dismisses, degrades) this man from his bo-aireship (i.e. from his position as *bo-aire* or chief)? ' My car-driver asked me one time :—' Can an inspector of National Schools be broke, sir? ' By which he meant could he be dismissed at any time without any cause.

Breedoge [*d* sounded like *th* in *bathe*]; a figure dressed up to represent St. Brigit, which was carried about from house to house by a procession of boys and girls in the afternoon of the 31st Jan. (the eve of the saint's festival), to collect small money contributions. With this money they got up a little rustic evening party with a dance next day, 1st Feb. ' Breedoge ' means ' little *Brighid* or *Brighit*,' *Breed* (or rather *Breedh*) representing the sound of *Brighid*, with *óg* the old diminutive feminine termination.

Brecham, the straw collar put on a horse's or an ass's neck : sometimes means the old-fashioned straw saddle or pillion. (Ulster.)

Brehon Law; the old native .law of Ireland. A judge or a lawyer was called a ' brehon.'

Brew; a margin, a brink : ' that lake is too shallow to fish from the brews': from the Irish *bru*, same sound and meaning. See Broo.

Brief; prevalent: ' fever is very brief.' Used all over the southern half of Ireland. Perhaps a mistake for *rife*.

Brillauns or brill-yauns, applied to the poor articles of furniture in a peasant's cottage. Dick O'Brien and Mary Clancy are getting married as soon as they can gather up the few *brill-yauns* of furniture. (South-east of Ireland.)

Brine-oge ; ' a young fellow full of fun and frolic.' (Carleton : Ulster.)

Bring : our peculiar use of this (for ' take ') appears in such phrases as :—' he brought the cows to the field': ' he brought me to the theatre.' (Hayden and Hartog.) See Carry.

Brock, brockish ; a badger. It is just the Irish *broc*.

Brock, brocket, brockey ; applied to a person heavily pock-marked. I suppose from *broc*, a badger. (Ulster.)

Brogue, a shoe : Irish *bróg*. Used also to designate the Irish accent in speaking English : for the old Irish thong-stitched brogue was considered so characteristically Irish that the word was applied to our accent ; as a clown is called a *cauboge* (which see : Munster).

Brohoge or bruhoge ; a small batch of potatoes roasted. See Brunoge.

Broken ; bankrupt : quite a common expression is :— Poor Phil Burke is ' broken horse and foot '; i.e. utterly bankrupt and ruined.

Broo, the edge of a potato ridge along which cabbages are planted. Irish *bru*, a margin, a brink.

Brosna, brusna, bresna ; a bundle of sticks for firing : a faggot. This is the Irish *brosna*, universally used in Ireland at the present day, both in Irish and English ; and used in the oldest Irish documents. In the Tripartite Life of St. Patrick, written in Irish ten centuries ago, we are told that when Patrick was a boy, his foster-mother sent him one day for a *brossna* of withered branches to make a fire.

Broth of a boy ; a *good* manly brave boy : the essence of manhood, as broth is the essence of meat.

Brough ; a ring or halo round the moon. It is the Irish *bruach*, a border.

Broughan ; porridge or oatmeal stirabout. Irish *brochán*. (Ulster.)

Bruggadauns [*d* sounded like *th* in *they*] ; the stalks of ferns found in meadows after mowing. (Kerry.)

Brulliagh ; a row, a noisy scuffle. (Derry.)

Brunoge ; a little batch of potatoes roasted in a fire made in the potato field at digging time : always dry, floury and palatable. (Roscommon.) Irish *bruithneóg*. See Brohoge.

Bruss or briss ; small broken bits mixed up with dust : very often applied to turf-dust. Irish *brus*, *bris*, same sounds and meaning. (South.)

Brutteen, brutin, bruteens; the Ulster words for caulcannon; which see. Irish *brüightin*.

Buckaun; the upright bar of a hinge on which the other part with the door hangs. Irish *bocán*.

Buckley, Father Darby, 68, 146.

Bucknabarra; any non-edible fungus. (Fermanagh.) See Pookapyle.

Buck teeth; superfluous teeth which stand out from the ordinary row. (Knowles : Ulster.)

Buddaree [*dd* sounded like *th* in *they*]; a rich purse-proud vulgar farmer. (Munster.) Irish.

Buff; the skin; to strip to one's buff is to strip naked. Two fellows going to fight with fists strip to their buff, i.e. naked from the waist up. (Munster.)

Buggaun (Munster), buggeen (Leinster); an egg without a shell. Irish *bog*, soft, with the dim. termination.

Bullaun, a bull calf. Irish, as in next word.

Bullavaun, bullavogue; a strong, rough, bullying fellow. From *bulla* the Irish form of *bull*. (Moran : Carlow.)

Bullaworrus; a spectral bull 'with fire blazing from his eyes, mouth, and nose,' that guards buried treasure by night. (Limerick.) Irish.

Bullia-bottha (or boolia-botha); a fight with sticks. (Simmons : Armagh.) Irish *buaileadh*, striking; and *bata*, a stick.

Bullagadaun [*d* sounded like *th* in *they*]; a short stout pot-bellied fellow. (Munster.) From Irish *bolg* [pron. bullog], a belly, and the dim. *dán*.

Bullshin, bullsheen; same as *Bullaun*.

Bum ; to cart turf to market : *bummer*, a person who does so as a way of living, like Billy Heffernan in 'Knocknagow.' Bum-bailiff, a bog bailiff. (Grainger : Arm.)   Used more in the northern half of Ireland than in the southern.

Bun ; the tail of a rabbit.   (Simmons : Arm.)   Irish *bun*, the end.

Bunnans ; roots or stems of bushes or trees. (Meath.) From Irish *bun* as in last word.

Bunnaun ; a long stick or wattle. (Joyce : Limerick.)

Bunnioch ; the last sheaf bound up in a field of reaped corn. The binder of this (usually a girl) will die unmarried. (MacCall : Wexford.)

Butt ; a sort of cart boarded at bottom and all round the sides, 15 or 18 inches deep, for potatoes, sand, &c. (Limerick.) In Cork any kind of horse-cart or donkey-cart is called a *butt*, which is a departure from the (English) etymology. In Limerick any kind of cart except a butt is called a *car* ; the word *cart* is not used at all.

Butthoon has much the same meaning as *potthalowng*, which see.   Irish *butún*, same sound and meaning. (Munster.)

Butter up ; to flatter, to cajole by soft sugary words, generally with some selfish object in view :—' I suspected from the way he was buttering me up that he came to borrow money.'

Byre : the place where the cows are fed and milked ; sometimes a house for cows and horses, or a farm-yard.

By the same token : this needs no explanation ; it is a survival from Tudor English. (Hayden and Hartog.)

Cabin-hunting ; going about from house to house to gossip. (South.)

Cabman's Answer, The, 208.

Cadday' [strong accent on -day] to stray idly about. As a noun an idle *stray* of a fellow.

Cadge ; to hawk goods for sale. (Simmons : Armagh.) To go about idly from house to house, picking up *a bit and a sup*, wherever they are to be had. (Moran : Carlow.)

Caffler ; a contemptible little fellow who gives saucy *cheeky* foolish talk. Probably a mispronunciation of *caviller*. (Munster.)

Cagger ; a sort of pedlar who goes to markets and houses selling small goods and often taking others in exchange. (Kinahan : South and West.)

Cahag ; the little cross-piece on the end of a spade-handle, or of any handle. (Mon.)

Cailey ; a friendly evening visit in order to have a gossip. There are usually several persons at a cailey, and along with the gossiping talk there are songs or music. Irish *céilidh*, same sound and meaning. Used all over Ireland, but more in the North than elsewhere.

Calleach na looha [Colleagh : accented on 2nd syll. in South ; on 1st in North] 'hag of the ashes.' Children—and sometimes *old children*—think that a little hag resides in the ashpit beside the fire. Irish *cailleach*, an old woman : *luaith*, ashes.

Calleach-rue (' red hag ') ; a little reddish brown fish about 4 inches long, plentiful in small streams. We boys thought them delicious when broiled on the turf-coals. We fished for them either with a loop-snare made of a single horsehair on the end of a twig, with which it was very hard to catch them ; for, as the boys used to say, ' they were cute little divels '—or directly—like the sportsmen of old—with a spear —the same spear being nothing but *an ould fork.*

Caish ; a growing pig about 6 months old. (Munster.)

Call ; claim, right : ' put down that spade ; you have no call to it.'

> ' Bedad,' says he, ' this sight is queer,
>   My eyes it does bedizen—O;
> What *call* have you marauding here,
>   Or how daar you leave your prison—O?'
>   (Repeal Song : 1843.)

Need, occasion : they lived so near each other that there was no call to send letters. ' Why are you shouting that way ? ' ' I have a good call to shout, and that blackguard running away with my apples.' Father O'Flynn could preach on many subjects :—' Down from mythology into thayology, Troth ! and conchology if he'd the call.' (A. P. Graves.) Used everywhere in Ireland in these several senses.

Call ; custom in business : Our new shopkeeper is getting great call, i.e. his customers are numerous. South.)

Cam or caum ; a metal vessel for melting resin to make *sluts* or long torches ; also used to melt metal for coining. (Simmons : Armagh.) Called a *grisset* in Munster. Usually of a curved shape : Irish *cam*, curved.

Candle. ' Jack Brien is a good scholar, but he couldn't hold a candle to Tom Murphy': i.e. he is very inferior to him. The person that holds a candle for a workman is a mere attendant and quite an inferior.

Cannags; the stray ears left after the corn has been reaped and gathered. (Morris: Mon.) Called *liscauns* in Munster.

Caper: oat-cake and butter. (Simmons: Armagh.)

Caravat and Shanavest; the names of two hostile factions in Kilkenny and all round about there, of the early part of last century. Like Three-year-old and Four-year-old. Irish *Caravat*, a cravat; and *Shanavest*, old vest: which names were adopted, but no one can tell why.

Card-cutter; a fortune-teller by card tricks. Card-cutters were pretty common in Limerick in my early days: but it was regarded as disreputable to have any dealings with them.

Cardia; friendship, a friendly welcome, additional time granted for paying a debt. (All over Ireland.) Ir. *cáirde*, same meanings.

Cardinal Points, 168.

Carleycue; a very small coin of some kind. Used like *keenoge* and *cross*. (Very general.)

Carn; a heap of anything; a monumental pile of stones heaped up over a dead person. Irish *carn*, same meanings.

Caroline or 'Caroline hat'; a tall hat. ('Knocknagow': all over Munster.)

Caroogh, an expert or professional card-player. (Munster.) Irish *cearrbhach*, same sound and meaning.

Carra, Carrie; a weir on a river. (Derry.) Irish *carra*, same meaning.

Carrigaholt in Clare, 145.

Carry; to lead or drive: 'James, carry down those cows to the river' (i.e. drive): 'carry the horse to the forge' (lead). 'I will carry my family this year to Youghal for the salt water.' (Kinahan: South, West, and North-west.)   See Bring.

Case: the Irish *cás*, and applied in the same way: 'It is a poor case that I have to pay for your extravagance.' *Nách dubhach bocht un cás bheith ag tuitim le ghrádh* : ' isn't it a poor case to be failing through love.'—Old Irish Song.   Our dialectical Irish *case*, as above, is taken straight from the Irish *cás* ; but this and the standard English *case* are both borrowed from Latin.

Cassnara ; respect, anything done out of respect: 'he put on his new coat for a *casnara*.' (Morris: South Mon.)

Castor oil was our horror when we were children. No wonder ; for this story went about of how it was made.   A number of corpses were hanging from hooks round the walls of the *factory*, and drops were continually falling from their big toes into vessels standing underneath.   This was castor oil.

Catin clay ; clay mixed with rushes or straws used in building the mud walls of cottages. (Simmons: Arm.)

Cat of a kind : they're 'cat of a kind,' both like each other and both objectionable.

Cat's lick ; used in and around Dublin to express exactly the same as the Munster *Scotch lick*, which see.   A cat has a small tongue and does not do much licking,

Caubeen ; an old shabby cap or hat : Irish *cáibin* : he wore a ' shocking bad caubeen.'

Cauboge ; originally an old hat, like caubeen ; but now applied—as the symbol of vulgarity—to an ignorant fellow, a boor, a bumpkin : ' What else could you expect from that cauboge ? ' (South.)

Caulcannon, Calecannon, Colecannon, Kalecannon ; potatoes mashed with butter and milk, with chopped up cabbage and pot-herbs. In Munster often made and eaten on Hallow Eve. The first syllable is the Irish *cál*, cabbage ; *cannon* is also Irish, meaning speckled.

Caur, kindly, good-natured, affable. (Morris : South Mon.)

Cawmeen ; a mote : ' there's a cawmeen in my eye.' (Moran : Carlow.) Irish with the diminutive.

Cawsha Pooka ; the big fungus often seen growing on old trees or elsewhere. From Irish *cáise*, cheese : the ' Pooka's cheese.' See Pooka and Pookapyle and Bucknabarra.

Cead míle fáilte [caidh meela faultha], a hundred thousand welcomes. Irish, and universal in Ireland as a salute.

Ceólaun [keolaun], a trifling contemptible little fellow. (Munster.)

Cess ; very often used in the combination *bad cess* (bad luck) :—' Bad cess to me but there's something comin' over me.' (Kickham : ' Knocknagow.') Some think this is a contraction of *success* ; others that it is to be taken as it stands—a *cess* or contribution ; which receives some little support from its use in Louth to mean 'a quantity of corn in for threshing,'

Chalk Sunday ; the first Sunday after Shrove Tuesday (first Sunday in Lent), when those young men who should have been married, but were not, were marked with a heavy streak of chalk on the back of the *Sunday coat*, by boys who carried bits of chalk in their pockets for that purpose, and lay in wait for the bachelors. The marking was done while the congregation were assembling for Mass : and the young fellow ran for his life, always laughing, and often singing the concluding words of some suitable doggerel such as :—' And you are not married though Lent has come !' This custom prevailed in Munster. I saw it in full play in Limerick : but I think it has died out. For the air to which the verses were sung, see my ' Old Irish Music and Songs,' p. 12.

Champ (Down) ; the same as ' caulcannon,' which see. Also potatoes mashed with butter and milk ; same as ' pandy,' which see.

Chanter ; to go about grumbling and fault-finding. (Ulster.)

Chapel : Church : Scallan, 143.

Chaw for *chew*, 97. ' Chawing the rag '; continually grumbling, jawing, and giving abuse. (Kinahan.)

Cheek ; impudence ; *brass* : cheeky ; presumptuous.

Chincough, whooping-cough : from *kink-cough*. See Kink.

Chittering ; constantly muttering .complaints.

(Knowles.)

Chook chook [the *oo* sounded rather short] ; a call for hens. It is the Irish *tiuc*, come.

Christian ; a human being as distinguished from one of the lower animals :—' That dog has nearly as much sense as a Christian.'

Chuff : full.—I'm chuffey after my dinner.' (MacCall : Wexford.)

Clabber, clobber, or clawber ; mud : thick milk. See Bonnyclabber.

Clamp ; a small rick of turf, built up regularly. (All through Ireland.)

Clamper ; a dispute, a wrangle. (Munster.) Irish *clampar*, same meaning.

Clarsha ; a lazy woman. (Morris : South Monaghan.)

Clart ; an untidy dirty woman, especially in preparing food. (Simmons : Armagh.)

Clash, to carry tales : Clashbag, a tale-bearer. (Simmons : Armagh.)

Classy ; a drain running through a byre or stableyard. (Morris : South Monaghan.) Irish *clais*, a trench, with the diminutive *y* added.

Clat ; a slovenly untidy person ; dirt, clay : 'wash the *clat* off your hands' : clatty ; slovenly, untidy— (Ulster) : called *clotty* in Kildare ;—a slattern.

Clatch ; a brood of chickens. (Ulster.) See Clutch.

Cleean [2-syll.] ; a relation by marriage—such as a father-in-law. Two persons so related are *cleeans*. Irish *cliamhan*, same sound and meaning.

Cleever ; one who deals in poultry ; because he carries them in a *cleeve* or large wicker basket. (Morris : South Monaghan.) Irish *cliabh* [cleeve], a basket.

Cleevaun ; a cradle : also a crib or cage for catching birds. The diminutive of Irish *cliabh* or cleeve, a wicker basket.

Clegg ; a horsefly. (Ulster and Carlow.)

Clehalpeen ; a shillelah or cudgel with a knob at the end. (South.) From Irish *cleath*, a wattle, and *ailpin* dim. of *alp*, a knob.

Clever is applied to a man who is tall, straight, and well made.

Clevvy ; three or four shelves one over another in a wall : a sort of small open cupboard like a dresser. (All over the South.)

Clibbin, clibbeen ; a young colt. (Donegal.) Irish *clibin*, same sound and meaning.

Clibbock ; a young horse. (Derry.)

Clift ; a light-headed person, easily roused and rendered foolishly excited. (Ulster.)

Clipe-clash : a tell-tale. (Ulster.) See Clash.

Clochaun, clochan ; a row of stepping-stones across a river. (General.) From Irish *cloch*, a stone, with the diminutive *án*.

Clock ; a black beetle. (South.)

Clocking hen ; a hen hatching. (General.) From the sound or *clock* she utters.

Clooracaun or cluracaun, another name for a leprachaun, which see.

Close ; applied to a day means simply warm :—' This is a very close day.'

Clout ; a blow with the hand or with anything. Also a piece of cloth, a rag, commonly used in the diminutive form in Munster—*cloutheen*. *Cloutheens* is specially applied to little rags used with an infant. *Clout* is also applied to a clownish person :—' It would be well if somebody would teach that *clout* some manners.'

Clove ; to clove flax is to *scutch* it—to draw each handful repeatedly between the blades of a ' cloving tongs,' so as to break off and remove the brittle husk, leaving the fibre smooth and free. (Munster.)

Clutch ; a brood of chickens or of any fowls : same as clatch. I suppose this is English : Waterton (an English traveller) uses it in his ' Wanderings '; but it is not in the Dictionaries of Chambers and Webster.

Cluthoge ; Easter eggs. (P. Reilly ; Kildare.)

Cly-thoran ; a wall or ditch between two estates. (Roscommon.) Irish *cladh* [cly], a raised dyke or fence ; *teóra*, gen. *teórann* [thoran], a boundary.

Cobby-house ; a little house made by children for play. (Munster.)

Cockles off the heart, 194.

Cog ; to copy surreptitiously ; to crib something from the writings of another and pass it off as your own. One schoolboy will sometimes copy from another :—' You cogged that sum.'

Coghil ; a sort of long-shaped pointed net. (Armagh.) Irish *cochal*, a net.

Coldoy ; a bad halfpenny : a spurious worthless article of jewellery. (Limerick.)

Colleen ; a young girl. (All over Ireland.) Irish *cailín*, same sound and meaning.

Colley ; the woolly dusty fluffy stuff that gathers under furniture and in remote corners of rooms. Light soot-smuts flying about.

Colloge ; to talk and gossip in a familiar friendly way. An Irish form of the Latin or English word ' colloquy.'

Collop ; a standard measure of grazing land, p. 177.

Collop ; the part of a flail that is held in the hand. (Munster.) See Boolthaun. Irish *colpa*.

Come-all-ye ; a nickname applied to Irish Folk Songs and Music ; an old country song ; from the beginning of many of the songs :—' Come all ye tender Christians,' &c. This name, intended to be reproachful, originated among ourselves, after the usual habit of many ' superior ' Irishmen to vilify their own country and countrymen and all their customs and peculiarities. Observe, this opening is almost equally common in English Folk-songs ; yet the English do not make game of them by nicknames. Irish music, which is thus vilified by some of our brethren, is the most beautiful Folk Music in the world.

Comether ; *come hether* or *hither*, 97.

Commaun, common ; the game of goaling or hurley. So called from the *commaun* or crooked-shaped stick with which it is played : Irish *cam* or *com*, curved or crooked ; with the diminutive—*camán*. Called *hurling* and *goaling* by English speakers in Ireland, and *shinney* in Scotland.

Commons ; land held in common by the people of a village or small district : see p. 177.

Comparisons, 136.

Conacre ; letting land in patches for a short period. A farmer divides a large field into small portions— $\frac{1}{4}$ acre, $\frac{1}{2}$ acre, &c.—and lets them to his poorer neighbours usually for one season for a single crop, mostly potatoes, or in Ulster flax. He generally undertakes to manure the whole field, and charges high rents for the little lettings. I saw this in practice more than 60 years ago in Munster. Irish *con*, common, and Eng. *acre*.

Condition ; in Munster, to ' change your condition ' is to get married.

Condon, Mr. John, of Mitchelstown, 155.

Conny, canny ; discreet, knowing, cute.

Contrairy, for *contrary*, but accented on second syll. ; cross, perverse, cranky, crotchety, 102.

Convenient : see Handy.

Cool : hurlers and football players always put one of their best players to *mind cool* or *stand cool*, i.e. to stand at their own goal or gap, to intercept the ball if the opponents should attempt to drive it through. Universal in Munster. Irish *cúl* [cool], the back. The full word is *cool-baur-ya* where ' baur-ya ' is the goal or gap. The man standing cool is often called ' the man in the gap' (see p. 182).

Cool ; a good-sized roll of butter. (Munster.)

Cooleen or coulin ; a fair-haired girl. This is the name of a celebrated Irish air. From *cúl* the back [of the head], and *fionn*, white or fair :—*cúil-fhionn*, [pron. cooleen or coolin].

Coonagh ; friendly, familiar, *great* (which see) :— ' These two are very *coonagh*.' (MacCall : Wexford.) Irish *cuaine*, a family.

Coonsoge, a bees' nest. (Cork.) Irish *cuansa* [coonsa], a hiding-place, with the diminutive *óg*.

Cooramagh ; kindly, careful, thoughtful, provident :— ' No wonder Mrs. Dunn would look well and happy with such a *cooramagh* husband.' Irish *curamach*, same meaning.

Coord [*d* sounded like *th* in *bathe*], a friendly visit to a neighbour's house. Irish *cuaird*, a visit. Coordeeagh, same meaning. (Munster.)

Cope-curley ; to stand on the head and throw the heels over ; to turn head over heels. (Ulster.)

Core : work given as a sort of loan to be paid back.

I send a man on *core* for a day to my neighbour:
when next I want a man he will send me one for
a day in return. So with horses: two one-horse
farmers who work their horses in pairs, borrowing
alternately, are said to be in *core*. Very common
in Munster. Irish *cobhair* or *cabhair* [core or
co-ir, 2-syll.] help, support.

Coreeagh; a man who has a great desire to attend
funerals—goes to every funeral that he can possibly reach. (Munster.) Same root as last.

Corfuffle; to toss, shake, confuse, mix up. (Derry.)

Correesk; a crane. (Kildare.) Irish *corr*, a bird of
the crane kind, and *riasc* [reesk], a marsh.

Cŏsher [the *o* long as in *motion*]; banqueting,
feasting. In very old times in Ireland, certain
persons went about with news from place to place,
and were entertained in the high class houses:
this was called *coshering*, and was at one time
forbidden by law. In modern times it means
simply a friendly visit to a neighbour's house to have
a quiet talk. Irish *cóisir*, a banquet, feasting.

Costnent. When a farm labourer has a cottage and
garden from his employer, and boards himself, he
lives *costnent*. He is paid small wages (called
costnent wages) as he has house and plot free.
(Derry.)

Cot; a small boat: Irish *cot*. See 'Irish Names of
Places,' I. 226, for places deriving their names
from *cots*.

Cowlagh; an old ruined house. (Kerry.) Irish
coblach [cowlagh].

Coward's blow; a blow given to provoke a boy to
fight or else be branded as a coward.

Cow's lick.   When the hair in front over the fore-head turns at the roots upward and backward, that is a *cow's lick*, as if a cow had licked it upwards. The idea of a cow licking the hair is very old in Irish literature.   In the oldest of all our miscellaneous Irish MSS.—The Book of the Dun Cow—Cuculainn's hair is so thick and smooth that king Laery, who saw him, says :—' I should imagine it is a cow that licked it.'

Cox, Mr. Simon, of Galbally, 156.

Craags ; great fat hands ; big handfuls.   (Morris : South Mon.)

Crab : a cute precocious little child is often called an *old crab*.   ' Crabjaw ' has the same meaning.

Cracked ; crazy, half mad.

Cracklins ; the browned crispy little flakes that remain after *rendering* or melting lard and pouring it off.   (Simmons : Armagh.)

Crahauns or Kirraghauns ; very small potatoes not used by the family : given to pigs.   (Munster.) Irish *creathán*.

Crans (always in pl.) ; little tricks or dodges. (Limk).

Crapper ; a half glass of whiskey.   (Moran : Carlow.)

Craw-sick ; ill in the morning after a drunken bout.

Crawtha ; sorry, mortified, pained.   (Limerick.) Irish *cráidhte* [crawtha], same meaning.

Crawthumper ; a person ostentatiously devotional.

Creelacaun : see Skillaun.

Creel ; a strong square wicker frame, used by itself for holding turf, &c., or put on asses' backs (in pairs), or put on carts for carrying turf or for taking calves, *bonnives*, &c., to market.   Irish *criol*. (All through Ireland.)

Creepy ; a small stool, a stool.　(Chiefly in Ulster.)

Crith ; hump on the back.　Irish *cruit*, same sound
and meaning.　From this comes *critthera* and
crittheen, both meaning a hunchback.

Cro, or cru : a house for cows.　(Kerry.)　Irish *cro*,
a pen, a fold, a shed for any kind of animals.

Croaked ; I am afraid poor Nancy is croaked, i.e.
doomed to death.　The raven croaks over the
house when one of the family is about to die.
(MacCall : Wexford.)

Croft ; a water bottle, usually for a bedroom at night.
You never hear *carafe* in Ireland : it is always *croft*.

Cromwell, Curse of, 166.

Crumel'ly.　(Limerick.)　More correctly *curr amilly*.
(Donegal.)　An herb found in grassy fields with
a sweet root that children dig up and eat.　Irish
' honey-root.'

Cronaun, croonaun ; a low humming air or song,
any continuous humming sound : ' the old woman
was cronauning in the corner.'

Cronebane, cronebaun ; a bad halfpenny, a worthless
copper coin.　From Cronebane in Co. Wicklow,
where copper mines were worked.

Croobeen or crubeen ; a pig's foot.　Pigs' croobeens
boiled are a grand and favourite viand among us
—all through Ireland.　Irish *crúb* [croob], a foot,
with the diminutive.

Croost ; to throw stones or clods from the hand :—
' Those boys are always *croosting* stones at my
hens.'　Irish *crústa* [croostha], a missile, a clod.

Croudy : see Porter-meal.

Crowl or Croil ; a dwarf, a very small person : the
smallest *bonnive* of the litter.　An Irish word.

Cruiskeen ; a little cruise for holding liquor.   Used
all over Ireland.

> ' In a shady nook one moonlight night
>   A *leprechaun* I spied ;
> With scarlet cap and coat of green,
>   A *cruiskeen* by his side.'

The *Cruiskeen Laun* is the name of a well-known
Irish air—the Scotch call it ' John Anderson
my Jo.' Irish *cruiscin*, a pitcher : *lán* [laun], full :
i.e. in this case full of *pottheen*.

Crusheen ; a stick with a flat crosspiece fastened at
bottom for washing potatoes in a basket.   Irish
cros, a cross, with the diminutive.   Also called a
boghaleen, from Irish *bachal*, a staff, with diminutive.   (Joyce : Limerick.)

Cuck ; a tuft : applied to the little tuft of feathers on
the head of some birds, such as plovers, some
hens and ducks, &c.   Irish *coc* : same sound and
meaning.   (General.)

Cuckles ; the spiky seed-pods of the thistle : thistle
heads.   (Limerick.)

Cuckoo spit ; the violet : merely the translation of
the Irish name, *sail-chuach*, spittle of cuckoos.
Also the name of a small frothy spittle-like substance often found on leaves of plants in summer,
with a little greenish insect in the middle of it.
(Limerick.)

Cugger-mugger ; whispering, gossiping in a low
voice : Jack and Bessie had a great *cugger-mugger*.
Irish *cogar*, whisper, with a similar duplication
meaning nothing, like tip-top, shilly-shally,
gibble-gabble, clitter-clatter, &c.   I think ' hugger-

mugger ' is a form of this : for *hugger* can't be
derived from anything, whereas *cugger* (*cogur*) is a
plain Irish word.

Cull ; when the best of a lot of any kind—sheep,
cattle, books, &c.—have been picked out, the bad
ones that are left—the refuse—are the *culls*.
(Kinahan : general.)

Culla-greefeen ; when foot or hand is ' asleep' with
the feeling of ' pins and needles.' The name is
Irish and means ' Griffin's sleep'; but why so
called I cannot tell. (Munster.)

Cup-tossing ; reading fortunes from tea-leaves thrown
out on the saucer from the tea-cup or teapot.
(General.)

Cur ; a twist : a *cur* of a rope. (Joyce : Limerick.)

Curate ; a common little iron poker kept in use to
spare the grand one : also a grocer's assistant.
(Hayden and Hartog.)

Curcuddiagh ; cosy, comfortable. (Maxwell : ' Wild
Sports of the West': Irish : Mayo.)

Curifixes ; odd *curious* ornaments or *fixtures* of any
kind. (General.) Peter Brierly, looking at the
knocker :—' I never see such *curifixes* on a *doore*
afore.' (Edw. Walsh : very general.)

Curragh ; a wicker boat covered formerly with hides
but now with tarred canvass. (See my ' Smaller
Social Hist. of Anc. Ireland.')

Current ; in good health : he is not current ; his
health is not current. (Father Higgins : Cork.)

Curwhibbles, currifibbles, currywhibbles ; any strange,
odd, or unusual gestures ; or any unusual twisting
of words, such as prevarication ; wild puzzles
and puzzling talk :—' The horsemen are in regular
currywhibles about something.' (R. D. Joyce.)

Cush ; a sort of small horse, from *Cushendall* in Antrim.

Cushlamochree ; pulse of my heart. Irish *Cuislĕ*, vein or pulse ; *mo*, my ; *croidhe* [cree], heart.

Cushoge ; a stem of a plant ; sometimes used the same as *traneen*, which see. (Moran : Carlow ; and Morris : Monaghan.)

Cut ; a county or barony cess tax ; hence Cutman, the collector of it. (Kinahan : Armagh and Donega .) 'The three black *cuts* will be levied.' (Seumas MacManus : Donegal.)

Daisy-picker ; a person who accompanies two lovers in their walk ; why so called obvious. Brought to keep off gossip.

Dalk, a thorn. (De Vismes Kane : North and South.) Irish *dealg* [dallog], a thorn.

Dallag [*d* sounded like *th* in *that*] ; any kind of covering to blindfold the eyes (Morris : South Monaghan) : 'blinding,' from Irish *dall*, blind.

Dallapookeen ; blindman's buff. (Kerry.) From Irish *dalladh* [dalla] blinding ; and *puicin* [pookeen], a covering over the eyes.

Daltheen [the *d* sounded like *th* in *that*], an impudent conceited little fellow : a diminutive of *dalta*, a foster child. The diminutive *dalteen* was first applied to a horseboy, from which it has drifted to its present meaning.

Dancing customs, 170, 172.

Dannagh ; mill-dust and mill-grains for feeding pigs. (Moran : Carlow : also Tip.) Irish *deanach*, same sound and meaning.

Dander [second *d* sounded like *th* in *hither*], to walk about leisurely : a leisurely walk.

Dandy ; a small tumbler ; commonly used for drinking punch.

Darradail or daradeel [the *d*'s sounded like *th* in *that*] a sort of long black chafer or beetle.   It raises its tail when disturbed, and has a strong smell of apples.   There is a religious legend that when our Lord was escaping from the Jews, barefoot, the stones were marked all along by traces of blood from the bleeding feet.   The daradail followed the traces of blood ; and the Jews following, at length overtook and apprehended our Lord.   Hence the people regard the daradail with intense hatred, and whenever they come on it, kill it instantly.   Irish *darbh-daol.*

Dark ; blind : ' a dark man.'   (Very general.)   Used constantly even in official and legal documents, as in workhouse books, especially in Munster.   (Healy.)

Darrol ; the smallest of the brood of pigs, fowl, &c. (Mayo.)   Irish *dearóil*, small, puny, wretched.

Davis, Thomas, vi. 83, &c.

Dead beat or dead *bet* ; tired out.

Dear ; used as a sort of intensive adjective :—' Tom ran for the dear life ' (as fast as he could).   (Crofton Croker.)   ' He got enough to remember all the dear days of his life.'   (' Dub. Pen. Journ.')

Dell ; a lathe.   Irish *deil*, same sound and meaning. (All over Munster.)

Devil's needle ; the dragon-fly.   Translation of the Irish name *snathad-a'-diabhail* [snahad-a-dheel].

Deshort [to rhyme with *port*] ; a sudden interruption, a surprise : ' I was taken at a *deshort.*'   (Derry.)

Devil, The, and his ' territory,' 56.

Dickonce ; one of the disguised names of the devil used in *white* cursing : ' Why then the dickonce take you for one gander.' (Gerald Griffin.)

Diddy ; a woman's pap or breast : a baby sucks its mother's diddy.   Diminutive of Irish *did*, same.

Dido ; a girl who makes herself ridiculous with fantastic finery.   (Moran : Carlow.)

Didoes (singular *dido*) ; tricks, antics : ' quit your didoes.   (Ulster.)

Dildron or dildern ; a bowraun, which see.

Dillesk, dulsk, dulse or dilse ; a sort of sea plant growing on rocks, formerly much used (when dried) as an article of food (as *kitchen*), and still eaten in single leaves as a sort of relish.   Still sold by basket-women in Dublin.   Irish *duilesc*.

Dip.   When the family dinner consisted of dry potatoes, i.e. potatoes without milk or any other drink, dip was often used, that is to say, gravy or broth, or water flavoured in any way in plates, into which the potato was dipped at each bit.   I once saw a man using dip of plain water with mustard in it, and eating his dinner with great relish.   You will sometimes read of 'potatoes and point,' namely, that each person, before taking a bite, *pointed* the potato at a salt herring or a bit of bacon hanging in front of the chimney : but this is mere fun, and never occurred in real life.

Disciple ; a miserable looking creature of a man.   Shane Glas was a long lean scraggy wretched looking fellow (but really strong and active), and another says to him—jibing and railing—' Away with ye, ye miserable *disciple*.   Arrah, by the hole

of my coat, after you dance your last jig upon
nothing, with your hemp cravat on, I'll coax yer
miserable carcase from the hangman to frighten
the crows with.' (Edw. Walsh in 'Pen. Journ.')

Disremember : to forget. Good old English; now
out of fashion in England, but common in Ireland.

Ditch. In Ireland a ditch is a raised fence or
earthen wall or mound, and a dyke (or *sheuch* as
they call it in Donegal and elsewhere in Ulster) is
a deep cutting, commonly filled with water. In
England both words mean exactly the reverse.
Hence ' hurlers on the ditch,' or ' the best hurlers
are on the ditch ' (where speakers of pure English
would use ' fence ') said in derision of persons who
are mere idle spectators sitting up on high watching the game—whatever it may be—and boasting
how they would *do the devil an' all* if they were
only playing. Applied in a broad sense to those
who criticise persons engaged in any strenuous
affair—critics who think they could do better.

Dollop; to adulterate : ' that coffee is dolloped.'

Donny; weak, in poor health. Irish *donaidhe*, same
sound and meaning. Hence *donnaun*, a poor
weakly creature, same root with the diminutive.
From still the same root is *donsy*, sick-looking.

Donagh-dearnagh, the Sunday before Lammas (1st
August). (Ulster.) Irish *Domnach*, Sunday; and
deireannach, last, i.e. last Sunday of the period
before 1st August.

Doodoge [the two *d*'s sounded like *th* in *thus*]; a big
pinch of snuff. |Limk.] Irish *dúdóg*.

Dooraght [*d* sounded as in the last word]; tender
care and kindness shown to a person. Irish

dúthracht, same sound and meaning. In parts of Ulster it means a small portion given over and above what is purchased (Simmons and Knowles); called elsewhere a *tilly*, which see. This word, in its sense of kindness, is very old; for in the Brehon Law we read of land set aside by a father for his daughter through *dooraght*.

Doorshay-daurshay [*d* in both sounded as *th* in *thus*], mere hearsay or gossip. The first part is Irish, representing the sound of *dubhairt-sé*, 'said he.' The second part is a mere doubling of the first, as we find in many English words, such as 'fiddle-faddle,' 'tittle-tattle' (which resembles our word). Often used by Munster lawyers in court, whether Irish-speaking or not, in depreciation of hearsay evidence in contradistinction to the evidence of looking-on. · Ah, that's all mere *doorshay-daurshay*.' Common all over Munster. The information about the use of the term in law courts I got from Mr. Maurice Healy. A different form is sometimes heard :—*D'innis bean dom gur innis bean di*, 'a woman told me that a woman told her.'

Dornoge [*d* sounded as in doodoge above]; a small round lump of a stone, fit to be cast from the hand. Irish *dorn*, the shut hand, with the dim. *óg.*

Double up ; to render a person helpless either in fight or in argument. The old tinker in the fair got a blow of an amazon's fist which 'sent him sprawling and *doubled* him up for the rest of the evening.' (Robert Dwyer Joyce : 'Madeline's Vow.')

Down in the heels ; broken down in fortune (one mark of which is the state of the heels of shoes).

Down blow; a heavy or almost ruinous blow of any kind :—' The loss of that cow was a down blow to poor widow Cleary.'

Downface; to persist boldly in an assertion (whether true or no): He downfaced me that he returned the money I lent him, though he never did.

Down-the-banks; a scolding, a reprimand, punishment of any kind.

Dozed : a piece of timber is dozed when there is a dry rot in the heart of it. (Myself for Limk.: Kane for North.)

Drad ; a grin or contortion of the mouth. (Joyce.)

Drag home. (Simmons ; Armagh : same as Hauling home, which see.)

Drass ; a short time, a turn :—' You walk a drass now and let me ride': 'I always smoke a drass before I go to bed of a night.' (' Collegians,' Limerick.)   Irish *dreas*, same sound and meaning.

Drench : a form of the English *drink*, but used in a peculiar sense in Ireland.   A *drench* is a philtre, a love-potion, a love-compelling drink over which certain charms were repeated during its preparation.   Made by boiling certain herbs (*orchis*) in water or milk, and the person drinks it unsuspectingly.   In my boyhood time a beautiful young girl belonging to a most respectable family ran off with an ill-favoured obscure beggarly diseased wretch.   The occurrence was looked on with great astonishment and horror by the people—no wonder ; and the universal belief was that the fellow's old mother had given the poor girl a *drench*.   To this hour I cannot make any guess at the cause of that astounding elopement : and it is not surprising that the people were driven to the supernatural for an explanation.

Dresser ; a set of shelves and drawers in a frame in a kitchen for holding plates, knives, &c.

Drisheen is now used in Cork as an English word, to denote a sort of pudding made of the narrow intestines of a sheep, filled with blood that has been cleared of the red colouring matter, and mixed with meal and some other ingredients. So far as I know, this viand and its name are peculiar to Cork, where *drisheen* is considered suitable for persons of weak or delicate digestion. (I should observe that a recent reviewer of one of my books states that drisheen is also made in Waterford.) Irish *dreas* or driss, applied to anything slender, as a bramble, one of the smaller intestines, &c.— with the diminutive.

Drizzen, a sort of moaning sound uttered by a cow. (Derry).

Drogh ; the worst and smallest bonnive in a litter. (Armagh.) Irish *droch*, bad, evil. (See Eervar.)

Droleen ; a wren : merely the Irish word *dreóilín*.

Drop ; a strain of any kind ' running in the blood.' A man inclined to evil ways ' has a bad drop ' in him (or ' a black drop '): a miser ' has a hard drop.' The expression carries an idea of heredity.

Drugget ; a cloth woven with a mixture of woollen and flaxen thread : so called from Drogheda where it was once extensively manufactured. Now much used as cheap carpeting.

Druids and Druidism, 178.

Drumaun ; a wide back-band for a ploughing horse,

with hooks to keep the traces in place. (Joyce : Limerick.)   From Irish *druim*, the back.

Drummagh ; the back strap used in yoking two horses. (Joyce : Limerick.) Irish *druim*, the back, with the termination -*ach*, equivalent to English -*ous* and -*y*.

Dry potatoes ; potatoes eaten without milk or any other drink.

Dry lodging ; the use of a bed merely, without food.

Drynaun-dun or drynan-dun [two *d*'s sounded like *th* in *that*] ; the blackthorn, the sloe-bush.   Irish *droigheanán* [drynan or drynaun], and *donn*, brown-coloured.

Ducks ; trousers of snow-white canvas, much used as summer wear by gentle and simple fifty or sixty years ago.

Dudeen [both *d*'s sounded like *th* in *those*] ; a smoking-pipe with a very short stem.   Irish *dúidín*, *dúd*, a pipe, with the diminutive.

Duggins ; rags : ' that poor fellow is all in duggins.' (Armagh.)

Dull ; a loop or eye on a string.   (Monaghan.)

Dullaghan [*d* sounded as *th* in *those*] ; a large trout. (Kane : Monaghan.)   An Irish word.

Dullaghan ; ' a hideous kind of hobgoblin generally met with in churchyards, who can take off and put on his head at will.   (From ' Irish Names of Places,' I. 193, which see for more about this spectre.   See Croker's ' Fairy Legends.')

Dullamoo [*d* sounded like *th* in *those*] ; a wastrel, a scapegrace, a *ne'er-do-weel*.   Irish *dul*, going ; *amudha* [amoo], astray, to loss :—*dullamoo*, ' a person going to the bad,' 'going to the dogs.'

Dundeen ; a lump of bread without butter. (Derry.)

Dunisheen ; a small weakly child. (Moran : Carlow.)
Irish *donaisin,* an unfortunate being ; from *donas,*
with diminutive. See Donny.

Dunner ; to knock loudly at a door. (Ulster.)

Dunt (sometimes *dunch*), to strike or butt like a cow
or goat with the head. A certain lame old man
(of Armagh) was nicknamed ' Dunt the pad (path ').
(Ulster.)

Durneen, one of the two handles of a scythe that
project from the main handle. Irish *doirnin,* same
sound and meaning : diminutive from *dorn,* the
fist, the shut hand.

Durnoge ; a strong rough leather glove, used on the
left hand by faggot cutters. (MacCall : Wexford.)
Dornoge, given above, is the same word but
differently applied.

Duty owed by tenants to landlords, 181.

Earnest ; ' in earnest ' is often used in the sense of
' really and truly ' :—' You're a man in earnest,
Cus, to strike the first blow on a day [of battle]
like this.' (R. D. Joyce.)

Eervar ; the last pig in a litter. This *bonnive* being
usually very small and hard to keep alive is often
given to one of the children for a pet ; and it is
reared in great comfort in a warm bed by the
kitchen fire, and fed on milk. I once, when a
child, had an eervar of my own which was the joy
of my life. Irish *iarmhar* [eervar], meaning
' something after all the rest ' ; the hindmost.
(Munster.) See Drogh for Ulster.

Elder ; a cow's udder. All over Ireland.

Elegant. This word is used among us, not in its proper sense, but to designate anything good or excellent of its kind:—An elegant penknife, an elegant gun: 'That's an elegant pig of yours, Jack?' Our milkman once offered me a present for my garden—' An elegant load of dung.'

> I haven't the *janius* for work,
> For 'twas never the gift of the Bradys;
> But I'd make a most *elegant* Turk,
> For I'm fond of tobacco and ladies.
>
> (LEVER.)

'How is she [the sick girl] coming on?'
'Elegant,' was the reply. ('Knocknagow.')
Elementary schools, 159.
Exaggeration and redundancy, 120.
Existence, way of predicating, 23.
Eye of a bridge; the arch.

Faireen (south), fairin (north); a present either given in a fair or brought from it. Used in another sense—a lasting injury of any kind:—' Poor Joe got a faireen that day, when the stone struck him on the eye, which I'm afraid the eye will never recover.' Used all over Ireland and in Scotland.

> Ah Tam, ah Tam, thou'lt get thy fairin',
> In hell they'll roast thee like a herrin'.
>
> (BURNS.)

Fair-gurthra; 'hungry grass.' There is a legend all through Ireland that small patches of grass grow here and there on mountains; and if a person in walking along happens to tread on one of them he is instantly overpowered with hunger so as to be quite unable to walk, and if help or food is not at hand he will sink down and perish. That persons are attacked and rendered helpless by sudden hunger on mountains in this manner is certain. Mr. Kinahan gives me an instance where he had to carry his companion, a boy, on his back a good distance to the nearest house: and Maxwell in 'Wild Sports of the West' gives others. But he offers the natural explanation: that a person is liable to sink suddenly with hunger if he undertakes a hard mountain walk with a long interval after food. Irish *feur*, grass; *gorta*, hunger.

Fairy breeze. Sometimes on a summer evening you suddenly feel a very warm breeze: that is a band of fairies travelling from one fort to another; and people on such occasions usually utter a short prayer, not knowing whether the 'good people' are bent on doing good or evil. (G. H. Kinahan.) Like the Shee-geeha, which see.

Fairy-thimble, the same as 'Lusmore,' which see.

Famished; distressed for want of something:—'I am famished for a smoke—for a glass,' &c.

Farbreaga; a scarecrow. Irish *fear*, a man: *breug* falsehood: a false or pretended man.

Farl; one quarter of a griddle cake. (Ulster.)

Faúmera [the *r* has the slender sound]; a big strolling beggarman or idle fellow. From the Irish *Fomor*. The *Fomors* or *Fomora* or Fomorians were one of the mythical colonies that came to Ireland (see any of my Histories of Ireland, Index): some accounts represent them as giants. In Clare the country people that go to the seaside in summer for the benefit of the 'salt water' are

called *Faumeras*. In Tramore they are called
olishes [o long]; because in the morning before
breakfast they go down to the strand and take a
good *swig* of the salt water—an essential part of
the cure—and when one meets another he (or she)
asks in Irish '*ar ólish*,' 'did you drink?' In
Kilkee the dogfish is called *Faumera*, for the dogfish is among the smaller fishes like what legend
represents the Fomorians in Ireland.

Faustus, Dr., in Irish dialect, 60.

Fear is often used among us in the sense of *danger*.
Once during a high wind the ship's captain neatly
distinguished it when a frightened lady asked
him :—' Is there any fear, sir ?' ' There's plenty
of fear, madam, but no danger.'

Feck or fack; a spade. From the very old Irish
word, *fec*, same sound and meaning.

Fellestrum, the flagger (marsh plant). Irish *feles-
trom*. (South.)

Fetch ; what the English call a *double*, a preter-
natural apparition of a living person, seen usually
by some relative or friend. If seen in the morning
the person whose fetch it is will have a long and
prosperous life : if in the evening the person will
soon die.

Finane or Finaun ; the white half-withered long
grass found in marshy or wet land. Irish *finn* or
fionn, white, with the diminutive.

Finely and poorly are used to designate the two
opposite states of an invalid. ' Well, Mrs. Lahy,
how is she ?' [Nora the poor sick little girl].
' Finely, your reverence,' Honor replied (going on
well). The old sinner Rody, having accidentally

shot himself, is asked how he is going on ;—
' Wisha, poorly, poorly ' (badly). (G. Griffin.)

Finger—to put a finger in one's eye ; to overreach
and cheat him by cunning :—' He'd be a clever
fellow that would put a finger in Tom's eye.'

First shot, in distilling pottheen ; the weak stuff that
comes off at the first distillation : also called
singlings.

Flahoolagh, plentiful ; ' You have a flahoolagh hand,
Mrs. Lyons ' : ' Ah, we got a flahoolagh dinner
and no mistake.' Irish *flaith* [flah], a chief, and
amhail [ooal], like, with the adjectival termination
ach : *flahoolagh*, ' chieftain-like.' For the old
Irish chiefs kept open houses, with full and plenty
—*launa-vaula*—for all who came. (South.)

Flipper ; an untidy man. (Limerick.)

Flitters ; tatters, rags :—' His clothes were all in
flitters.'

Flog ; to beat, to exceed :—' That flogs Europe '
(' Collegians '), i.e. it beats Europe : there's nothing
in Europe like it.

Fluke, something very small or nothing at all.
' What did you get from him ? ' ' Oh I got flukes
(or ' flukes in a hand-basket ')—meaning nothing.
Sometimes it seems to mean a small coin, like
cross and *keenoge*. ' When I set out on that journey
I hadn't a fluke.' (North and South.)

Fockle ; a big torch made by lighting a sheaf of
straw fixed on a long pole : fockles were usually
lighted on St. John's Eve. (Limerick.) It is
merely the German word *fackel*, a torch, brought
to Limerick by the Palatine colony. (See p. 65.)

Fog-meal ; a great meal or big feed : a harvest dinner.

Fooster; hurry, flurry, fluster, great fuss. Irish *fústar*, same sound and meaning. (Hayden and Hartog.)

> ' Then Tommy jumped about elate,
> Tremendous was his *fooster*—O ;
> Says he, " I'll send a message straight
> To my darling Mr. Brewster—O !" '
>
> (Repeal Song of 1843.)

Forbye ; besides. (Ulster.)

For good ; finally, for ever : ' he left home for good.'

Fornent, fornenst, forenenst ; opposite : he and I sat fornenst each other in the carriage.

> ' Yet here you strut in open day
> Fornenst my house so freely—O.'
>
> (Repeal Song of 1843.)

An old English word, now obsolete in England, but very common in Ireland.

Foshla ; a marshy weedy rushy place ; commonly applied to the ground left after a cut-away bog. (Roscommon.)

Four bones ; ' Your own four bones,' 127.

Fox ; (verb) to pretend, to feign, to sham : ' he's not sick at all, he's only foxing.' Also to cut short the ears of a dog.

Frainey ; a small puny child :—' Here, eat this bit, you little *frainey*.'

Fraughans ; whortleberries. Irish *fraoch*, with the diminutive. See Hurt.

Freet ; a sort of superstition or superstitious rite. (Ulster.)

Fresh and Fresh :—' I wish you to send me the butter every morning : I like to have it fresh and fresh.

This is English gone out of fashion : I remember seeing it in Pope's preface to ' The Dunciad.'

Frog's jelly ; the transparent jelly-like substance found in pools and ditches formed by frogs round their young tadpoles, 121.

Fum ; soft spongy turf. (Ulster.) Called *soosaun* in Munster.

Gaatch [*aa* long as in *car*], an affected gesture or movement of limbs body or face : *gaatches* ; assuming fantastic ridiculous attitudes. (South.)

Gad ; a withe : ' as tough as a gad.' (Irish *gad*, 60.)

Gadderman ; a boy who puts on the airs of a man ; a mannikin or *manneen*, which see. (Simmons : Armagh.)

Gaffer ; an old English word, but with a peculiar application in Ireland, where it means a boy, a young chap. ' Come here, gaffer, and help me.'

Gag ; a conceited foppish young fellow, who tries to figure as a swell.

Gah'ela or gaherla ; a little girl. (Kane : Ulster.) Same as *girsha*.

Gaileen ; a little bundle of rushes placed under the arms of a beginner learning to swim. (Joyce : Limerick.) When you support the beginner's head keeping it above water with your hands while he is learning the strokes : that we used to designate ' *giving a gaileen*.'

Galbally, Co. Limerick, 156.

Galoot : a clownish fellow.

Galore ; plenty, plentiful. Irish adverb *go leór*, 4.

Gankinna ; a fairy, a leprachaun. (Morris : South Mon.) Irish *gann*, small.

Gannoge ; an undefined small quantity. (Antrim.)
Irish *gann*, small, with diminutive *óg*.

Garden, in the South, is always applied to a field of
growing potatoes. ' In the land courts we never
asked "How many acres of potatoes?"; but "How
many acres of garden?"' (Healy.) A usual inquiry
is ' How are your gardens going on?' meaning
' How are your potato crops doing?'

Garlacom ; a lingering disease in cows believed to
be caused by eating a sort of herb. (P. Moran :
Meath.)

Garland Sunday ; the first Sunday in August (sometimes called Garlick Sunday.)

Garron, garraun ; an old worn-out horse. (Irish
gearrán.)

Gash ; a flourish of the pen in writing so as to
form an ornamental curve, usually at the end.
(Limerick.)

Gatha ; an effeminate fellow who concerns himself
in women's business : a *Sheela*. (Joyce : Limerick.)

Gatherie ; a splinter of bog-deal used as a torch.
(Moran : Carlow.) Also a small cake (commonly
smeared with treacle) sold in the street on market
days. Irish *geataire* [gatthera], same meanings.

Gaug ; a sore crack in the heel of a person who goes
barefooted. (Moran : Carlow.) Irish *gág* [gaug],
a cleft, a crack.

Gaulsh ; to loll. (MacCall : Wexford.)

Gaunt or gant ; to yawn. (Ulster.)

Gaurlagh ; a little child, a baby : an unfledged bird.
Irish *gárlach*, same sound and meanings.

Gawk ; a tall awkward fellow. (South.)

Gawm, gawmoge; a soft foolish fellow. (South.) Irish *gám*, same meaning. See Gommul.

Gazebo; a tall building; any tall object; a tall awkward person.

Gazen, gazened; applied to a wooden vessel of any kind when the joints open by heat or drought so that it leaks. (Ulster.)

Gallagh-gunley; the harvest moon. (Ulster.) *Gallagh* gives the sound of Irish *gealach*, the moon, meaning whitish, from *geal*, white.

Geck; to mock, to jeer, to laugh at. (Derry.)

Geenagh, geenthagh; hungry, greedy, covetous. (Derry.) Irish *gionach* or *giontach*, gluttonous.

Geens; wild cherries. (Derry.)

Gentle; applied to a place or thing having some connexion with the fairies—haunted by fairies. A thornbush where fairies meet is a ' gentle bush': the hazel and the foxglove (fairy-thimble) are gentle plants.

Geócagh; a big strolling idle fellow. (Munster.) Irish *geocach*, same sound and meaning.

Geosadaun or Yosedaun [*d* in both sounded like *th* in *they*]; the yellow rag-weed : called also boliaun [2-syll.] and booghalaun.

Get; a bastard child. (North and South.)

Gibbadaun; a frivolous person. (Roscommon.) From the Irish *giob*, a scrap, with the diminutive ending *dán* : a *scrappy* trifling-minded person.

Gibbol [*g* hard as in *get*]; a rag : your jacket is all hanging down in gibbols.' (Limerick.) Irish *giobal*, same sound and meaning.

Giddhom; restlessness. In Limerick it is applied to cows when they gallop through the fields with

tails cocked out, driven half mad by heat and flies:
'The cows are galloping with giddhom.' Irish
giodam, same sound and meaning.

Gill-gowan, a corn-daisy. (Tyrone.) From Irish
geal, white, and *gowan*, the Scotch name for a daisy.

Girroge [two *g*'s sounded as in *get*, *got*]. Girroges
are the short little drills where the plough runs
into a corner. (Kildare and Limerick.) Irish
gearr, short, with the diminutive *óg* : *girroge*, any
short little thing.

Girsha ; a little girl. (North and South.) Irish
geirrseach [girsagh], from *gearr*, short or small,
with the feminine termination *seach*.

Gistra [*g* sounded as in *get*], a sturdy, active old
man. (Ulster.) Irish *giostaire*, same sound and
meaning.

Gladiaathor [*aa* long as in *car*] ; a gladiator, a
fighting quarrelsome fellow : used as a verb
also :—' he went about the fair *gladiaatherin*,' i.e.
shouting and challenging people to fight him.

Glaum, glam ; to grab or grasp with the whole
hand ; to maul or pull about with the hands.
Irish *glám* [glaum], same meaning.

Glebe ; in Ireland this word is almost confined to
the land or farm attached to a Protestant rector's
residence : hence called *glebe-land*. See p. 143.

Gleeag ; a small handful of straw used in plaiting
straw mats : a sheaf of straw threshed. (Kildare
and Monaghan.)

Gleeks : to give a fellow the gleeks is to press the
forefingers into the butt of the ears so as to cause
pain : a rough sort of play. (Limerick.)

Glenroe, Co. Limerick, 68, 146.

Gliggeen ; a voluble silly talker. (Munster.) Irish *gluigin* [gliggeen], a little bell, a little tinkler : from *glog*, same as *clog*, a bell.

Gliggerum ; applied to a very bad old worn-out watch or clock. (Limerick.)

Glit ; slimy mud ; the green vegetable (*ducksmeat*) that grows on the surface of stagnant water. (Simmons : Armagh.)

Gloit ; a blockhead of a young fellow. (Knowles.)

Glory be to God ! Generally a pious exclamation of thankfulness, fear, &c. : but sometimes an ejaculation of astonishment, wonder, admiration, &c. Heard everywhere in Ireland.

Glower ; to stare or glare at : ' what are you glowerin' at ! ' (Ulster.)

Glugger [*u* sounded as in *full*] ; empty noise ; the noise made by shaking an addled egg. Also an addled egg. Applied very often in a secondary sense to a vain empty foolish boaster. (Munster.)

Glunter : a stupid person. (Knowles : Ulster.)

Goaling : same as Hurling, which see.

Gob ; the mouth including lips : ' Shut your gob.' Irish *gob*, same meaning. Scotch, ' greedy *gab*.' (Burns.)

Gobshell ; a big spittle direct from the mouth. (Limerick.) From Irish *gob*, the mouth, and *seile* [shella], a spittle.

Gobs or jackstones ; five small round stones with which little girls play against each other, by throwing them up and catching them as they fall ; ' there are Nelly and Sally playing gobs.'

Gods and goddesses of Pagan Ireland, 177.

Godspeed : see Back of God-speed.

God's pocket. Mr. Kinahan writes to me:—'The
first time I went to the Mullingar hotel I had a
delicate child, and spoke to the landlady as to
how he was to be put up [during the father's
absence by day on outdoor duty]. "Oh never
fear sir," replied the good old lady, "the poor
child will be *in God's pocket* here." ' Mr. K. goes
on to say:—I afterwards found that in all that
part of Leinster they never said 'we will make
you comfortable,' but always 'you will be in God's
pocket,' or 'as snug as in God's pocket.' I heard
it said of a widow and orphans whose people
were kind to them, that they were in 'God's
pocket.' Whether Seumas MacManus ever came
across this term I do not know, but he has something very like it in 'A Lad of the O'Friels,'
viz., 'I'll make the little girl as happy as if she
was in *Saint Peter's pocket.*'

Goggalagh, a dotard. (Munster.) Irish *gogail*, the
cackling of a hen or goose; also doting; with the
usual termination *ach*.

Going on; making fun, joking, teasing, chaffing,
bantering:—' Ah, now I see you are only *going on*
with me.' 'Stop your *goings on*.' (General.)

Golder [*d* sounded like *th* in further]; a loud sudden
or angry shout. (Patterson: Ulster.)

Goleen; an armful. See Gwaul.

Gombeen man; a usurer who lends money to small
farmers and others of like means, at ruinous
interest. The word is now used all over Ireland.
Irish *goimbín* [gombeen], usury.

Gommul, gommeril, gommula, all sometimes
shortened to *gom*; a simple-minded fellow, a half

fool. Irish *gamal, gamaille, gamairle, gamarail*, all same meaning. (*Gamal* is also Irish for a camel.) Used all over Ireland.

Good deed ; said of some transaction that is a well-deserved punishment for some wrong or unjust or very foolish course of action. Bill lends some money to Joe, who never returns it, and a friend says:—' 'Tis a good deed Bill, why did you trust such a schemer ? ' Barney is bringing home a heavy load, and is lamenting that he did not bring his ass :—' 'Tis a good deed : where was I coming without Bobby ?' (the ass). (' Knocknagow ') ' I'm wet to the skin': reply :—' 'Tis a good deed: why did you go out without your overcoat ? '

Good boy : in Limerick and other parts of Munster, a young fellow who is good—strong and active—at all athletic exercises, but most especially if he is brave and tough in fighting, is ' a good boy.' The people are looking anxiously at a sailing boat labouring dangerously in a storm on the Shannon, and one of them remarks :—' 'Tis a good boy that has the rudder in his hand.' (Gerald Griffin.)

Good people ; The fairies. The word is used merely as *soft sawder*, to *butter them up*, to curry favour with them—to show them great respect at least from the teeth out—lest they might do some injury to the speaker.

Googeen [two *g*'s as in *good* and *get*] ; a simple soft-minded person. (Moran: Carlow.) Irish *guag*, same meaning, with the diminutive : *guaigín*.

Gopen, gowpen ; the full of the two hands used together. (Ulster.) Exactly the same meaning as *Lyre* in Munster, which see.

Gor; the coarse turf or peat which forms the surface of the bog. (Healy : for Ulster.)

Gorb ; a ravenous eater, a glutton. (Ulster.)

Gorsoon: a young boy. It is hard to avoid deriving
this from French *garçon*, all the more as it has no
root in Irish. Another form often used is *gossoon*,
which is derived from Irish:—*gas*, a stem or stalk,
a young boy. But the termination *oon* or *ūn* is
suspicious in both cases, for it is not a genuine
Irish suffix at all.

Gossip ; a sponsor in baptism.

Goster ; gossipy talk. Irish *gastairĕ*, a prater, a
chatterer.) ' Dermot go 'long with your goster.'
(Moore—in his youth.)

Gouloge ; a stick with a little fork of two prongs at
the end, for turning up hay, or holding down furze
while cutting. (South.) Used in the North often
in the form of *gollog*. Irish *gabhal* [gowl], a fork,
with the dim. *óg*.

Gounau ; housewife [huzzif] thread, strong thread
for sewing, pack thread. Irish *gabhshnáth*
(Fr. Dinneen), same sound and meaning : from
snáth, a thread : but how comes in *gabh* ? In one
of the Munster towns I knew a man who kept a
draper's shop, and who was always called *Gounau*,
in accordance with the very reprehensible habit
of our people to give nicknames.

Goureen-roe : a snipe, a jacksnipe. (Munster.)
Irish *gabhairin-reó*, the ' little goat of the frost '
(reó, frost): because on calm frosty evenings you
hear its quivering sound as it flies in the twilight,
very like the sound emitted by a goat.

Gra, grah ; love, fondness, liking. Irish *grádh*

[graw]. ' I have great gra for poor Tom.' I asked an Irishman who had returned from America and settled down again here and did well :—' Why did you come back from America?' 'Ah,' he replied, ' I have great *gra* for the old country.'

Graanbroo ; wheat boiled in new milk and sweetened : a great treat to children, and generally made from their own gleanings or *liscauns*, gathered in the fields. Sometimes called *brootheen*. (Munster.) The first from Irish *grán*, grain, and *brúgh*, to break or bruise, to reduce to pulp, or cook, by boiling. *Brootheen* (also applied to mashed potatoes) is from *brúgh*, with the diminutive.

Graanoge, graan-yoge [*aa* in both long like *a* in *car*], a hedgehog. Irish *gráineóg*, same sound.

Graanshaghaun [*aa* long as in *car*]; wheat (in grain) boiled. (Joyce: Limerick.) In my early days what we called *graanshaghaun* was wheat in grains, not boiled, but roasted in an iron pot held over the fire, the wheat being kept stirred till done.

Graffaun ; a small axe with edge across like an adze for grubbing or *graffing* land, i.e. rooting out furze and heath in preparation for tillage. Used all through the South. ' This was the word used in Co. Cork law courts.' (Healy.) Irish *grafán*, same sound and meaning.

Graip or grape ; a dung-fork with three or four prongs. Irish *grápa*.

Grammar and Pronunciation, 74.

Grammel; to grope or fumble or gather with both hands. (Derry.)

Graves, Mr. A. P., 58, &c.

Grawls ; children. Paddy Corbett, thinking he is

ruined, says of his wife :—' God comfort poor
Jillian and the grawls I left her.' (Edward
Walsh.) 'There's Judy and myself and the poor
little grawls.' (Crofton Croker: p. 155.)

Grawvar; loving, affectionate :—' That's a grawver
poor boy.' (Munster.) Irish *grádhmhar*, same
sound and meaning : from *grádh*, love.

Grazier ; a young rabbit. (South and West.)

Great; intimate, closely acquainted :—' Tom Long
and Jack Fogarty are very great.' (All over
Ireland.) ' Come gie's your hand and sae we're
greet.' (Burns.)

Greedy-gut ; a glutton ; a person who is selfish
about stuffing himself, wishing to give nothing to
anyone else. Gorrane Mac Sweeny, when his
mistress is in want of provisions, lamenting that
the eagles (over Glengarriff) were devouring the
game that the lady wanted so badly, says :—' Is
it not the greatest pity in life . . . . that these
greedy-guts should be after swallowing the game,
and my sweet mistress and her little ones all the
time starving.' (Caesar Otway in ' Pen. Journ.')

Greenagh ; a person that hangs round hoping to get
food (Donegal and North-West): a ' Watch-pot.'

Greesagh ; red hot embers and ashes. ' We roasted
our potatoes and eggs in the greesagh.' (All
over Ireland.) Irish *griosach*, same sound.

Greet ; to cry. ' Tommy was greetin' after his
mother.' (Ulster.)

Greth ; harness of a horse : a general name for all
the articles required when yoking a horse to the
cart. (Knowles: Ulster.)

Griffin, Gerald, author of ' The Collegians,' 5, &c.

Grig (greg in Sligo) : a boy with sugarstick holds it out to another and says, ' grig, grig,' to triumph over him. Irish *griog*, same sound and meaning.

Grinder ; a bright-coloured silk kerchief worn round the neck. (Edward Walsh : all over Munster.)

Gripe ; a trench, generally beside a high ditch or fence. ' I got down into the gripe, thinking to [hide myself].' (Crofton Croker.)

Griskin or greeskeen ; a small bit of meat cut off to be roasted—usually on the coals. Irish *griscin*.

Grisset ; a shallow iron vessel for melting things in, such as grease for dipping rushes, resin for dipping torches (*sluts* or *paudioges*, which see), melting lead for various purposes, white metals for coining, &c. If a man is growing rapidly rich :—' You'd think he had the grisset down.'

Groak or groke ; to look on silently—like a dog— at people while they are eating, hoping to be asked to eat a bit. (Derry.)

Grogue ; three or four sods of turf standing on end, supporting each other like a little pyramid on the bog to dry. (Limerick.) Irish *gruag*, same meaning.

Groodles ; the broken bits mixed with liquid left at the bottom of a bowl of soup, bread and milk, &c.

Group or grup ; a little drain or channel in a cow-house to lead off the liquid manure. (Ulster.)

Grue or grew ; to turn from with disgust :—' He grued at the physic.' (Ulster).

Grug ; sitting on one's grug means sitting on the heels without touching the ground. (Munster.) Same as Scotch *hunkers*. ' Sit down on your grug and thank God for a seat.'

Grumagh or groomagh ; gloomy, ill-humoured :—

'I met Bill this morning looking very *grumagh*.' (General.) From Irish *gruaim* [*grooim*], gloom, ill-humour, with the usual suffix *-ach*, equivalent to English *-y* as in *gloomy*.

Grumpy ; surly, cross, disagreeable. (General.)

Gubbadhaun ; a bird that follows the cuckoo. (Joyce.)

Gubbaun ; a strap tied round the mouth of a calf or foal, with a row of projecting nail points, to prevent it sucking the mother. From Irish *gob*, the mouth, with the diminutive. (South.)

Gubbalagh ; a mouthful. (Munster.) Irish *goblach*, same sound and meaning. From *gob*, the mouth, with the termination *lach*.

Gullion ; a sink-pool. (Ulster.)

Gulpin ; a clownish uncouth fellow. (Ulster.)

Gulravage, gulravish ; noisy boisterous play. (North-east Ulster.)

Gunk; a 'take in,' a 'sell'; as a verb, to 'take in,' to cheat. (Ulster.)

Gushers ; stockings with the soles cut off. (Morris : Monaghan.) From the Irish. Same as triheens.

Gurry ; a *bonnive*, a young pig. (Morris : Mon.)

Gutter ; wet mud on a road (*gutters* in Ulster).

Gwaul [*l* sounded as in *William*]; the full of the two arms of anything : 'a gwaul of straw.' (Munster.) In Carlow and Wexford, they add the diminutive, and make it *goleen*. Irish *gabháil*.

Hain ; to hain a field is to let it go to meadow, keeping the cows out of it so as to let the grass grow : possibly from *hayin'*. (Waterford : Healy.) In Ulster *hain* means to save, to economise.

Half a one ; half a glass of whiskey. One day a poor blind man walked into one of the Dublin branch banks, which happened to be next door to a public-house, and while the clerks were looking on, rather puzzled as to what he wanted, he slapped two pennies down on the counter ; and in no very gentle voice :—' Half a one ! '

Half joke and whole earnest ; an expression often heard in Ireland which explains itself. ' Tim told me—half joke and whole earnest—that he didn't much like to lend me his horse.'

Hand ; to make a hand of a person is to make fun of him ; to humbug him : Lowry Looby, thinking that Mr. Daly is making game of him, says :— ' 'Tis making a hand of me your honour is.' (Gerald Griffin.) Other applications of *hand* are ' You made a bad hand of that job,' i.e. you did it badly. If a man makes a foolish marriage : ' He made a bad hand of himself, poor fellow.'

Hand-and-foot ; the meaning of this very general expression is seen in the sentence ' He gave him a hand-and-foot and tumbled him down.'

Hand's turn ; a very trifling bit of work, an occa-sion :—' He won't do a hand's turn about the house' : ' he scolds me at every hand's turn,' i.e. on every possible occasion.

Handy ; near, convenient :—' The shop lies handy to me' ; an adaptation of the Irish *láimh le* (meaning *near*). *Láimh le Corcaig*, lit. *at hand with Cork*— near Cork. This again is often expressed *con-venient to Cork*, where *convenient* is intended to mean simply *near*. So it comes that we in Ireland regard *convenient* and *near* as exactly synonymous, which they are not. In fact on almost every possible occasion, we—educated and uneducated—use *convenient* when *near* would be the proper word. An odd example occurs in the words of the old Irish folk-song :—

> ' A sailor courted a farmer's daughter,
> Who lived *convaynient* to the Isle of Man.'

Hannel; a blow with the spear or spike of a pegging-top (or ' castle-top') down on the wood of another top. Boys often played a game of tops for a certain number of hannels. At the end of the game the victor took his defeated opponent's top, sunk it firmly down into the grassy sod, and then with his own top in his hand struck the other top a number of hannels with the spear of his own to injure it as much as possible. ' Your castle-tops came in for the most hannels.' (' Knocknagow.')

Hap; to wrap a person round with any covering, to tuck in the bedclothes round a person. (Ulster.)

Hard word (used always with *the*); a hint, an inkling, a tip, a bit of secret information :— ' They were planning to betray and cheat me, but Ned gave me the hard word, and I was prepared for them, so that I defeated their schemes.'

Hare; to make a hare of a person is to put him down in argument or discussion, or in a contest of wit or cunning; to put him in utter confusion. ' While you were speaking to the little boy that made a hare of you.' (Carleton in Ir. Pen. Journ.)

> ' Don't talk of your Provost and Fellows of Trinity,
> Famous for ever at Greek and Latinity,
> Faix and the divels and all at Divinity—
> Father O'Flynn 'd make hares of them all !'
>   (A. P. GRAVES.)

Harvest; always used in Ireland for autumn:—
' One fine day in harvest.' (Crofton Croker.)

Hauling home; bringing home the bride, soon after
the wedding, to her husband's house. Called also
a 'dragging-home.' It is always made the
occasion of festivity only next in importance to
the wedding. For a further account, and for a
march played at the Hauling home, see my 'Old
Irish Folk Music and Songs,' p. 130.

Hausel; the opening in the iron head of an axe,
adze, or hammer, for the handle. (Ulster.)

Haverel: a rude coarse boor, a rough ignorant
fellow. (Moran: Carlow.)

Havverick; a rudely built house, or an old ruined
house hastily and roughly restored:—' How can
people live in that old havverick?' (Limerick.)

Hayden, Miss Mary, M.A., 5, &c.

Healy, Mr. Maurice, 178, &c.

Head or harp; a memorial of the old Irish coinage,
corresponding with English *head or tail*. The old
Irish penny and halfpenny had the king's head on
one side and the Irish harp on the other. ' Come
now, head or harp,' says the person about to throw
up a halfpenny of any kind.

Heard tell; an expression used all throughout
Ireland:—' I heard tell of a man who walked to
Glendalough in a day.' It is old English.

Heart-scald; a great vexation or mortification.
(General.) Merely the translation of *scallach-
croidhe* [scollagh-cree], *scalding* of the heart.

Hearty; tipsy, exhilarated after a little ' drop.'

Hedge schools, 149.

T

Higgins, The Rev. Father, p. 244, and elsewhere.

Hinch ; the haunch, the thigh. To hinch a stone is to *jerk* (or *jurk* as they say in Munster), to hurl it from under instead of over the shoulder. (Ulster.)

Hinten ; the last sod of the ridge ploughed. (Ulster.)

Ho ; equal. Always used with a negative, and also in a bad sense, either seriously or in play. A child spills a jug of milk, and the mother says :—' Oh Jacky, there's no *ho* to you for mischief' (no equal to you). The old woman says to the mischievous gander :—' There's no ho with you for one gander.' (Gerald Griffin : 'The Coiner.') This *ho* is an Irish word : it represents the sound of the Irish prefix *cho* or *chomh*, equal, as much as, &c. 'There's no ho to Jack Lynch' means there's no one for whom you can use *cho* (equal) in comparing him with Jack Lynch.

Hobbler ; a small cock of fresh hay about 4 feet high. (Moran : Carlow.)

Hobby ; a kind of Irish horse, which, three or four centuries ago, was known all over Europe ' and held in great esteem for their easy amble : and from this kind of horse the Irish light-armed bodies of horse were called hobellers.' (Ware. See my ' Smaller Social History of Ancient Ireland,' p. 487.) Hence a child's toy, a hobby-horse. Hence a favourite pursuit is called a ' hobby.'

Hoil ; a mean wretched dwelling : an uncomfortable situation. (Morris : South Monaghan.)

Hollow ; used as an adverb as follows :—' Jack Cantlon's horse beat the others hollow in the race' : i.e. beat them utterly.

Holy show : ' You're a holy show in that coat,' i.e. it makes quite a show of you ; makes you look ridiculous. (General.)

Holy well ; a well venerated on account of its association with an Irish saint : in most cases retaining the name of the saint :—' Tober-Bride,' St. Bride's or Brigit's well. In these wells the early saints baptised their converts. They are found all through Ireland, and people often pray beside them and make their *rounds*. (See ' Smaller Social History of Ancient Ireland.')

Hool or hooley ; the same as a Black swop.

Hot-foot ; at once, immediately :—' Off I went hot-foot.' ' As soon as James heard the news, he wrote a letter hot-foot to his father.'

Houghle ; to wobble in walking. (Armagh.)

Hugger-mugger : see Cugger-mugger.

Huggers or hogars, stockings without feet. (Ulster.)

Hulk ; a rough surly fellow. (Munster.) A bad person. (Simmons : Armagh.) Irish *olc*, bad.

Hungry-grass : see Fair-gurtha.

Hunker-slide ; to slide on ice sitting on the hunkers (or as they would say in Munster, sitting on one's *grug*) instead of standing up straight : hence to act with duplicity : to shirk work :—' None of your hunker-sliding for me.' (Ulster.)

Hurling ; the common game of ball and hurley or *commaun*. The chief terms (besides those mentioned elsewhere) are :—*Puck*, the blow of the hurley on the ball : The *goals* are the two gaps at opposite sides of the field through which the players try to drive the ball. When the ball is thrown high up between two players with their commauns ready drawn to try which will strike it on its way down : that is *high-rothery*. When two adjacent parishes or districts contended (instead of two small parties at an ordinary match), that was *scoobeen* or 'conquering goal' (Irish *scuab*, a broom : *scoobeen, sweeping* the ball away). I have seen at least 500 on each side engaged in one of these *scoobeens* ; but that was in the time of the eight millions—before 1847. Sometimes there were bad blood and dangerous quarrels at scoobeens. See Borick, Sippy, Commaun, and Cool. (For the ancient terms see my 'Smaller Social History of Ancient Ireland,' p. 513.) For examples of these great contests, see Very Rev. Dr. Sheehan's ' Glenanaar,' pp. 4, 231.

Hurt : a whortleberry : hurts are *fraughans*, which see. From *whort*. (Munster.)

Husho or rather huzho ; a lullaby, a nurse-song, a cradle-song ; especially the chorus, consisting of a sleepy *cronaun* or croon—like ' shoheen-sho Loo-lo-lo,' &c. Irish *suantraighe* [soontree]. 'The moaning of a distant stream that kept up a continual *cronane* like a nurse *hushoing*.' ' My mother was hushoing my little sister, striving to quieten her.' (Both from Crofton Croker.) ' The murmur of the ocean *huzhoed* me to sleep.' (Irish Folk Song :— ' M'Kenna's Dream.')

Idioms ; influence of the Irish language on, 4 :— derived from Irish, 23.

If ; often used in the sense of *although*, *while*, or some such signification, which will be best understood from the following examples :—A Dublin jarvey who got sixpence for a long drive, said in a rage :—' I'm in luck to-day ; but *if I am*, 'tis blazing *bad* luck.'   ' Bill ran into the house, and if he did, the other man seized him round the waist and threw him on his back.'

If that.   This is old English, but has quite disappeared from the standard language of the present day, though still not unfrequently heard in Ireland :—' If that you go I'll go with you.'

> ' *If* from Sally *that* I get free,
> My dear I love you most tenderlie.'
> > (Irish Folk Song—' Handsome Sally.')

> ' And *if that* you wish to go further
> Sure God He made Peter His own,
> The keys of His treasures He gave him,
> To govern the old Church of Rome.'
> > (Old Irish Folk Song.)

Inagh' or in-yah' [both strongly accented on second syll.] ; a satirical expression of dissent or disbelief, like the English *forsooth*, but much stronger.   A fellow boasting says :—' I could run ten miles in an hour ' : and another replies, ' You could *inah*' : meaning ' Of course I don't believe a word of it.' A man coming back from the other world says to a woman :—' I seen your [dead] husband there too, ma'am ; ' to which she replies :—' My husband *inah*.' (Gerald Griffin : ' Collegians.') Irish *an eadh*, same sound and meaning.

Inch ; a long strip of level grassy land along a river. Very general. Irish *inis* [innish], of the same family as Lat. *insula* : but *inis* is older than *insula* which is a diminutive and consequently a derived form. ' James, go out and drive the cows down to the inch.'

Insense' ; to make a person understand :—' I can't

insense him into his letters.' ' I insensed him into the way the job was to be done.' [Accent on -sense'.]

In tow with ; in close acquaintance with, courting. John is in tow with Jane Sullivan.

Ire, sometimes *ira* ; children who go barefoot sometimes get *ire* in the feet ; i.e. the skin chapped and very sore. Also an inflamed spot on the skin rendered sore by being rubbed with some coarse seam, &c.

Irish language ; influence of, on our dialect, 1, 23.

Jackeen ; a nickname for a conceited Dublin citizen of the lower class.

Jack Lattin, 172.

Jap or jop ; to splash with mud. (Ulster.)

Jaw ; impudent talk : *jawing* ; scolding, abusing :—

> ' He looked in my face and he gave me some jaw,
>   Saying " what brought you over from Erin-go-braw ? " '
>   (Irish Folk Song.)

Jingle ; one of Bianconi's long cars.

Johnny Magorey ; a hip or dog-haw ; the fruit of the dog-rose. (Central and Eastern counties.)

Join ; to begin at anything ; ' the child joined to cry '; ' my leg joined to pain me '; ' the man joined to plough.' (North.)

Jokawn ; an oaten stem cut off above the joint, with a tongue cut in it, which sounds a rude kind of music when blown by the mouth. (Limerick.) Irish *geocán*, same sound and meaning.

Jowlter, fish-jowlter ; a person who hawks about fish through the country, to sell. (South.)

Just : often used as a final expletive—more in

Ulster than elsewhere :—' Will you send anyone ? '
' Yes, Tommy just.'   ' Where are you going now? '
' To the fair just.'

Keenagh or keenagh-lee: mildew often seen on
cheese, jam, &c. In a damp house everything
gets covered with *keenagh-lee*. Irish *caonach*, moss ;
caonach-lee, mildew : *lee* is Irish *liagh* [lee], grey.
(North and North-West of Ireland.)

Keeping : a man is *on his keeping* when he is hiding
away from the police, who are on his track for
some offence. This is from the Irish *coiméad*,
keeping ; *air mo choiméad*, ' on my keeping.'

Keeroge ; a beetle or clock. Irish *ciar* [keer],
dark, black, with the diminutive *óg*: *keeroge*,
' black little fellow.'

Kelters, money, coins : ' He has the kelthers,'
said of a rich man. *Yellow kelters*, gold money :
' She has the kelthers ' : means she has a large
fortune. (Moran : Carlow.)

Kemp or camp; to compete : two or more persons
kemp against each other in any work to determine
which will finish first. (Ulster.) See Carleton's
story, ' The Rival Kempers.'

Keolaun ; a contemptible little creature, boy or man.
(South and West.)

Keowt ; a low contemptible fellow.

Kepper; a slice of bread with butter, as distinguished
from a *dundon*, which see.

Kesh ; a rough bridge over a river or morass, made
with poles, wickerwork, &c.—overlaid with bushes
and *scraws* (green sods). Understood all through
Ireland. A small one over a drain in a bog is

often called in Tipperary and Waterford a *kishoge*, which is merely the diminutive.

Kib ; to put down or plant potatoes, each seed in a separate hole made with a spade.   Irish *ciob*, same sound and meaning.

Kickham, Charles, author of ' Knocknagow,' 5, &c.

Kiddhoge, a wrap of any kind that a woman throws hastily over her shoulders. (Ulster.) Irish *cuideóg*, same sound and sense here.

Kilfinane, Co. Limerick, 147.

Killeen ; a quantity :—' That girl has a good killeen of money.   (Ulster.)   Irish *cillín* [killeen].

Killeen ; an old churchyard disused except for the occasional burial of unbaptised infants.   Irish *cill*, a church, with the diminutive *in*.

Kimmeen ; a sly deceitful trick; kimmeens or kymeens, small crooked ways :—' Sure you're not equal to the *kimmeens* of such complete deceivers at all at all.'   (Sam Lover in Ir. Pen. Mag.)   Irish *com*, crooked ; diminutive *cuimin* [kimmeen].

Kimmel-a-vauleen ; uproarious fun.   Irish *cimel- a'-mháilín*, literally ' rub-the-bag.'   There is a fine Irish jig with this name.   (South.)

Kink ; a knot or short twist in a cord.

Kink ; a fit of coughing or laughing : ' they were in kinks of laughing.'   Hence *chincough*, for whooping-cough, i.e. *kink*-cough.   I know a holy well that has the reputation of curing whooping-cough, and hence called the ' Kink-well.'

Kinleen or keenleen, or kine-leen ; a single straw or corn stem.   (South.)   Irish *caoinlin*, same sound.

Kinleen-roe ; an icicle : the same word as last with the addition of *reo* [roe], frost : ' frost-stem.'

Kinnatt', [1st syll. very short ; accent on 2nd syll. : to rhyme with *cat*] ; an impertinent conceited impudent little puppy.

Kippen or kippeen ; any little bit of stick : often used as a sort of pet name for a formidable cudgel or shillelah for fighting. Irish *cip* [kip], a stake or stock, with the diminutive.

Kish ; a large square basket made of wattles and wickerwork used for measuring turf or for holding turf on a cart. Sometimes (South) called a *kishaun*. Irish *cis* or *ciseán*, same sounds and meanings : also called *kishagh*.

Kishtha ; a treasure : very common in Connaught, where it is often understood to be hidden treasure in a fort under the care of a leprachaun. Irish *ciste*, same sound and meaning.

Kitchen ; any condiment or relish eaten with the plain food of a meal, such as butter, dripping, &c. A very common saying in Tyrone against any tiresome repetition is :—' Butter to butter is no kitchen.' As a verb ; to use sparingly, to economise :—' Now kitchen that bit of bacon for you have no more.'

Kitthoge or kitthagh ; a left-handed person. Understood through all Ireland. Irish *ciotóg*, *ciotach*, same sounds and meaning.

Kitterdy ; a simpleton, a fool. (Ulster.)

Knauvshauling [the *k* sounded distinctly] ; grumbling, scolding, muttering complaints. (Limerick.) From Irish *cnamh* [knauv : *k* sounded], a bone, the jawbone. The underlying idea is the same as when we speak of a person giving *jaw*. See Jaw.

' Knocknagow ' : see Kickham.

Kybosh ; some sort of difficulty or ' fix ' :—' He put the kybosh on him : he defeated him.' (Moran : Carlow.)

Kyraun, keeraun ; a small bit broken off from a sod of turf. Irish *caor*, or with the diminutive, *caorán*, same sound and meaning.

Laaban ; a rotten sterile egg (Morris : for South Monaghan): same as *Glugger*, which see. Irish *láb* or *láib*, mire, dirt, with diminutive.

Lad ; a mischievous tricky fellow :—' There's no standing them lads.' (Gerald Griffin.)

Lagheryman or Logheryman. (Ulster.) Same as Leprachaun, which see.

Lambaisting ; a sound beating. Quite common in Munster.

Langel ; to tie the fore and the hind leg of a cow or goat with a spancel or fetter to prevent it going over fences. (Ulster.) Irish *langal*, same sound and meaning.

Lapcock ; an armful or roll of grass laid down on the sward to dryfor hay. (Ulster.)

Lark-heeled ; applied to a person having long sharp heels. See Saulavotcheer.

Larrup ; to wallop, to beat soundly. (Donegal and South.)

Lashings, plenty: lashings and leavings, plenty and to spare : specially applied to food at meals. (General.)

Lassog, a blaze of light. (Morris : South Monaghan.) From Irish *las*, light, with the diminutive.

Lauchy ; applied to a person in the sense of pleasant, good-natured, lovable. Irish *láchaiidhe*, same sound and sense. (Banim : general in the South.) ' He's a *lauchy* boy.'

Laudy-daw ; a pretentious fellow that sets up to be a great swell. (Moran : Carlow ; and South.)

Launa-vaula ; full and plenty :—There was launa-vaula at the dinner. Irish *lán-a-mhála* (same sound), ' full bags.'

Lazy man's load. A lazy man takes too many things in one load to save the trouble of going twice, and thereby often lets them fall and breaks them.

Learn is used for *teach* all over Ireland, but more in Ulster than elsewhere. Don't forget to ' larn the little girl her catechiz.' (Seumas Mac Manus.) An old English usage : but dead and gone in England now.

Leather ; to beat:—' I gave him a good leathering,' i.e., a beating, a thrashing. This is not derived, as might be supposed, from the English word *leather* (tanned skin), but from Irish, in which it is of very old standing :—*Letrad* (modern *leadradh*), cutting, hacking, lacerating : also a champion fighter, a warrior, a *leatherer*. (Corm. Gloss.—9th cent.) Used all through Ireland.

Leather-wing ; a bat. (South.)

Lee, the Very Rev. Patrick, V. F., of Kilfinane, 148.

Lebbidha ; an awkward, blundering, half-fool of a fellow. (South.) Irish *leibide*, same sound and meaning.

Leg bail ; a person gives (or takes) *leg bail* when he runs away, absconds. (General.)

Lend ; loan. Ned came ' for the *lend* of the ould mare.' (' Knocknagow.') Often used in the following way :—' Come and lend a hand,' i.e., give some help. ' Our shooting party comes off to-morrow : will you *lend* your gun ' : an invitation to join the party. (Kinahan.)

Leprachaun ; a sort of fairy, called by several names
in different parts of Ireland :—luricaun, cluricaun,
lurragadaun, loghryman, luprachaun.   This last
is the nearest to the Gaelic original, all the preceding anglicised forms being derived from it.
Luprachaun itself is derived by a metathesis from
Irish *luchorpán*, from *lu*, little, and *corpán*, the dim.
of *corp*, a body :—' weeny little body.' The reader
will understand all about this merry little chap
from the following short note and song written by
me and extracted from my ' Ancient Irish Music '
(in which the air also will be found).   The leprachaun is a very tricky little fellow, usually dressed
in a green coat, red cap, and knee-breeches, and
silver shoe-buckles, whom you may sometimes see
in the shades of evening, or by moonlight, under
a bush ; and he is generally making or mending a
shoe : moreover, like almost all fairies, he would
give the world for *pottheen*.   If you catch him and
hold him, he will, after a little threatening, show
you where treasure is hid, or give you a purse in
which you will always find money.   But if you
once take your eyes off him, he is gone in an
instant ; and he is very ingenious in devising tricks
to induce you to look round.   It is very hard to
catch a leprachaun, and still harder to hold him.
I never heard of any man who succeeded in
getting treasure from him, except one, a lucky
young fellow named MacCarthy, who, according
to the peasantry, built the castle of Carrigadrohid
near Macroom in Cork with the money.   Every
Irishman understands well the terms *cruiskeen* and
mountain dew, some indeed a little too well ; but

for the benefit of the rest of the world, I think it
better to state that a *cruiskeen* is a small jar, and
that *mountain dew* is *pottheen* or illicit whiskey.

In a shady nook one moonlight night,
 A leprachaun I spied ;
With scarlet cap and coat of green ;
 A cruiskeen by his side.
'Twas tick tack tick, his hammer went,
 Upon a weeny shoe ;
And I laughed to think of a purse of gold ;
 But the fairy was laughing too.

With tip-toe step and beating heart,
 Quite softly I drew nigh :
There was mischief in his merry face ;—
 A twinkle in his eye.
He hammered and sang with tiny voice,
 And drank his mountain dew :
And I laughed to think he was caught at last :—
 But the fairy was laughing too.

As quick as thought I seized the elf ;
 ' Your fairy purse !' I cried ;
'The purse !' he said—'' 'tis in her hand—
 'That lady at your side !'
I turned to look : the elf was off !
 Then what was I to do ?
O, I laughed to think what a fool I'd been ;
 And the fairy was laughing too.

Let out; a spree, an entertainment. (General.)
'Mrs. Williams gave a great let out.'

Libber; this has much the same meaning as *flipper*,
which see : an untidy person careless about his
dress and appearance—an easy-going *ould sthreel*
of a man. I have heard an old fellow say,
regarding those that went before him—father,

grandfather, &c.—that they were 'ould *aancient* libbers,' which is the Irish peasant's way of expressing Gray's 'rude forefathers of the hamlet.'

Lief; willing: 'I had as lief be working as not.' 'I had liefer': I had rather. (General.) This is an old English word, now fallen out of use in England, but common here.

Lifter; a beast that is so weak from starvation (chiefly in March when grass is withered up) that it can hardly stand and has to be lifted home from the hill-pasture to the stable. (Kinahan: Connemara.)

Light; a little touched in the head, a little crazed:—
'Begor sir if you say I know nothing about sticks your head must be getting light in earnest.' (Robert Dwyer Joyce.)

Likely; well-looking: 'a likely girl'; 'a *clane* likely boy.'

Likes; 'the likes of you': persons or *a person* like you or in your condition. Very common in Ireland. 'I'll not have any dealings with the likes of him.' Colonel Lake, Inspector General of Constabulary in last century, one afternoon met one of his recruits on the North Circular Road, Dublin, showing signs of liquor, and stopped him. 'Well, my good fellow, what is your name please?' The recruit replied:—'Who are you, and what right have you to ask my name?' 'I am Colonel Lake, your inspector general.' The recruit eyed him closely:—'Oh begor your honour, if that's the case it's not right for the likes of me to be talking to the likes of you': on which he turned round and took leg bail on the spot like a deer, leaving

the inspector general standing on the pathway.
The Colonel often afterwards told that story with
great relish.

Linnaun-shee or more correct *Lannaun-shee*; a
familiar spirit or fairy that attaches itself to a
mortal and follows him. From Irish *leannán*, a
lover, and *sidh* [shee], a fairy: *lannaun-shee*, 'fairy-
lover.'

Linnie; a long shed—a sort of barn—attached to a
a farm house for holding farm-yard goods and
articles of various kinds—carts, spades, turnips,
corn, &c. (Munster.) Irish *lann-iotha*, lit. 'corn-
house.'

Lint; in Ulster, a name for flax.

Linthern or lenthern; a small drain or sewer
covered with flags for the passage of water, often
under a road from side to side. (Munster.) Irish
lintreán, *linntreach* [lintran, lintragh].

Liscauns; gleanings of corn from the field after
reaping: 'There's Mary gathering *liscauns*.'
(South.) Irish.

Loanen; a lane, a *bohereen*. (Ulster.)

Lob; a quantity, especially of money or of any
valuable commodity:—' 'Tis reported that Jack
got a great lob of money with his wife.' A person
is trying to make himself out very useful or of
much consequence, and another says satirically—
generally in play :—' Oh what a *lob* you are !'

Lock; a quantity or batch of anything—generally
small:—a lock of straw; a lock of sheep. (General.)

Logey; heavy or fat as applied to a person. (Moran:
Carlow.) Also the fireplace in a flax-kiln.

Lone; unmarried :—'A lone man'; 'a lone woman.'

Long family ; a common expression for a large family.

Lood, loodh, lude ; ashamed : ' he was lude of himself when he was found out.' (South.)

Loody ; a loose heavy frieze coat. (Munster.)

Loof ; the open hand, the palm of the hand. (Ulster.) Irish *lámh* [lauv], the hand.

Loo-oge or lu-oge ; the eel-fry a couple of inches long that come up the southern Blackwater periodically in myriads, and are caught and sold as food. (Waterford : Healy.) Irish *luadhóg*, same sound and meaning.

Loose leg ; when a person is free from any engagement or impediment that bound him down—' he has a loose leg '—free to act as he likes. ' I have retired from the service with a pension, so that now I have a loose leg.' The same is often said of a prisoner discharged from jail.

Lord ; applied as a nickname to a hunchback. The hunchback Danny Mann in ' The Collegians ' is often called ' Danny the lord.'

Losset ; a kneading tray for making cakes.

Lossagh ; a sudden blaze from a turf fire. Irish *las* [loss], a blaze, with the usual termination *ach*.

Lossoge ; a handful or little bundle of sticks for firing. (Mayo.) Irish *las* [loss], fire, a blaze, with the diminutive termination.

Low-backed car ; a sort of car common in the southern half of Ireland down to the middle of the last century, used to bring the country people and their farm produce to markets. Resting on the shafts was a long flat platform placed lengthwise and sloping slightly downwards towards the back, on which were passengers and goods. Called trottle-car in Derry.

Loy ; a spade. Used in the middle of Ireland all across from shore to shore. Irish *láighe*, same sound and meaning.

Luck-penny ; a coin given by the seller to the buyer after a bargain has been concluded : given to make sure that the buyer will have luck with the animal or article he buys.

Ludeen or loodeen [*d* sounded like *th* in *then*]; the little finger. Irish *lúidín*, same sound and meaning. From *lu*, little, with the diminutive termination.

Lu-oge : see Loo-oge.

Luscan ; a spot on the hillside from which the furze and heath have been burned off. (Wicklow and round about.) From Irish *losc* to burn : *luscan*, 'burned little spot.'

Lusmore ; fairy-thimble, fairy-finger, foxglove, *Digitalis purpurea* ; an herb of mighty power in fairy lore. Irish *lus*, herb ; *mór*, great; ' mighty herb.'

Lybe ; a lazy fellow. (MacCall : Wex.) See Libber.

Lyre ; the full of the two hands used together : a beggar usually got a *lyre* of potatoes. (Munster : same as *gopen* in Ulster.) Irish *ladhar*, same sound and meaning.

MacManus, Seumas, 5, &c.

Mad ; angry. There are certain Irish words, such as *buileamhail*, which might denote either *mad* or very *angry* : hence in English you very often hear :—' Oh the master is very mad with you,' i.e. angry. ‘Excessively angry’ is often expressed this way in dialect language :—‘The master is blazing mad about that accident to the mare.’ But even this expression is classical Irish ; for we read in the Irish Bible that Moses went away from Pharaoh, *air lasadh le feirg*, ‘blazing with anger.’ ‘Like mad’ is often used to denote very quickly or energetically : Crofton Croker speaks of people who were ‘dancing like mad.’ This expression is constantly heard in Munster.

Maddha-brishtha ; an improvised tongs, such as would be used with a fire in the fields, made from a strong twig bent sharp. (Derry.) Irish *maide* [maddha], a stick ; *briste*, broken :—‘broken stick.’

Maddhiaghs or muddiaghs; same as last, meaning simply ‘sticks’: the two ends giving the idea of plurality. (Armagh.)

Maddhoge or middhoge ; a dagger. (North and South.) Irish *meadóg* or *miodóg*.

Made ; fortunate :—‘ I’m a made man ’ (or ‘ a *med* man ’), meaning ‘ my fortune is made.’ (Crofton Croker—but used very generally.)

Mag ; a swoon :—‘ Light of grace,’ she exclaimed, dropping in a *mag* on the floor. (Edward Walsh : used all over Munster.)

Maisled ; speckled ; a lazy young fellow’s shins get maisled from sitting before the fire. (Knowles : Ulster.)

Make; used in the South in the following way :—
‘ This will make a fine day ’: ‘ That cloth will make a fine coat ’: ‘ If that fellow was shaved he’d make a handsome young man ’ (Irish folk-song) : ‘ That Joe of yours is a clever fellow : no doubt he’ll

make a splendid doctor.' The noun *makings* is applied similarly :—' That young fellow is the makings of a great scholar.'

Man above. In Irish God is often designated *an Fear suas* or *an t-É suas* (' the Man above,' ' the Person above ') : thus in Hardiman's ' Irish Minstrelsy ' (I. 228) :—*Comarc an t-É tá shuas ort* : ' the protection of the Person who is above be on thee ' : *an Fear suas* occurs in the Ossianic Poems. Hence they use this term all through the South :—' As cunning as he is he can't hide his knavery from *the Man above*.'

Man in the gap, 182.

Mankeeper ; used North and South as the English name of the little lizard called in Irish ' Art-loochra,' which see.

Mannam ; my soul : Irish *m'anam*, same sound and meaning :—' Mannam on ye,' used as an affectionate exclamation to a child. (Scott : Derry.)

Many ; ' too many ' is often used in the following way, when two persons were in rivalry of any kind, whether of wit, of learning, or of strength :—' James was too many for Dick,' meaning he was an overmatch for him.

Maol, Mail, Maileen, Moileen, Moilie (these two last forms common in Ulster ; the others elsewhere) ; a hornless cow. Irish *Maol* [mwail], same meaning. Quite a familiar word all through Ireland.

Mau-galore ; nearly drunk : Irish *maith* [mau], good : *go leór*, plenty : ' purty well I thank you,' as the people often say : meaning almost the same as Burns's ' I was na fou but just had plenty.' (Common in Munster.)

One night Jacky was sent out, much against his will, for an armful of turf, as the fire was getting low ; and in a moment afterwards, the startled famil heard frantic yells. Just as they jumped up Jacky rushed in still yelling with his whole throat.

' What's the matter—what's wrong !'

' Oh I saw the divel ! '

' No you didn't, you fool, 'twas something else you saw.'

' No it wasn't, 'twas the divel I saw—didn't I know him well !'

' How did you know him—did you see his horns ?'

' I didn't: he had no horns—he was a *mwail* divel—sure that's how I knew him !'

They ran out of course ; but the *mwail* divel was gone, leaving behind him, standing up against the turf-rick, the black little *Maol* Kerry cow.

Margamore ; the ' Great Market ' held in Derry immediately before Christmas or Easter. (Derry.) Irish *margadh* [marga], a market, *mór* [more], great.

Martheen ; a stocking with the foot cut off. (Derry.) Irish *mairtin*, same sound and meaning. *Martheens* are what they call in Munster *triheens*, which see.

Mass, celebration of, 144.

Mauleen ; a little bag : usually applied in the South to the little sack slung over the shoulder of a potato-planter, filled with the *potato-sets* (or *skillauns*), from which the setter takes them one by one to plant them. In Ulster and Scotland, the word is *mailin*, which is sometimes applied to a purse :——

' A *mailin* plenished (filled) fairly.' (Burns.)

Maum ; the full of the two hands used together

"Mau-galore" entry is misplaced. See p.291.

(Kerry) ; the same as *Lyre* and *Gopan*, which see. Irish *Mám*, same sound and meaning.

Mavourneen ; my love. (Used all through Ireland.) Irish *Mo-mhúirnin*, same sound and meaning. See Avourneen.

May-day customs, 170.

Méaracaun [mairacaun] ; a thimble. Merely the Irish *méaracán*, same sound and meaning : from *méar*, a finger, with the diminutive termination *cán*. Applied in the South to the fairy-thimble or fox-glove, with usually a qualifying word :— Meara-caun-shee (*shee*, a fairy—fairy thimble) or Meara caun-na-man-shee (where na-man-shee is the Irish *na-mban-sidhe*, of the *banshees* or fairy-women). ' Lusmore,' another name, which see.

Mearing ; a well-marked boundary—but not neces-sarily a raised *ditch*—a fence between two farms, or two fields, or two bogs. Old English.

Mease : a measure for small fish, especially herrings : —' The fisherman brought in ten mease of her-rings.' Used all round the Irish coast. It is the Irish word *mias* [meece], a dish.

Mee-aw ; a general name for the potato blight. Irish *mi-adh* [mee-aw], ill luck: from Irish *mi*, bad, and *ádh*, luck. But *mee-aw* is also used to designate ' misfortune' in general.

Meela-murder ; ' a thousand murders ' : a general exclamation of surprise, alarm, or regret. The first part is Irish—*mile* [meela], a thousand ; the second is of course English.

Meelcar' [*car* long like the English word *car*] ; also called *meelcartan* ; a red itchy sore on the sole of the foot just at the edge. It is believed by the

people to be caused by a red little flesh-worm, and
hence the name *miol* [meel], a worm, and *cearr*
[car], an old Irish word for red :—Meel-car,
'red-worm.'   (North and South.)

Meeraw; ill luck.   (Munster.)   From Irish *mi*, ill,
and ráth [raw], luck :—' There was some *meeraw*
on the family.

Melder of corn; the quantity sent to the mill and
ground at one time.   (Ulster.)

Memory of History and of Old Customs, 143.

Merrow; a mermaid.   Irish *murrughagh* [murrooa],
from *muir*, the sea.   She dives and travels under
sea by means of a hood and cape called *cohuleen-
dru*: *cochall*, a hood and cape (with diminutive
termination); *druádh*, druidical: ' magical cape.'

Midjilinn or middhilin; the thong of a flail. (Morris :
South Monaghan.)

Mihul or mehul [*i* and *e* short]; a number of men
engaged in any farm-work, especially corn-reaping
still used in the South and West.   It is the very
old Irish word *meithel*, same sound and meaning.

Mills.   The old English game of ' nine men's morris '
or ' nine men's merrils ' or *mills* was practised in
my native place when I was a boy.   We played
it on a diagram of three squares one within
another, connected by certain straight lines, each
player having nine counters.   It is mentioned
by Shakespeare (' Midsummer-Night's Dream ').   I
learned to be a good player, and could play it
still if I could meet an antagonist.   How it
reached Limerick I do not know.   A few years
ago I saw two persons playing mills in a hotel
in Llandudno; and my heart went out to them.

Mind ; often used in this way :—' Will you write that letter to-day ?' ' No : I won't mind it to-day : I'll write it to-morrow.'

Minnikin ; a very small pin.

Minister ; always applied in Ireland to a Protestant clergyman.

Miscaun, mescaun, mescan, miscan ; a roll or lump of butter. Irish *mioscán* [miscaun]. Used all over Ireland.

Mitch ; to play truant from school.

Mitchelstown, Co. Cork, 155.

Moanthaun; boggy land. Moantheen; a little bog. (Munster.) Both dims. of Irish *móin*, a bog.

Molly ; a man who busies himself about women's affairs or does work that properly belongs to women. (Leinster.) Same as *sheela* in the South.

Moneen ; a little *moan* or bog ; a green spot in a bog where games are played. Also a sort of jig dance-tune : so called because often danced on a green *moneen*. (Munster.)

Month's Mind ; Mass and a general memorial service for the repose of the soul of a person, celebrated a month after death. The term was in common use in England until the change of religion at the Reformation ; and now it is not known even to English Roman Catholics. (Woollett.) It is in constant use in Ireland, and I think among Irish Catholics everywhere. But the practice is kept up by Catholics all over the world. Mind, ' Memory.'

Mootch : to move about slowly and meaninglessly : without intelligence. A mootch is a slow stupid person. (South.)

Moretimes ; often used as corresponding to *sometimes* :
'Sometimes she employs herself at sewing, and
moretimes at knitting.'

Mor-yah ; a derisive expression of dissent to drive
home the untruthfulness of some assertion or
supposition or pretence, something like the
English 'forsooth,' but infinitely stronger :—A
notorious schemer and cheat puts on airs of piety
in the chapel and thumps his breast in great
style ; and a spectator says :—Oh how pious and
holy Joe is growing—*mar-yah !* 'Mick is a great
patriot, mor-yah !—he'd sell his country for half a
crown.' Irish *mar-sheadh* [same sound], 'as it
were.'

Mossa ; a sort of assertive particle used at the
opening of a sentence, like the English *well*,
indeed : carrying little or no meaning. 'Do you
like your new house ?'—'Mossa I don't like it
much.' Another form of *wisha*, and both
anglicised from the Irish *má'seadh*, used in Irish in
much the same sense.

Mountain dew ; a fanciful and sort of pet name for
pottheen whiskey : usually made in the *mountains*.

Mounthagh, mounthaun ; a toothless person.
(Munster.) From the Irish *mant* [mounth], the
gum, with the terminations. Both words are
equivalent to *gummy*, a person whose mouth is
all gums.

Moutre. In very old times a mill-owner commonly
received as payment for grinding corn one-tenth
of the corn ground—in accordance with the
Brehon Law. This custom continued to recent
times—and probably continues still—in Ulster,

where the quantity given to the miller is called *moutre*, or *muter*, or *mooter*.

Mulharten ; a flesh-worm : a form of meelcartan. See Meelcar.

Mullaberta ; arbitration. (Munster.) Merely the Irish *moladh-beirte*, same sound and meaning : in which *moladh* [mulla] is 'appraisement'; and *beirtĕ*, gen. of *beart*, ' two persons ' :—lit. ' appraisement of two.' The word mullaberta has however in recent times drifted to mean a loose unbusinesslike settlement. (Healy.)

Mummers, 171.

Murray, Mr. Patrick, schoolmaster of Kilfinane, 153, 154, and under ' Roasters,' below.

Murrogh O'Brien, Earl of Inchiquin, 165.

Musicianer for musician is much in use all over Ireland. Of English origin, and used by several old English writers, among others by Collier.

Nab ; a knowing old-fashioned little fellow. (Derry.)

Naboc'lesh ; never mind. (North and South.) Irish *ná-bac-leis* (same sound), ' do not stop to mind it,' or ' pass it over.'

Nail, paying on the nail, 183.

Naygur ; a form of *niggard* : a wretched miser :—

> ' I certainly thought my poor heart it would bleed
> To be trudging behind that old naygur.'
>> (Old Munster song ; ' The Spalpeen's Complaint' :
>> from ' Old Irish Folk Music and Songs.')

> ' In all my ranging and serenading,
> I met no naygur but humpy Hyde.'
>> (See ' Castlehyde ' in my ' Old Irish Music and Songs.')

Nicely : often used in Ireland as shown here :—
'Well, how is your [sick] mother to-day ?' 'Oh
she's nicely,' or ' doing nicely, thank you' ; i.e.
getting on very well—satisfactorily. A still
stronger word is *bravely.* ' She's doing bravely
this morning ' ; i.e. extremely well—better than
was expected.

Nim or nym ; a small bit of anything. (Ulster.)

Noggin ; a small vessel, now understood to hold two
glasses ; also called naggin. Irish *noigin.*

Nose ; to pay through the nose ; to pay and be made
to pay, against your grain, the full sum without
delay or mitigation.

Oanshagh ; a female fool, corresponding with oma-
daun, a male fool. Irish *óinseach*, same sound
and meaning : from *ón*, a fool, and *seach*, he
feminine termination.

Offer ; an attempt :—' I made an offer to leap the
fence but failed.

Old English, influence of, on our dialect, 6.

Oliver's summons, 184.

On or upon ; in addition to its functions as explained
at pp. 27, 28, it is used to express obligation :—
' Now I put it *upon* you to give Bill that message for
me ': one person meeting another on Christmas Day
says :—' My Christmas box *on* you,' i.e. ' I put it
as an obligation on you to give me a Christmas
box.'

Once ; often used in this manner :—' Once he promises
he'll do it ' (Hayden and Hartog) : ' Once you pay
the money you are free,' i.e. *if* or *when* you pay.

O'Neills and their war-cry, 179.

Oshin [sounded nearly the same as the English word ocean] ; a weakly creature who cannot do his fair share of work. (Innishowen, Donegal.)

Out ; used, in speaking of time, in the sense of *down* or *subsequently* :—'His wife led him a mighty uneasy life from the day they married *out*.' (Gerald Griffin : Munster.) 'You'll pay rent for your house for the first seven years, and you will have it free from that *out*.'

Out ; to call a person *out of his name* is to call him by a wrong name.

Out ; ' be off out of that ' means simply *go away*.

Out ; ' I am out with him ' means I am not on terms with him—I have fallen out with him.

Overright ; opposite, in front of : the same meaning as *forenenst* ; but *forenenst* is English, while over-right is a wrong translation from an Irish word— *ós-cómhair*. *Os* means over, and *comhair* opposite : but this last word was taken by speakers to be *cóir* (for both are sounded alike), and as *cóir* means *right* or just, so they translated *os-comhair* as if it were *ós-cóir*, ' over-right.' (Russell : Munster.)

Paddhereen ; a prayer : dim. of Latin *Pater* (*Pater Noster*). *Paddereen Paurtagh*, the Rosary : from Irish *páirteach*, sharing or partaking : because usually several join in it.

Páideóge [paudh-yoge] ; a torch made of a wick dipped in melted rosin (Munster) : what they call a *slut* in Ulster.

Paghil or pahil ; a lump or bundle, 108. (Ulster.)

Palatines, 65.

Palleen ; a rag : a torn coat is ' all in *paleens*.' (Derry.)

Palm ; ' the yew-tree, 184.

Pampooty ; a shoe made of untanned hide. (West.)

Pandy ; potatoes mashed up with milk and butter. (Munster.)

Pannikin ; now applied to a small tin drinking-vessel : an old English word that has fallen out of use in England, but is still current in Ireland : applied down to last century to a small earthenware pot used for boiling food.   These little vessels were made at Youghal and Ardmore (Co. Waterford). The earthenware pannikins have disappeared, their place being supplied by tinware. (Kinahan.)

Parisheen ; a foundling ; one brought up in childhood by the *parish*. (Kildare.)

Parson ; was formerly applied to a Catholic parish priest : but in Ireland it now always means a Protestant minister.

Parthan ; a crab-fish. (Donegal.)   Merely the Irish *partan*, same sound and meaning.

Parts ; districts, territories :—' Prince and plinny-pinnytinshary of these parts ' (King O'Toole and St. Kevin) : ' Welcome to these parts.' (Crofton Croker.)

Past ; ' I wouldn't put it *past* him,' i.e. I think him bad or foolish enough (to do it).

Past ; more than : ' Our landlord's face we rarely see past once in seven years '—Irish Folk Song.

Pattern (i.e. *patron*) ; a gathering at a holy well or other relic of a saint on his or her festival day, to pray and perform *rounds* and other devotional acts in honour of the patron saint.   (General.)

Pattha ; a pet, applied to a young person who is brought up over tenderly and indulged too much :—

' What a *pattha* you are ! ' This is an extension
of meaning ; for the Irish *peata* [pattha] means
merely a *pet*, nothing more.

Pelt ; the skin :—' He is in his pelt,' i.e. naked.

Penal Laws, 144, and elsewhere through the book.

Personable ; comely, well-looking, handsome :—
' Diarmid Bawn the piper, as personable a looking
man as any in the five parishes.' (Crofton Croker :
Munster.)

Pickey ; a round flat little stone used by children in
playing *transe* or Scotch-hop. (Limerick.)

Piggin ; a wooden drinking-vessel. It is now called
pigin in Irish ; but it is of English origin.

Pike ; a pitchfork ; commonly applied to one with
two prongs. (Munster.)

Pike or croppy-pike ; the favourite weapon of the
rebels of 1798 : it was fixed on a very long handle,
and had combined in one head a long sharp spear,
a small axe, and a hook for catching the enemy's
horse-reins.

Pillibeen or pillibeen-meeg ; a plover. (Munster.)
' I'm king of Munster when I'm in the bog, and
the *pillibeens* whistling about me.' (' Knocknagow.') Irish *pilibin-miog*, same sound and meaning.

Pindy flour ; flour that has begun to ferment slightly
on account of being kept in a warm moist place.
Cakes made from it were uneatable as they were
soft and clammy and slightly sour. (Limerick.)

Pinkeen ; a little fish, a stickleback : plentiful in
small streams. Irish *pincin*, same sound and
meaning. See Scaghler.

Piper's invitation ; ' He came on the piper's invitation,' i.e. uninvited. (Cork.) A translation of

Irish *cuireadh-píobaire* [curra-peebara]. Pipers sometimes visited the houses of well-to-do people and played—to the great delight of the boys and girls—and they were sure to be well treated. But that custom is long since dead and gone.

Pish minnaan' [the *aa* long as *a* in *car*] ; common wild peas. (Munster.) They are much smaller— both plant and peas — than the cultivated pea, whence the above anglicised name, which has the same sound as the Irish *pise-mionnáin*, ' kid's peas.'

Pishmool ; a pismire, an ant. (Ulster.)

Pishoge, pisheroge, pishthroge ; a charm, a spell, witchcraft :—' It is reported that someone took Mrs. O'Brien's butter from her by *pishoges*.'

Place ; very generally used for house, home, homestead :—' If ever you come to Tipperary I shall be very glad to see you at *my place*.' This is a usage of the Irish language ; for the word *baile* [bally], which is now used for *home*, means also, and in an old sense, a place, a spot, without any reference to home.

Plaikeen ; an old shawl, an old cloak, any old covering or wrap worn round the shoulders. (South.)

Plantation ; a colony from England or Scotland settled down or *planted* in former times in a district in Ireland from which the rightful old Irish owners were expelled, 7, 169, 170.

Plaumause [to rhyme with *sauce*] ; soft talk, plausible speech, flattery—conveying the idea of insincerity. (South.) Irish *plámás*, same sound and meaning.

Plauzy ; full of soft, flattering, *plausible* talk. Hence

the noun *pláusoge* [plauss-oge], a person who is plauzy. (South.)

Plerauca ; great fun and noisy revelry. Irish *pléaráca*, same sound and meaning.

Pluddogh ; dirty water. (MacCall : Wexford.) From Irish *plod* [pludh], a pool of dirty water, with the termination *ach*.

Pluvaun ; a kind of soft weed that grows excessively on tilled moory lands and chokes the crop. (Moran : Carlow.)

Poll-talk ; backbiting : from the *poll* of the head : the idea being the same as in *back*biting.

Polthogue ; a blow ; a blow with the fist. Irish *palltóg*, same sound and meaning.

Pooka ; a sort of fairy : a mischievous and often malignant goblin that generally appears in the form of a horse, but sometimes as a bull, a buckgoat, &c. The great ambition of the pooka horse is to get some unfortunate wight on his back ; and then he gallops furiously through bogs, marshes, and woods, over rocks, glens, and precipices ; till at last when the poor wretch on his back is nearly dead with terror and fatigue, the pooka pitches him into some quagmire or pool or briar-brake, leaving him to extricate himself as best he can. But the goblin does not do worse : he does not kill people. Irish *púca*. Shakespeare has immortalised him as Puck, the goblin of 'A Midsummer-Night's Dream.'

Pookapyle, also called Pookaun ; a sort of large fungus, the toadstool. Called also *causha pooka*. All these names imply that the Pooka has something to do with this poisonous fungus. See Causha-pooka (pooka's cheese).

Pookeen; a play—blindman's buff: from Irish *púic*, a veil or covering, from the covering put over the eyes. Pookeen is also applied in Cork to a cloth muzzle tied on calves or lambs to prevent sucking the mother. The face-covering for blindman's buff is called *pookoge*, in which the dim. *óg* is used instead of *in* or *een*. The old-fashioned *coal-scuttle* bonnets of long ago that nearly covered the face were often called *pookeen* bonnets. It was of a bonnet of this kind that the young man in Lóver's song of ' Molly Carew ' speaks :—

> Oh, *lave* off that bonnet or else I'll *lave* on it
> The loss of my wandering sowl :—

because it hid Molly's face from him.

Poor mouth ; making the poor mouth is trying to persuade people you are very poor—making out or pretending that you are poor.

Poor scholars, 151, 157.

Poreens ; very small potatoes—mere *crachauns* (which see)—any small things, such as marbles, &c. (South : *porrans* in Ulster.)

Porter-meal : oatmeal mixed with porter. Seventy or eighty years ago, the carters who carried bags of oatmeal from Limerick to Cork (a two-day journey) usually rested for the night at Mick Lynch's public-house in Glenosheen, They often took lunch or dinner of porter-meal in this way :— Opening the end of one of the bags, the man made a hollow in the oatmeal into which he poured a quart of porter, stirring it up with a spoon : then he ate an immense bellyful of the mixture. But those fellows could digest like an ostrich.

In Ulster, oatmeal mixed in this manner with buttermilk, hot broth, &c., and eaten with a spoon, is called *croudy*

Potthalowng; an awkward unfortunate mishap, not very serious, but coming just at the wrong time. When I was a boy 'Jack Mullowney's *potthalowng*' had passed into a proverb. Jack one time went *courting*, that is, to spend a pleasant evening with the young lady at the house of his prospective father-in-law, and to make up the match with the old couple. He wore his best of course, body-coat, white waistcoat, caroline hat (tall silk), and *ducks* (ducks, snow-white canvas trousers.) All sat down to a grand dinner given in his honour, the young couple side by side. Jack's plate was heaped up with beautiful bacon and turkey, and white cabbage swimming in fat, that would make you lick your lips to look at it. Poor Jack was a bit sheepish; for there was a good deal of banter, as there always is on such occasions. He drew over his plate to the very edge of the table; and in trying to manage a turkey bone with knife and fork, he turned the plate right over into his lap, down on the ducks.

The marriage came off all the same; but the story went round the country like wildfire; and for many a long day Jack had to stand the jokes of his friends on the *potthalowng*. Used in Munster. The Irish is *patalong*, same sound and meaning; but I do not find it in the dictionaries.

Pottheen; illicit whiskey: always distilled in some remote lonely place, as far away as possible from the nose of a gauger. It is the Irish word *poitin* [pottheen], little pot. We have partly the same term still; for everyone knows the celebrity of *pot*-still whiskey: but this is *Parliament* whiskey, not *pottheen*, see p. 174.

Power; a large quantity, a great deal: Jack Hickey has a power of money: there was a *power of cattle in the fair yesterday*: there's a power of ivy on that old castle. Miss Grey, a small huckster who kept a little vegetable shop, was one day showing off her rings and bracelets to our servant. 'Oh Miss Grey,' says the girl, 'haven't you a terrible lot of them.' 'Well Ellen, you see I want them all, for I go into *a power of society*.' This is an old English usage as is shown by this extract from Spenser's ' View ' : —' Hee also [Robert Bruce] sent over his said brother Edward, with a power of Scottes and Red-Shankes into Ireland.' There is a corresponding Irish expression (*neart airgid*, ap o wer of money), but I think this is translated from English rather than the reverse. The same idiom exists in Latin with the word *vis* (power): but examples will not be quoted, as they would take up a power of space.

Powter [*t* sounded like *th* in *pith*]; to root the ground like a pig; to root up potatoes from the ground with the hands. (Derry.)

Prashagh, more commonly called prashagh-wee; wild cabbage with yellow blossoms, the rape plant. Irish *praiseach-bhuidhe* [prashagh-wee], yellow cabbage. *Praiseach* is borrowed from Latin *brassica*.

Prashameen; a little group all clustered together :— ' The children sat in a prashameen on the floor.' I have heard this word a hundred times in Limerick among English speakers : its Irish form should be *praisimin*, but I do not find it in the dictionaries.

Prashkeen ; an apron. Common all over Ireland. Irish *praiscin*, same sound and meaning.

Prawkeen ; raw oatmeal and milk (Mac Call : South Leinster.) See Porter-meal.

Prepositions, incorrect use of, 26, 32, 44.

Presently ; at present, now :—'I'm living in the country presently.' A Shakespearian survival :— Prospero :—' Go bring the rabble.' Ariel :—' Presently?' [i.e. shall I do so now?] Prospero :—' Ay, with a wink.' Extinct in England, but preserved and quite common in Ireland.

Priested ; ordained : ' He was priested last year.'

Priest's share ; the soul. A mother will say to a refractory child :—' I'll knock the priest's share out of you.' (Moran : Carlow.)

Professions hereditary, 172.

Pronunciation, 2, 91 to 104.

Protestant herring : Originally applied to a bad or a stale herring : but in my boyhood days it was applied, in our neighbourhood, to almost anything of an inferior quality :—' Oh that butter is a Protestant herring.' Here is how it originated :—Mary Hewer of our village had been for time out of mind the only huckster who sold salt herrings, sending to Cork for a barrel from time to time, and making good profit. At last Poll Alltimes sent for a barrel and set up an opposition shop, taking away a large part of Mary's custom. Mary was a Catholic and Poll a Protestant : and then our herrings became sharply distinguished as Catholic herrings and Protestant herrings : each party eating herrings

x 2

of their own creed.   But after some time a horrible
story began to go round—whispered at first under
people's breath—that Poll found *the head of a black*
with long hair packed among the herrings half way
down in her barrel.   Whether the people believed
it or not, the bare idea was enough ; and Protestant
herrings suddenly lost character, so that poor Poll's
sale fell off at once, while Mary soon regained all
her old customers.   She well deserved it, if anyone
ever deserved a reward for a master-stroke of
genius.   But I think this is all ' forgotten lore'
in the neighbourhood now.

Proverbs, 105.

Puck; to play the puck with anything : a softened
equivalent of *playing the devil*.   *Puck* here means
the Pooka, which see.

Puck ; a blow :—' He gave him a puck of a stick
on the head.'   More commonly applied to a punch
or blow of the horns of a cow or goat.   ' The cow
gave him a puck (or pucked him) with her horns and
knocked him down.'   The blow given by a hurler
to the ball with his *caman* or hurley is always called
a *puck*.   Irish *poc*, same sound and meaning.

Puckaun ; a he-goat. (South.)   Irish *poc*, a he-goat,
with the diminutive.

Puke ; a poor puny unhealthy-looking person.

Pulling a cord (or *the cord*) ; said of a young man
and a young woman who are courting :—' Miss
Anne and himself that's pulling the cord.'
(' Knocknagow.')

Pulloge ; a quantity of hidden apples : usually hidden
by a boy who steals them. (Limerick.)   Diminutive of the Irish *poll*, a hole.

Pusheen ; the universal word for a kitten in Munster :
a diminutive of the English word *puss* ; exactly
equivalent to *pussy*.

Puss [*u* sounded as in *full*] ; the mouth and lips,
always used *in dialect* in an offensive or con-
temptuous sense :—' What an ugly *puss* that fellow
has.' ' He had a puss on him,' i.e. he looked
sour or displeased—with lips contracted. I heard
one boy say to another :—' I'll give you a *skelp*
(blow) on the puss.' (General.) Irish *pus*, the
mouth, same sound.

Pusthaghaun ; a puffed up conceited fellow. The
corresponding word applied to a girl is *pusthoge*
(MacCall : Wexford) : the diminutive termination
aun or *chaun* being masculine and *óg* feminine.
Both are from *pus* the mouth, on account of the
consequential way a conceited person squares up
the lips.

Quaw or quagh ; a *quag* or quagmire :—' I was
unwilling to attempt the *quagh*.' (Maxwell : ' Wild
Sports' : Mayo, but used all over Ireland.) Irish
caedh [quay], for which and for the names derived
from it, see ' Irish Names of Places ' : II. 396.

Quality ; gentlemen and gentlewomen as distinguished from the common people. Out of use in
England, but general in Ireland :—' Make room for
the quality.'

Queer, generally pronounced *quare*; used as an
intensive in Ulster :—This day is quare and hot
(very hot) ; he is quare and sick (very sick) : like
fine and fat elsewhere (see p. 89).

Quin or quing ; the swing-tree, a piece of wood used

to keep the chains apart in ploughing to prevent
them rubbing the horses. (Cork and Kerry.) Irish
cuing [quing], a yoke.

Quit: in Ulster ' quit that' means *cease from that* :—
' quit your crying.'   In Queen's County they say
rise out of that.

Rabble ; used in Ulster to denote a fair where workmen congregate on the hiring day to be hired by
the surrounding farmers.   See Spalpeen.

Rack.   In Munster an ordinary comb is called a
rack : the word *comb* being always applied and
confined to a small close fine-toothed one.

Rackrent ; an excessive rent of a farm, so high as to
allow to the occupier a bare and poor subsistence.
Not used outside Ireland except so far as it has
been recently brought into prominence by the
Irish land question.

Rag on every bush ; a young man who is caught by
and courts many girls but never proposes.

Raghery ; a kind of small-sized horse ; a name given
to it from its original home, the island of Rathlin
or Raghery off Antrim.

Rake ; to cover up with ashes the live coals of a turf
fire, which will keep them alive till morning :—
' Don't forget to rake the fire.'

Randy ; a scold.   (Kinahan : general.)

Rap ; a bad halfpenny : a bad coin :—' He hasn't a
rap in his pocket.'

Raumaush or raumaish ; *romance* or fiction, but now
commonly applied to foolish senseless brainless
talk.   Irish *rámás* or *rámáis*, which is merely
adapted from the word *romance*.

Raven's bit; a beast that is going to die. (Kinahan.)

Rawney; a delicate person looking in poor health ; a poor sickly-looking animal. (Connaught.)   Irish *ránaidhe*, same sound and meaning.

Reansha ; brown bread : sometimes corrupted to *range*-bread. (MacCall : Wexford.)

Red or redd ; clear, clear out, clear away :—Redd the road, the same as the Irish *Fág-a-ballagh*, ' clear the way.'   If a girl's hair is in bad tangles, she uses a *redding-comb* first to open it, and then a finer comb.

Redden ; to light: ' Take the bellows and redden the fire.'   An Irishman hardly ever *lights* his pipe : he *reddens* it.

Redundancy, 52, 130.

Ree ; as applied to a horse means restive, wild, almost unmanageable.

Reek ; a rick :—A reek of turf : so the Kerry mountains, ' MacGillicuddy's Reeks.'

Reel-foot ; a club-foot, a deformed foot. (Ulster.) ' Reel-footed and hunch-backed forbye, sir.' (Old Ulster song.)

Reenaw'lee ; a slow-going fellow who dawdles and delays and hesitates about things.   (Munster.) Irish *rianálaidhe*, same sound and meaning : from *rian*, a way, track, or road : *rianalaidhe*, a person who wanders listlessly along the *way*.

Reign.   This word is often used in Munster, Leinster, and Connaught, in the sense of to occupy, to be master of : ' Who is in the Knockea farm?' ' Mr. Keating reigns there now.'   ' Who is your landlord ?' ' The old master is dead and his son Mr. William reigns over us now.' ' Long may

your honour [the master] reign over us.' (Crofton
Croker.)   In answer to an examination question,
a young fellow from Cork once answered me,
'Shakespeare reigned in the sixteenth century.'
This usage is borrowed from Irish, in which the
verb *riaghail* [ree-al] means both to rule (as a
master), and to reign (as a king), and as in many
other similar cases the two meanings were con-
founded in English.   (Kinahan and myself.)

Relics of old decency.   When a man goes down in
the world he often preserves some memorials of
his former rank — a ring, silver buckles in his
shoes, &c. — ' the relics of old decency.'

Revelagh ; a long lazy gadding fellow.   (Morris :
Monaghan.)

Rib ; a single hair from the head.   A poet, praising a young lady, says that ' every golden *rib* of
her hair is worth five guineas.'   Irish *ruibe* [ribbe],
same meaning.

Rickle ; a little heap of turf peats standing on ends
against each other.   (Derry.)   Irish *ricil*, same
sound and meaning.

Riddles, 185.

Ride and tie.   Two persons set out on a journey
having one horse.   One rides on while the
other sets out on foot after him.   The first man,
at the end of a mile or two, ties up the horse at the
roadside and proceeds on foot.   When the second
comes to the horse he mounts and rides till he is
one or two miles ahead of his comrade and then
ties. And so to the end of the journey. A common
practice in old times for courier purposes ; but not
in use now, I think.

Rife, a scythe-sharpener, a narrow piece of board punctured all over and covered with grease on which fine sand is sprinkled. Used before the present emery sharpener was known. (Moran: Carlow.) Irish *riabh* [reev], a long narrow stripe.

Right or wrong : often heard for *earnestly* : ' he pressed me right or wrong to go home with him.'

Ringle-eyed ; when the iris is light-coloured, and the circle bounding it is very marked, the person is *ringle-eyed*. (Derry.)

Rings ; often used as follows :—' Did I sleep at all ?' ' Oh indeed you did—you *slept rings round you*.'

Rip ; a coarse ill-conditioned woman with a bad tongue. (General.)

Roach lime ; lime just taken from the kiln, burnt, *before* being slaked and while still in the form of stones. This is old English from French *roche*, a rock, a stone.

Roasters ; potatoes kept crisping on the coals to be brought up to table hot at the end of the dinner— usually the largest ones picked out. But the word *roaster* was used only among the lower class of people : the higher classes considered it vulgar. Here is how Mr. Patrick Murray (see p. 154) describes them about 1840 in a parody on Moore's ' One bumper at parting' (a *lumper*, in Mr. Murray's version, means a big potato) :—

> ' One *lumper* at parting, though many
>   Have rolled on the board since we met,
> The biggest the hottest of any
>   Remains in the round for us yet.'

In the higher class of houses they were peeled and brought up at the end nice and brown in a dish. About eighty years ago a well-known military gentleman of Baltinglass in the County Wicklow—whose daughter told me the story—had on one occasion a large party of friends to dinner. On the very day of the dinner the waiter took ill, and the stable boy—a big coarse fellow—had to be called in, after elaborate instructions. All went well till near the end of the dinner, when the fellow thought things were going on rather slowly. Opening the diningroom door he thrust in his head and called out in the hearing of all :— ' Masther, are ye ready for the *roasthers*? ' A short time ago I was looking at the house and diningroom where that occurred.

Rocket ; a little girl's frock. (Very common in Limerick.) It is of course an old application of the English-French *rochet*.

Rodden ; a *bohereen* or narrow road. (Ulster.) It is the Irish *róidín*, little road.

Roman ; used by the people in many parts of Ireland for *Roman Catholic*. I have already quoted what the Catholic girl said to her Protestant lover : —' Unless that you turn a *Roman* you ne'er shall get me for your bride.' Sixty or seventy years ago controversial discussions—between a Catholic on the one hand and a Protestant on the other— were very common. I witnessed many when I was a boy—to my great delight. Garrett Barry, a Roman Catholic, locally noted as a controversialist, was arguing with Mick Cantlon, surrounded by a group of delighted listeners. At last Garrett, as a final clincher, took up the Bible, opened it at a certain place, and handed it to his opponent, with :

—' Read that heading out for us now if you please.'
Mick took it up and read ' St. Paul's Epistle to the
Romans.'   ' Very well,' says Garrett : ' now can
you show me in any part of that Bible, ' St. Paul's
Epistle to the *Protestants* ' ?   This of course was a
down blow ; and Garrett was greeted with a great
hurrah by the Catholic part of his audience.   This
story is in ' Knocknagow,' but the thing occurred
in my neighbourhood, and I heard about it long
before ' Knocknagow ' was written.

Rookaun ; great noisy merriment. Also a drinking-
bout. (Limerick.)

Room. In a peasant's house the *room* is a special
apartment distinct from the kitchen or living-room,
which is not a ' room ' in this sense at all. I
slept in the kitchen and John slept in the ' room.'
(Healy and myself : Munster.)

Round coal ; coal in lumps as distinguished from
slack or coal broken up small and fine.

Ruction, ructions ; fighting, squabbling, a fight, a
row. It is a memory of the *Insurrection* of 1798,
which was commonly called the ' Ruction.'

Rue-rub ; when a person incautiously scratches an
itchy spot so as to break the skin : that is *rue-rub.*
(Derry.)   From *rue*, regret or sorrow.

Rury ; a rough hastily-made cake or bannock.
(Morris : Monaghan.)

Rut ; the smallest bonnive in a litter. (Kildare and
Carlow.)

Saluting, salutations, 14.

Sapples ;   soap suds :   *sapple,* to wash in suds.
(Derry.)

Saulavotcheer ; a person having *lark-heels*. (Limerick.) The first syll. is Irish ; *sál* [saul], heel.

Sauvaun ; a rest, a light doze or nap. (Munster.) Irish *sámhán*, same sound and meaning, from *sámh* [sauv], pleasant and tranquil.

Scagh ; a whitethorn bush. (General.) Irish *sceach*, same sound and meaning.

Scaghler : a little fish—the pinkeen or thornback : Irish *sceach* [scagh], a thorn or thornbush, and the English termination *ler*.

Scald : to be *scalded* is to be annoyed, mortified, sorely troubled, vexed. (Very general.) Translated from one or the other of two Irish words, *loisc* [lusk], to burn ; and *scall*, to *scald*. Finn Bane says :—' Guary being angry with me he scorched me (*romloisc*), burned me, *scalded* me, with abuse.' (' Colloquy.') ' I earned that money hard and 'tis a great *heart-scald* (*scollach-croidhe*) to me to lose it.' There is an Irish air called ' The *Scalded* poor man.' (' Old Irish Music and Songs.')

Scalder, an unfledged bird (South): *scaldie* and *scaulthoge* in the North. From the Irish *scal* (bald), from which comes the Irish *scalachán*, an unfledged bird.

Scallan ; a wooden shed to shelter the priest during Mass, 143, 145.

Scalp, scolp, scalpeen ; a rude cabin, usually roofed with *scalps* or grassy sods (whence the name). In the famine times—1847 and after—a scalp was often erected for any poor wanderer who got stricken down with typhus fever : and in that the people tended him cautiously till he recovered or died. (Munster.) Irish *scailp* [scolp].

Scalteen : see Scolsheen.

Scollagh-cree ; ill-treatment of any kind. (Moran : Carlow.) Irish *scallach-croidhe*, same sound and meaning : a ' heart scald ' ; from *scalladh*, scalding, and *croidhe*, heart.

Scollop ; the bended rod pointed at both ends that a thatcher uses to fasten down the several straw-wisps. (General.) Irish *scolb* [scollub].

Scolsheen or scalteen ; made by boiling a mixture of whiskey, water, sugar, butter and pepper (or cara-way seeds) in a pot : a sovereign cure for a cold. In the old mail-car days there was an inn on the road from Killarney to Mallow, famous for scolsheen, where a big pot of it was always kept ready for travellers. (Kinahan and Kane.) Sometimes the word *scalteen* was applied to unmixed whiskey burned, and used for the same purpose. From the Irish *scall*, burn, singe, *scald*.

Sconce ; to chaff, banter, make game of :—' None of your sconcing.' (Ulster.)

Sconce ; to shirk work or duty. (Moran : Carlow.)

Scotch Dialect : influence of, on our Dialect, 6, 7.

Scotch lick ; when a person goes to clean up any-thing—a saucepan, a floor, his face, a pair of shoes, &c.—and only half does it, he (or she) has given it a *Scotch lick*. General in South. In Dublin it would be called a ' cat's lick' : for a cat has only a small tongue and doesn't do much in the way of licking.

Scout ; a reproachful name for a bold forward girl.

Scouther ; to burn a cake on the outside before it is fully cooked, by over haste in baking :—burned outside, half raw inside. Hence ' to scouther ' means to do anything hastily and incompletely. (Ulster.)

Scrab ; to scratch :—' The cat near scrabbed his eyes out.' (Patterson : Ulster.) In the South it is *scraub* :—' He scraubed my face.'

Scrab ; to gather the stray potatoes left after the regular crop, when they are afterwards turned out by plough or spade.

Scraddhin ; a scrap ; anything small—smaller than usual, as a small potato : applied contemptuously to a very small man, exactly the same as the Southern *sprissaun*. Irish *scraidin*, same sound and meaning. (East Ulster.)

Scran ; ' bad scran to you,' an evil wish like ' bad luck to you,' but much milder : English, in which *scran* means broken victuals, food-refuse, fare— very common. (North and South.)

Scraw ; a grassy sod cut from a grassy or boggy surface and often dried for firing ; also called *scrahoge* (with diminutive *óg*). Irish *scrath, scrathóg*, same sounds and meaning.

Screenge ; to search for. (Donegal and Derry.)

Scunder or Scunner ; a dislike ; to take a dislike or disgust against anything. (Armagh.)

Scut ; the tail of a hare or rabbit : often applied in scorn to a contemptible fellow :—' He's just a scut and nothing better.' The word is Irish, as is shown by the following quotation :—' The billows [were] conversing with the *scuds* (sterns) and the beautiful prows [of the ships]. (Battle of Moylena : and note by Kuno Meyer in ' Rev. Celt.') (General.)

Seeshtheen ; a low round seat made of twisted straw.

(Munster.)   Irish *suidhistin*, same sound and meaning : from *suidhe* [see], to sit, with diminutive.

Set : all over Ireland they use *set* instead of *let* [a house or lodging].   A struggling housekeeper failed to let her lodging, which a neighbour explained by :—' Ah she's no good at *setting*.'

Set ; used in a bad sense, like *gang* and *crew* :— ' They're a dirty set.'

Settle bed ; a folding-up bed kept in the kitchen : when folded up it is like a sofa and used as a seat. (All over Ireland.)

Seven'dable [accent on *ven*], very great, *mighty great* as they would say :—' Jack gave him a *sevendable* thrashing.'   (North.)

Shaap [the *aa* long as in *car*] ; a husk of corn, a pod. (Derry.)

Shamrock or Shamroge ; the white trefoil (*Trifolium repens*).   The Irish name is *seamar* [shammer], which with the diminutive makes *seamar-óg* [shammer-oge], shortened to *shamrock*.

Shanachus, shortened to *shanagh* in Ulster, a friendly conversation.   ' Grandfather would like to have a shanahus with you.'   (' Knocknagow.')   Irish *seanchus*, antiquity, history, an old story.

Shandradan' [accented strongly on *-dan*] ; an old rickety rattle-trap of a car.   The first syllable is Irish *sean* [shan], old.

Shanty : a mean hastily put up little house. (General.)   Probably from Irish *sean*, old, and *tigh* [tee], a house.

Shaugh ; a turn or smoke of a pipe.   (General.) Irish *seach*, same sound and meaning.

Shaughraun ; wandering about : to be *on the shaugh-raun* is to be out of employment and wandering idly about looking for work.   Irish *seachrán*, same sound and meaning.

Shebeen or sheebeen ; an unlicensed public-house or alehouse where spirits are sold on the sly. (Used all over Ireland.) Irish *sibin*, same sound and meaning.

Shee ; a fairy, fairies ; also meaning the place where fairies live, usually a round green little hill or elf-mound having a glorious palace underneath : Irish *sidhe*, same sound and meanings.   *Shee* often takes the diminutive form — *sheeoge*.

Shee-geeha ; the little whirl of dust you often see moving along the road on a calm dusty day : this is a band of fairies travelling from one *lis* or elf-mound to another, and you had better turn aside and avoid it.   Irish *sidhe-gaoithe*, same sound and meaning, where *gaoithe* is wind : ' wind-fairies' : called ' fairy-blast ' in Kildare.

Sheehy, Rev. Father, of Kilfinane, 147.

Sheela ; a female Christian name (as in ' Sheela Ni Gyra ').   Used in the South as a reproachful name for a boy or a man inclined to do work or interest himself in affairs properly belonging to women.   See ' Molly.'

Sheep's eyes : when a young man looks fondly and coaxingly on his sweetheart he is ' throwing sheep's eyes ' at her.

Sherral ; an offensive term for a mean unprincipled fellow. (Moran : South Mon.)

Sheugh or Shough ; a deep cutting, elsewhere called a ditch, often filled with water. (Seumas MacManus : N.W. Ulster.)

Shillelah ; a handstick of oak, an oaken cudgel for fighting. (Common all over Ireland.) From a district in Wicklow called Shillelah, formerly noted for its oak woods, in which grand shillelahs were plentiful.

Shingerleens [shing-erleens] ; small bits of finery ; ornamental tags and ends—of ribbons, bow-knots, tassels, &c.—hanging on dress, curtains, furniture, &c. (Munster.)

Shire ; to pour or drain off water or any liquid, quietly and without disturbing the solid parts remaining behind, such as draining off the whey-like liquid from buttermilk.

Shlamaan' [*aa* like *a* in *car*] ; a handful of straw, leeks, &c. (Morris: South Monaghan.)

Shoggle ; to shake or jolt. (Derry.)

Shoneen ; a *gentleman* in a small way : a would-be gentleman who puts on superior airs. Always used contemptuously.

Shook ; in a bad way, done up, undone :—' I'm shook by the loss of that money ' : 'he was shook for a pair of shoes.'

Shooler ; a wanderer, a stroller, a vagrant, a tramp, a rover : often means a mendicant. (Middle and South of Ireland.) From the Irish *siubhal* [shool], to walk, with the English termination *er* : lit. ' walker.'

Shoonaun ; a deep circular basket, made of twisted rushes or straw, and lined with calico ; it had a cover and was used for holding linen, clothes, &c. (Limerick and Cork.) From Irish *sibhinn* [shiven], a rush, a bulrush : of which the diminutive *siubhnán* [shoonaun] is our word : signifying 'made of rushes.' Many a shoonaun I saw in my day; and I remember meeting a man who was a shoonaun maker by trade.

Short castle or short castles; a game played by two persons on a square usually drawn on a slate with the two diagonals: each player having three counters. See Mills.

Shore; the brittle woody part separated in bits and dust from the fibre of flax by scutching or *cloving*. Called *shores* in Monaghan.

Shraff, shraft; Shrovetide: on and about Shrove Tuesday :—'I bought that cow last shraff.'

Shraums, singular shraum; the matter that collects about the eyes of people who have tender eyes: matter running from sore eyes. (Moran: Carlow.) Irish *sream* [sraum]. Same meaning.

Shrule; to rinse an article of clothing by pulling it backwards and forwards in a stream. (Moran: Carlow.) Irish *srúil*, a stream.

Shrough; a rough wet place; an incorrect anglicised form of Irish *srath*, a wet place, a marsh.

Shuggy-shoo; the play of see-saw. (Ulster.)

Shurauns; any plants with large leaves, such as hemlock, wild parsnip, &c. (Kinahan: Wicklow.)

Sighth (for sight); a great number, a large quantity. (General.) 'Oh Mrs. Morony haven't you a *sighth* of turkeys': 'Tom Cassidy has a sighth of money.' This is old English. Thus in a Quaker's diary of 1752 :—' There was a great sight of people passed through the streets of Limerick.' This expression is I think still heard in England, and is very much in use in America. Very general in Ireland.

Sign ; a very small quantity—a trace. Used all over Ireland in this way :—' My gardens are *every sign* as good as yours ' : ' he had no sign of drink on him ' : ' there's no sign of sugar in my tea ' (Hayden and Hartog) : ' look out to see if Bill is coming ' : ' no—there's no sign of him.' This is a translation from the Irish *rian*, for which see next entry.

Sign's on, sign is on, sign's on it ; used to express the result or effect or proof of any proceeding :—' Tom Kelly never sends his children to school, and sign's on (or sign's on it) they are growing up like savages ' : ' Dick understands the management of fruit trees well, and sign's on, he is making lots of money by them. This is a translation from Irish, in which *rian* means *track, trace, sign* : and ' sign's on it ' is *ta a rian air* (' its sign is on it ').

Silenced : a priest is silenced when he is suspended from his priestly functions by his ecclesiastical superiors : ' unfrocked.'

Singlings : the weak pottheen whiskey that comes off at the first distillation : agreeable to drink but terribly sickening. Also called ' First shot.'

Sippy ; a ball of rolled *sugans* (i.e. hay or straw ropes), used instead of a real ball in hurling or football. (Limerick.) Irish *suipigh*, same sound and meaning. A diminutive of *sop*, a wisp.

Skeeagh [2-syll.] ; a shallow osier basket, usually for potatoes. (South.)

Skeedeen ; a trifle, anything small of its kind ; a small potato. (Derry and Donegal.) Irish *scidin*, same sound and meaning.

Skellig, Skellig List—On the Great Skellig rock in the Atlantic, off the coast of Kerry, are the ruins of a monastery, to which people at one time went on pilgrimage—and a difficult pilgrimage it was. The tradition is still kept up in some places, though in an odd form; in connection with the custom that marriages are not solemnised in Lent, i.e. after Shrove Tuesday. It is well within my memory that—in the south of Ireland—young persons who should have been married before Ash-Wednesday, but were not, were supposed to set out on pilgrimage to Skellig on Shrove Tuesday night : but it was all a make-believe. Yet I remember witnessing occasionally some play in mock imitation of the pilgrimage. It was usual for a local bard to compose what was called a ' Skellig List '—a jocose rhyming catalogue of the unmarried men and women of the neighbour-hood who went on the sorrowful journey—which was circulated on Shrove Tuesday and for some time after. Some of these were witty and amus-ing : but occasionally they were scurrilous and offensive doggerel. They were generally too long for singing ; but I remember one—a good one too—which—when I was very young—I heard sung to a spirited air. It is represented here by a single verse, the only one I remember. (See also ' Chalk Sunday,' p. 234, above.)

> As young Rory and Moreen were talking,
>   How Shrove Tuesday was just drawing near ;
> For the tenth time he asked her to marry ;
>   But says she :—' Time enough till next year.'

'Then ochone I'm going to Skellig :
    O Moreen, what will I do ?
'Tis the woeful road to travel ;
    And how lonesome I'll be without you !'*

Here is a verse from another :—

Poor Andy Callaghan with doleful nose
Came up and told his tale of many woes :—
Some lucky thief from him his sweetheart stole,
Which left a weight of grief upon his soul :
With flowing tears he sat upon the grass,
And roared sonorous like a braying ass.

Skelly ; to aim askew and miss the mark ; to squint.
    (Patterson : all over Ulster.)
Skelp ; a blow, to give a blow or blows ; a piece cut
    off :—' Tom gave Pat a skelp' : ' I cut off a skelp
    of the board with a hatchet.' To run fast :—
    ' There's Joe skelping off to school.'
Skib ; a flat basket :—' We found the people col-
    lected round a skibb of potatoes.'   (' Wild Sports
    of the West.')
Skidder, skiddher ; broken thick milk, stale and
    sour. (Munster.)
Skillaun. The piece cut out of a potato to be used
    as seed, containing one germinating *eye*, from
    which the young stalk grows. Several skillauns
    will be cut from one potato ; and the irregular
    part left is a *skilloge* (Cork and Kerry), or a
    creelacaun (Limerick). Irish *sciollán*, same sound
    and meaning.
Skit ; to laugh and giggle in a silly way :—' I'll be

* From my ' Old Irish Folk Music and Songs,' p. 56, in which
also will be found the beautiful air of this.

bail they didn't skit and laugh.' (Crofton Croker.)
'Skit and laugh,' very common in South.

Skite; a silly frivolous light-headed person. Hence
Blatherumskite (South), or (in Ulster), blether-
umskite.

Skree; a large number of small things, as a skree
of potatoes, a skree of chickens, &c. (Morris:
South Monaghan.)

Skull-cure for a bad toothache. Go to the nearest
churchyard alone by night, to the corner where
human bones are usually heaped up, from which
take and bring away a skull. Fill the skull with
water, and take a drink from it: that will cure
your toothache.

Sky farmer; a term much used in the South with
several shades of meaning: but the idea underlying all is a farmer without land, or with only
very little—having broken down since the time
when he had a big farm—who often keeps a cow
or two grazing along the roadsides. Many of
these struggling men acted as intermediaries
between the big corn merchants and the large
farmers in the sale of corn, and got thereby a
percentage from the buyers. A 'sky farmer' has
his farm *in the sky*.

Slaan [*aa* long as the *a* in *car*] ; a sort of very sharp
spade, used in cutting turf or peat. Universal in
the South.

Slack-jaw; impudent talk, continuous imperti-
nences :—'I'll have none of your slack-jaw.'

Slang; a narrow strip of land along a stream, not
suited to cultivation, but grazed. (Moran: Carlow.)

Sleeveen; a smooth-tongued, sweet-mannered, sly,

guileful fellow. Universal all over the South and Middle. Irish *slighbhín*, same sound and meaning; from *sligh*, a way: *binn*, sweet, melodious: ' a *sweet-mannered* fellow.'

Slewder, sluder [*d* sounded like *th* in *smooth*]; a wheedling coaxing fellow: as a verb, to wheedle. Irish *slígheadóir* [sleedore], same meaning.

Sliggin; a thin flat little stone. (Limerick.) Irish. Primary meaning *a shell*.

Sling-trot; when a person or an animal is going along [not walking but] trotting or running along at a leisurely pace. (South.)

Slinge [slinj]; to walk along slowly and lazily. In some places, playing truant from school. (South.)

Slip; a young girl. A young pig, older than a *bonnive*, running about almost independent of its mother. (General.)

Slipe; a rude sort of cart or sledge without wheels used for dragging stones from a field. (Ulster.)

Slitther; a kind of thick soft leather: also a ball covered with that leather, for hurling. (Limerick.)

Sliver; a piece of anything broken or cut off, especially cut off longitudinally. An old English word, obsolete in England, but still quite common in Munster.

Slob; a soft fat quiet simple-minded girl or boy :— ' Your little Nellie is a quiet poor slob': used as a term of endearment.

Sloke, sloak, sluke, sloukaun; a sea plant of the family of *laver* found growing on rocks round the coast, which is esteemed a table delicacy—dark-coloured, almost black; often pickled and eaten with pepper, vinegar, &c. Seen in all the Dublin fish shops. The name, which is now known all over the Three Kingdoms, is anglicised from Irish *sleabhac, sleabhacán* [slouk, sloukaun].

Slug; a drink: as a verb, to drink:—'Here take a little slug from this and 'twill do you good.' Irish *slog* to swallow by drinking. (General.) Whence *slugga* and *sluggera*, a cavity in a river-bed into which the water is *slugged* or swallowed.

Slugabed; a sluggard. (General in Limerick.) Old English, obsolete in England:—' Fie, you slug-a-bed.' (' Romeo and Juliet.')

Slush; to work and toil like a slave: a woman who toils hard. (General.)

Slut; a torch made by dipping a long wick in resin. (Armagh.) Called a *paudheoge* in Munster.

Smaadher [*aa* like *a* in *car*]; to break in pieces. Jim Foley was on a *pooka's* back on the top of an old castle, and he was afraid he'd ' tumble down and be *smathered* to a thousand pieces.' (Ir. Mag.)

Smalkera; a rude home-made wooden spoon.

Small-clothes; kneebreeches. (Limerick.) So called to avoid the plain term *breeches*, as we now often say *inexpressibles*.

Small farmer; has a small farm with small stock of cattle: a struggling man as distinguished from a ' strong ' farmer.

Smeg, smeggeen, smiggin; a tuft of hair on the chin. (General.) Merely the Irish *smeig, smeigin*; same sounds and meaning.

Smithereens; broken fragments after a smash, 4.

Smullock [to rhyme with *bullock*]; a fillip of the finger. (Limerick.) Irish *smallóg*, same meaning.

Smur, smoor, fine thick mist. (North.)   Irish *smúr*, mist.

Smush [to rhyme with *bush*]: anything reduced to fine small fragments, like straw or hay, dry peat-mould in dust, &c.

Smush, used contemptuously for the mouth, a hairy mouth :—' I don't like your ugly *smush*.'

Snachta-shaidhaun : dry powdery snow blown about by the wind.   Irish *sneachta*, snow, and *séideán*, a breeze. (South.)

Snaggle-tooth ; a person with some teeth gone so as to leave gaps.

Snap-apple ; a play with apples on Hallow-eve, where big apples are placed in difficult positions and are to be caught by the teeth of the persons playing. Hence Hallow-Eve is often called ' Snap-apple night.'

Snauvaun ; to move about slowly and lazily.   From Irish *snámh* [snauv], to swim, with the diminutive :—Moving slowly like a person swimming.

Sned ; to clip off, to cut away, like the leaves and roots of a turnip.   Sned also means the handle of a scythe.

Snig ; to cut or clip with a knife :—' The shoots of that apple-tree are growing out too long : I must snig off the tops of them.'

Snish ; neatness in clothes. (Morris : Carlow.)

Snoboge; a rosin torch. (Moran : Carlow.) Same as *slut* and *paudheoge*.

Snoke ; to scent or snuff about like a dog. (Derry.)

So. This has some special dialectical senses among us. It is used for *if* :—' I will pay you well *so* you do the work to my liking.'   This is old English :—' I am content *so* thou wilt have it so.'

('Rom. and Jul.') It is used as a sort of emphatic expletive carrying accent or emphasis:—'Will you keep that farm?' 'I will *so*,' i.e. 'I will for certain.' 'Take care and don't break them' (the dishes): 'I won't *so*.' ('Collegians.') It is used in the sense of 'in that case':—'I am not going to town to-day': 'Oh well I will not go, *so*'—i.e. 'as you are not going.'

Sock; the tubular or half-tubular part of a spade or shovel that holds the handle. Irish *soc*.

Soft day; a wet day. (A usual salute.)

Soil; fresh-cut grass for cattle.

Sold; betrayed, outwitted:—'If that doesn't frighten him off you're sold' (caught in the trap, betrayed, ruined. Edw. Walsh in Ir. Pen. Journal).

Something like; excellent:—'That's something like a horse,' i.e. a fine horse and no mistake.

Sonaghan; a kind of trout that appears in certain lakes in November, coming from the rivers. (Prof. J. Cooke, M.A., of Dublin: for Ulster):—Irish *samhain* [sowan], November: *samhnachán* with the diminutive *án* or *chán*, 'November-fellow.'

Sonoohar; a good wife, a good partner in marriage; a good marriage: generally used in the form of a wish:—'Thankee sir and sonoohar to you.' Irish *sonuachar*, same sound and meaning.

Sonsy; fortunate, prosperous. Also well-looking and healthy:—'A fine *sonsy* girl.' Irish *sonas*, luck; *sonasach*, *sonasaigh*, same sound and meaning.

Soogan, sugan, sugaun; a straw or hay rope twisted by the hand.

Soss; a short trifling fall with no harm beyond a smart shock. (Moran: Carlow.)

Sough ;　a whistling　or sighing　noise　like　that
of the wind through　trees.　'Keep a calm sough'
means keep quiet, keep silence.　(Ulster.)

Soulth;　'a formless luminous apparition.'　(W. B.
Yeats.)　Irish *samhailt* [soulth], a ghost, an apparition;　*lit.* a 'likeness,' from *samhai* [sowel], like.

Sources of Anglo-Irish Dialect, 1.

Sowans, sowens ;　a sort of flummery or gruel usually
made and eaten　on Hallow Eve.　Very general
in Ulster and Scotland;　merely the Irish word
samhain, the first　of November ;　for Hallow Eve
is really a November　feast, as being the eve of the
first of that month.　In old times in Ireland, the
evening went with the coming night.

Spalpeen.　Spalpeens were labouring men—reapers,
mowers, potato-diggers, &c.—who travelled about
in　the　autumn　seeking　employment　from　the
farmers, each with his spade, or　his scythe, or his
reaping-hook.　They congregated in the towns on
market and　fair　days, where the　farmers of the
surrounding districts came to hire them.　Each
farmer brought　home his　own men, fed them on
good potatoes and milk, and　sent them to sleep in
the barn on dry straw—a bed—as one of them said
to me—'a bed fit for a lord, let alone a spalpeen.'
The word *spalpeen* is　now　used in　the　sense of
a low rascal.　Irish *spailpin*, same sound and
meaning.　(See my 'Old Irish Folk Music and
Songs,' p. 216 ; and for the Ulster term see Rabble
above.

Spaug ;　a big clumsy foot :—'You put your ugly
spaug down on my handkerchief.'　Irish *spág*, same
sound and sense.

Speel ; to climb. (Patterson : Ulster.)

Spink ; a sharp rock, a precipice. (Tyrone.) *Splink* in Donegal. Irish *spinnc* and *splinnc*, same sounds and meaning.

Spit; the soil dug up and turned over, forming a long trench as deep as the spade will go. 'He dug down three spits before he came to the gravel.'

Spoileen ; a coarse kind of soap made out of scraps of inferior grease and meat : often sold cheap at fairs and markets. (Derry and Tyrone.) Irish *spóilín*, a small bit of meat.

Spoocher ; a sort of large wooden shovel chiefly used for lifting small fish out of a boat. (Ulster.)

Spreece ; red-hot embers, chiefly ashes. (South.) Irish *spris*, same sound and meaning. Same as *greesagh.*

Sprissaun ; an insignificant contemptible little chap. Irish *spriosán* [same sound], the original meaning of which is a twig or spray from a bush. (South.)

'To the devil I pitch ye ye set of sprissauns.'

(Old Folk Song, for which see my 'Ancient Irish Music,' p. 85.)

Sprong : a four-pronged manure fork. (MacCall : South-east counties.)

Spruggil, spruggilla ; the craw of a fowl. (Morris : South Monaghan.) Irish *sprogal* [spruggal], with that meaning and several others.

Sprunge [sprunj], any animal miserable and small for its age. (Ulster.)

Spuds ; potatoes.

Spunk ; tinder, now usually made by steeping

brown paper in a solution of nitre ; lately gone
out of use from the prevalence of matches. Often
applied in Ulster and Scotland to a spark of fire :
' See is there a spunk of fire in the hearth.' Spunk
also denotes spirit, courage, and dash.   ' Hasn't
Dick great spunk to face that big fellow, twice his
size ?'

> ' I'm sure if you had not been drunk
>   With whiskey, rum, or brandy—O,
> You would not have the gallant spunk
>   To be half so bold or manly—O.'
>
> (Old Irish Folk Song.)

Irish *sponnc.*

Spy farleys ; to pry into secrets : to visit a house,
in order to spy about what's going on.   (Ulster.)

Spy-Wednesday ; the Wednesday before Easter.
According to the religious legend it got the name
because on the Wednesday before the Crucifixion
Judas was spying about how best he could deliver
up our Lord.   (General.)

Squireen ; an Irish gentleman in a small way who
apes the manners, the authoritative tone, and the
aristocratic bearing of the large landed proprietors.
Sometimes you can hardly distinguish a squireen
from a *half-sir* or from a *shoneen.*   Sometimes the
squireen was the son of the old squire : a worthless
young fellow, who loafed about doing nothing,
instead of earning an honest livelihood : but he
was too grand for that.   The word is a diminutive
of *squire,* applied here in contempt, like many
other diminutives.   The class of squireen is
nearly extinct : ' Joy be with them.'

Stackan ; the stump of a tree remaining after the

tree itself has been cut or blown down. (Simmons : Armagh.)   Irish *staic*, a stake, with the diminutive.

Stad ; the same as *sthallk*, which see.

Stag ; a potato rendered worthless or bad by frost or decay.

Stag ; a cold-hearted unfeeling selfish woman.

Stag ; an informer, who turns round and betrays his comrades :—' The two worst informers against a private [pottheen] distiller, barring a *stag*, are a smoke by day and a fire by night.' (Carleton in ' Ir. Pen. Journ.') ' Do you think me a *stag*, that I'd inform on you.'   (Ibid.)

Staggeen [the *t* sounded like *th* in *thank*], a worn-out worthless old horse.

Stand to or by a person, to act as his friend ; to stand *for* an infant, to be his sponsor in baptism.   The people hardly ever say, ' I'm his godfather,' but ' I stood for him.'

Stare ; the usual name for a starling (bird) in Ireland.

Station.   The celebration of Mass with confessions and Holy Communion in a private house by the parish priest or one of his curates, for the convenience of the family and their neighbours, to enable them the more easily to receive the sacraments.   Latterly the custom has been falling into disuse.

Staukan-vorraga [*t* sounded like *th* in *thorn*], a small high rick of turf in a market from which portions were continually sold away and as continually replaced : so that the *sthauca* stood always in the people's way.   Applied also to a big awkward fellow always visiting when he's not wanted, and

always in the way. (John Davis White, of Clonmel.)
Irish *stáca 'n mharga* [sthaucan-vorraga], the
'market stake or stack.'

Stelk or stallk; mashed potatoes mixed with beans
or chopped vegetables. (North.)

Sthallk; a fit of sulk in a horse—or in a child.
(Munster.) Irish *stailc*, same sound and meaning.

Sthoakagh; a big idle wandering vagabond fellow.
(South.) Irish *stócach*, same sound and meaning.

Sthowl; a jet or splash of water or of any liquid.
(South.) Irish *steall*, same sound and meaning.

Stim or stime; a very small quantity, an *iota*, an
atom, a particle :—' You'll never have a stim of
sense ' (' Knocknagow ') : ' I couldn't see a stim in
the darkness.'

Stook; a shock of corn, generally containing twelve
sheaves. (General.) Irish *stuaic*, same sound and
meaning, with several other meanings.

Stoon; a fit, the worst of a fit: same as English
stound : a sting of pain :—' Well Bridget how is
the toothache ?' 'Ah well sir the stoon is off.'
(De Vismes Kane : Ulster.)

Store pig ; a pig nearly full grown, almost ready to
be fattened. (Munster.)

Str. Most of the following words beginning with
str are derived from Irish words beginning with
sr. For as this combination *sr* does not exist in
English, when an Irish word with this beginning
is borrowed into English, a *t* is always inserted
between the *s* and *r* to bring it into conformity with
English usage and to render it more easily pronounced by English-speaking tongues. See this
subject discussed in ' Irish Names of Places,'

vol. i., p. 60.   Moreover the *t* in *str* is almost always sounded the same as *th* in *think, thank*.

Straar or sthraar [to rhyme with *star*]; the rough straddle which supports the back band of a horse's harness—coming between the horse's back and the band.   (Derry.)   The old Irish word *srathar* [same sound], a straddle, a pack-saddle.

Straddy; a street-walker, an idle person always sauntering along the streets.   There is a fine Irish air named 'The Straddy' in my 'Old Irish Music and Songs,' p. 310.   From Irish *sráid*, a street.

Strahane, strahaun, *struhane*; a very small stream like a mill stream or an artificial stream to a pottheen still.   Irish *sruth* [sruh] stream, with dim.

Strammel; a big tall bony fellow.   (Limerick.)

Strap; a bold forward girl or woman; the word often conveys a sense slightly leaning towards lightness of character.

Strath; a term used in many parts of Ireland to denote the level watery meadow-land along a river. Irish *srath*.

Stravage [to rhyme with *plague*]; to roam about idly:—He is always *stravaging* the streets.' In Ulster it is made *stavage*.

Streel; a very common word all through Ireland to denote a lazy untidy woman—a slattern : often made *streeloge* in Connaught, the same word with the diminutive.   As a verb, *streel* is used in the sense of to drag along in an untidy way:—'Her dress was streeling in the mud.'   Irish *sril* [sreel], same meanings.

Streel is sometimes applied to an untidy slovenly-looking man too, as I once heard it applied under odd circumstances when I was very young. Bartholomew Power was long and lanky, with his clothes hanging loose on him. On the morning when he and his newly-married wife— whom I knew well, and who was then no chicken— were setting out for his home, I walked a bit of the way with the happy bride to take leave of her. Just when we were about to part, she turned and said to me—these were her very words—' Well Mr. Joyce, you know the number of nice young men I came across in my day (naming half a dozen of them), and,' said she—nodding towards the bride-groom, who was walking by the car a few perches in front—' isn't it a heart-scald that at the end of all I have now to walk off with that streel of a devil.'

Strickle ; a scythe-sharpener covered with emery. (Simmons : Armagh.)

Strig ; the *strippings* or milk that comes last from a cow. (Morris : South Monaghan.)

Striffin ; the thin pellicle or skin on the inside of an egg-shell. (Ulster.)

Strippings ; the same as strig, the last of the milk that comes from the cow at milking—always the richest. Often called in Munster *sniug*.

Stroansha ; a big idle lazy lump of a girl, always gadding about. Irish *stróinse*, same sound and meaning.

Strock'ara [accent on *strock*-] ; a very hard-working man. (Munster.) Irish *stracaire*, same sound and meaning, with several other meanings.

Strong ; well in health, without any reference to muscular strength. ' How is your mother these times? ' ' She's very strong now thank God.'

z

Strong farmer ; a very well-to-do prosperous farmer, with a large farm and much cattle. In contradistinction to a 'small farmer.'

Stroup or stroop ; the spout of a kettle or teapot or the lip of a jug. (Ulster.)

Strunt ; to sulk. (Simmons : Armagh.) Same as *sthallk* for the South.

Stum ; a sulky silent person. (Antrim and Down.)

Stumpy ; a kind of coarse heavy cake made from grated potatoes from which the starch has been squeezed out : also called muddly. (Munster.)

Sturk, stirk, sterk ; a heifer or bullock about two years old : a pig three or four months old. Often applied to a stout low-sized boy or girl. Irish *store*.

Sugan ; a straw or hay rope : same as soogan.

Sugeen ; water in which oatmeal has been steeped : often drunk by workmen on a hot day in place of plain water. (Roscommon.) From Ir. *sugh*, juice.

Sulter ; great heat [of a day] : a word formed from *sultry* :—' There's great *sulther* to-day.'

Summachaun ; a soft innocent child. (Munster.) Irish *somachán*, same sound and meaning. In Connaught it means a big ignorant puffed up booby of a fellow.

Sup ; one mouthful of liquid : a small quantity drunk at one time. This is English :—' I took a small sup of rum.' (' Robinson Crusoe.') ' We all take a sup in our turn.' (Irish Folk Song.)

Sure ; one of our commonest opening words for a sentence : you will hear it perpetually among gentle and simple : ' Don't forget to lock up the fowls.' 'Sure I did that an hour ago.' ' Sure

you won't forget to call here on your way back?'
' James, sure I sold my cows.'

Swan-skin ; the thin finely-woven flannel bought in
shops ; so called to distinguish it from the coarse
heavy home-made flannel. (Limerick.)

Swearing, 66.

Tally-iron or tallin-iron ; the iron for *crimping* or
curling up the borders of women's caps. A corruption of *Italian-iron*.

Targe ; a scolding woman, a *barge*. (Ulster.)

Tartles : ragged clothes; torn pieces of dress.
(Ulster.)

Taste ; a small bit or amount of anything :—' He has
no taste of pride ': ' Aren't you ashamed of yourself?' ' Not a taste': ' Could you give me the
least taste in life of a bit of soap?'

Tat, tait ; a tangled or matted wad or mass of hair
on a girl or on an animal. ' Come here till I
comb the *tats* out of your hair. (Ulster.) Irish
tath [tah]. In the anglicised word the aspirated
t (th), which sounds like *h* in Irish, is restored to
its full sound in the process of anglicisation in
accordance with a law which will be found
explained in ' Irish Names of Places,' vol. i.,
pp. 42–48.

Teem ; to strain off or pour off water or any liquid.
To *teem* potatoes is to pour the water off them
when they are boiled. In a like sense we say it
is *teeming* rain. Irish *taom*, same sound and sense.

Ten commandments. ' She put her ten commandments on his face,' i.e. she scratched his face with
her ten finger-nails. (MacCall : Wexford.)

z 2

Tent ; the quantity of ink taken up at one time by a pen.

Terr ; a provoking ignorant presumptuous fellow. (Moran : Carlow.)

Thacka, thuck-ya, thackeen, thuckeen ; a little girl. (South.) Irish *toice, toicin* [thucka, thuckeen].

Thaheen ; a handful of flax or hay. Irish *tath, taithin* [thah, thaheen], same meaning. (Same Irish word as Tat above : but in *thaheen* the final *t* is aspirated to *h*, following the Irish word.)

Thauloge : a boarded-off square enclosure at one side of the kitchen fire-place of a farmhouse, where candlesticks, brushes, wet boots, &c., are put. (Moran : Carlow.)

Thayvaun or theevaun ; the short beam of the roof crossing from one rafter to the opposite one. (South.) Irish *taobh* [thaiv], a 'side,' with the diminutive.

Theeveen ; a patch on the side of a shoe. (General.) Irish *taobh* [thaiv], a side with the dim. *een* ; taoibhin [theeveen], ' little side.'

Thick ; closely acquainted : same meaning as ' Great,' which see. ' Dick is very thick with Joe now.'

Thiescaun thyscaun, [thice-caun], or thayscaun : a quantity of anything, as a small load of hay drawn by a horse : 'When you're coming home with the cart from the bog, you may as well bring a little *thyscaun* of turf. (South.) Irish *taoscán* [thayscaun], same meaning.

Think long : to be longing for anything—home, friends, an event, &c. (North.) 'I am thinking long till I see my mother.'

Thirteen. When the English and Irish currencies were different, the English shilling was worth thirteen pence in Ireland : hence a shilling was called a *thirteen* in Ireland :—' I gave the captain six thirteens to ferry me over to Parkgate.' (Irish Folk Song.)

Thivish ; a spectre, a ghost. (General.) Irish *taidhbhse* [thivshe], same meaning.

Thole ; to endure, to bear :—' I had to thole hardship and want while you were away.' (All over Ulster.)

Thon, thonder ; yon, yonder :—' Not a tree or a thing only thon wee couple of poor whins that's blowing up thonder on the rise.' (Seumas MacManus, for North-West Ulster.)

Thoun'thabock : a good beating. Literally ' strong tobacco: Ir. *teann-tabac* [same sound]. 'If you don't mind your business, I'll give you thounthabock.'

Thrape or threep ; to assert vehemently, boldly, and in a manner not to brook contradiction. Common in Meath and from that northward.

Thrashbag ; several pockets sewed one above another along a strip of strong cloth for holding thread, needles, buttons, &c., and rolled up when not in use. (Moran : Carlow.)

Thraulagh, or thaulagh ; a soreness or pain in the wrist of a reaper, caused by work. (Connaught.) Irish—two forms—*trálach* and *tádhlach* [thraulagh, thaulagh.]

Three-na-haila ; mixed up all in confusion :—' I must arrange my books and papers : they are all *three-na-haila.*' (South.) Irish *trí n-a chéile*, ' through each other.' The translation ' through-other ' is universal in Ulster.

Three-years-old and Four-years-old; the names of two hostile factions in the counties of Limerick, Tipperary, and Cork, of the early part of last century, who fought whenever they met, either individually or in numbers, each faction led by its redoubtable chief. The weapons were sticks, but sometimes stones were used. We boys took immense delight in witnessing those fights, keeping at a safe distance however for fear of a stray stone. Three-years and Four-years battles were fought in New Pallas in Tipperary down to a few years ago.

Thrisloge; a long step in walking, a long jump. (Munster.) Irish *trioslóg*, same sound.

Throllop; an untidy woman, a slattern, a *streel*. (Banim : very general in the South.)

Thurmus, thurrumus; to sulk from food. (Munster.) Irish *toirmesc* [thurrumask], same meaning :— 'Billy won't eat his supper : he is *thurrumusing*.'

Tibb's-Eve; 'neither before nor after Christmas,' i.e., never : 'Oh you'll get your money by Tibb's-Eve.'

Till; used in many parts of Ireland in the sense of 'in order that' :—'Come here Micky *till* I comb your hair.'

Tilly ; a small quantity of anything given over and above the quantity purchased. Milkmen usually give a tilly with the pint or quart. Irish *tuilledh*, same sound and meaning. Very general.

Tinges ; goods that remain long in a draper's hands. (Moran : Carlow.)

Togher [toher] ; a road constructed through a bog or swamp ; often of brambles or wickerwork covered over with gravel and stones.

Tootn-egg [3-syll.], a peculiar-shaped brass or white-metal button, having the stem fastened by a conical-shaped bit of metal. I have seen it explained as *tooth-and-egg*; but I believe this to be a guess. (Limerick.)

Tory-top; the seed cone of a fir-tree. (South.)

Towards; in comparison with :—' That's a fine horse towards the one you had before.'

Tradesman; an artisan, a working mechanic. In Ireland the word is hardly ever applied to a shopkeeper.

Trake; a long tiresome walk : ' you gave me a great trake for nothing.' (Ulster.)

Tram or tram-cock; a hay-cock—rather a small one. (Moran : Carlow.)

Trams; the ends of the cart shafts that project behind. (North.) Called *heels* in the South.

Trance; the name given in Munster to the children's game of Scotch hop or pickey.

Traneen or trawneen : a long slender grass-stalk, like a knitting-needle. Used all over Ireland. In some places *cushoge*.

Travel; used in Ulster for walking as distinguished from driving or riding :—' Did you drive to Derry ? ' ' Oh no, I travelled.'

Trice; to make an agreement or bargain. (Simmons : Armagh.)

Triheens : a pair of stockings with only the legs : the two feet cut off. It is the Irish *troigh* [thro], a foot, with the diminutive—*troighthin* [triheen]. In Roscommon this word is applied to the handle of a loy or spade which has been broken and patched together again. (Connaught and Munster.)

Trindle ; the wheel of a wheelbarrow. (Morris for South Monaghan.)

Trinket ; a small artificial channel for water : often across and under a road. (Simmons and Patterson : East Ulster.) See Linthern.

Turf ; peat for fuel : used in this sense all over Ireland. We hardly ever use the word in the sense of 'Where heaves the *turf* in many a mouldering heap.'

Turk ; an ill-natured surly boorish fellow.

Twig ; to understand, to discern, to catch the point : —' When I hinted at what I wanted, he twigged me at once.' Irish *tuig* [twig], to understand.

Ubbabo ; an exclamation of wonder or surprise ; —' Ubbabo,' said the old woman, ' we'll soon see to that.' (Crofton Croker.)

Ullagone ; an exclamation of sorrow ; a name applied to any lamentation :—' So I sat down . . . and began to sing the Ullagone.' (Crofton Croker.) 'Mike was ullagoning all day after you left.' (Irish.)

Ullilu ; an interjection of sorrow equivalent to the English *alas* or *alack and well-a-day*. (Irish.)

Unbe-knownst ; unknown, secret. (De Vismes Kane for Monaghan : but used very generally.)

Under has its peculiar uses :—' She left the fish out under the cats, and the jam out under the children.' (Hayden and Hartog : for Dublin and its neighbourhood : but used also in the South.)

Under-board ; ' the state of a corpse between death and interment.' (Simmons : Armagh.) ' From the board laid on the breast of the corpse, with a plate of snuff and a Bible or Prayerbook laid on it.' (S. Scott, Derry.)

Variety of Phrases, A, 185.

Venom, generally pronounced *vinnom*; energy :—
'He does his work with great venom.' An attempted translation from an Irish word that bears
more than one meaning, and the wrong meaning
is brought into English :—viz. *neim* or *neimh*, literally *poison, venom*, but figuratively *fierceness, energy*.
John O'Dugan writes in Irish (500 years ago) :—
Ris gach ndruing do niad a neim : 'against every tribe
they [the Clann Ferrall] exert their *neim*' (literally
their *poison*, but meaning their energy or bravery).
So also the three sons of Fiacha are endowed *coisin
neim* 'with fierceness,' lit. with *poison* or *venom*.
(Silva Gadelica.) In an old Irish tale a lady
looks with intense earnestness on a man she
admires: in the Irish it is said ' She put *nimh a
súl* on him, literally the '*venom* of her eyes,'
meaning the keenest glance of her eyes.

Hence over a large part of Ireland, especially
the South, you will hear : ' Ah, Dick is a splendid
man to hire : he works with such *venom*.' A
countryman (Co. Wicklow), speaking of the new
National Teacher :—' Indeed sir he's well enough,
but for all that he hasn't the *vinnom* of poor
Mr. O'Brien : ' i.e. he does not teach with such
energy.

Very fond ; when there is a long spell of rain,
frost, &c., people say :—' It is very fond of the
rain,' &c.

Vcteen ; a person who is a *devotee* in religion :
nearly always applied in derision to one who
is excessively and ostentatiously devotional.
(General.)

Wad : a wisp of straw or hay pressed tightly together. A broken pane in a window is often stuffed with a wad of straw. 'Careless and gay, like a wad in a window': old saying. (General.)

Walsh, Edward, 5, &c.

Wangle ; the handful of straw a thatcher grasps in his left hand from time to time while thatching, twisted up tight at one end. By extension of meaning applied to a tall lanky weak young fellow. (Moran : middle eastern counties.)

Wangrace; oatmeal gruel for sick persons. (Simmons: Armagh.)

Want ; often used in Ulster in the following way :— 'I asked Dick to come back to us, for we couldn't want him,' i.e. couldn't do without him.'

Wap ; a bundle of straw ; as a verb, to make up straw into a bundle. (Derry and Monaghan.)

Warrant ; used all over Ireland in the following way—nearly always with *good*, *better*, or *best*, but sometimes with *bad* :—' You're a good warrant (a good hand) to play for us [at hurling] whenever we ax you.' (' Knocknagow.') ' She was a good warrant to give a poor fellow a meal when he wanted it': ' Father Patt gave me a tumbler of *rale* stiff punch, and the divel a better warrant to make the same was within the province of Connaught.' (' Wild Sports of the West.')

Watch-pot ; a person who sneaks into houses about meal times hoping to get a bit or to be asked to join.

Way. 'A dairyman's *way*, a labourer's *way*, means the privileges or perquisites which the dairyman or labourer gets, in addition to the main contract. A *way* might be grazing for a sheep, a patch of land for potatoes, &c.' (Healy : for Waterford.)

Wearables ; articles of clothing. In Tipperary they call the old-fashioned wig ' Dwyer's wearable.'

Weather-blade, in Armagh, the same as ' Goureen-roe' in the South, which see.

Wee (North), weeny (South) ; little.

Well became. ' When Tom Cullen heard himself insulted by the master, well became him he up and defied him and told him he'd stay no longer inhis house.' ' Well became' here expresses approval of Tom's action as being the correct and becoming thing to do. I said to little Patrick ' I don't like to give you any more sweets you're so near your dinner'; and well became him he up and said :— ' Oh I get plenty of sweets at home before my dinner.' ' Well became Tom he paid the whole bill.'

Wersh, warsh, worsh ; insipid, tasteless, needing salt or sugar. (Simmons and Patterson : Ulster.)

Wet and dry ; ' Tom gets a shilling a day, wet and dry'; i.e. constant work and constant pay in all weathers. (General.)

Whack : food, sustenance :—' He gets 2*s.* 6*d.* a day and his *whack.*'

Whassah or fassah ; to feed cows in some unusual place, such as along a lane or road : to herd them in unfenced ground. The food so, given is also called *whassah.* (Moran : for South Mon.) Irish *fásach,* a wilderness, any wild place.

Whatever ; at any rate, anyway, anyhow : usually put in this sense at the end of a sentence :— ' Although she can't speak on other days of

the week, she can speak on Friday, whatever.'
('Collegians.')   'Although you wouldn't take
anything else, you'll drink this glass of milk,
whatever.' (Munster.)

Curious, I find this very idiom in an English book
recently published: 'Lord Tweedmouth. Notes
and Recollections,' viz. :—'We could not cross
the river [in Scotland], but he would go [across]
whatever.'   The writer evidently borrowed this
from the English dialect of the Highlands, where
they use *whatever* exactly as we do. (William
Black: 'A Princess of Thule.')   In all these cases,
whether Irish or Scotch, *whatever* is a translation
from the Gaelic *ar mhodh ar bith* or some such
phrase.

Wheeling.   When a fellow went about flourishing
a cudgel and shouting out defiance to people to
fight him—shouting for his faction, side, or district, he was said to be 'wheeling':—'Here's for
Oola!' 'here's *three years!*' 'here's Lillis!'
(Munster.)   Sometimes called *hurrooing.*   See
'Three-years-old.'

Wheen ; a small number, a small quantity :—'I was
working for a wheen o' days': 'Ill eat a wheen of
these gooseberries.' (Ulster.)

Whenever is generally used in Ulster for *when* :—
'I was in town this morning and whenever I came
home I found the calf dead in the stable.'

Which.   When a person does not quite catch what
another says, there is generally a query :—'eh?'
'what?' or 'what's that you say?'   Our people
often express this query by the single word
'which?'   I knew a highly educated and highly

placed Dublin official who always so used the word. (General.)

Whipster; a bold forward romping impudent girl. (Ulster.) In Limerick it also conveys the idea of a girl inclined to *whip* or steal things.

Whisht, silence: used all over Ireland in such phrases as 'hold your whisht' (or the single word 'whisht'), i.e., be silent. It is the Gaelic word *tost*, silence, with the first *t* aspirated as it ought to be, which gives it the sound of *h*. They pronounce it as if it were written *thuist*, which is exactly sounded *whisht*. The same word—taken from the Gaelic of course—is used everywhere in Scotland:—When the Scottish Genius of Poetry appeared suddenly to Burns (in 'The Vision') :— 'Ye needna doubt, I held my whisht!'

Whisper, whisper here; both used in the sense of 'listen,' 'listen to me':—'Whisper, I want to say something to you,' and then he proceeds to say it, not in a whisper, but in the usual low conversational tone. Very general all over Ireland. 'Whisper' in this usage is simply a translation of *cogar* [cogger], and 'whisper here' of *cogar annso*; these Irish words being used by Irish speakers exactly as their dialectical English equivalents are used in English : the English usage being taken from the Irish.

White-headed boy or white-haired boy; a favourite, a person in favour, whether man or boy:—'Oh you're the white-headed boy now.'

Whitterit or whitrit ; a weasel. (Ulster.)

Whose owe? the same as 'who owns?':—'Whose owe is this book?' Old English. My correspondent states that this was a common construction in Anglo-Saxon. (Ulster.)

Why; a sort of terminal expletive used in some of the Munster counties:—'Tom is a strong boy why': 'Are you going to Ennis why?' 'I am going to Cork why.'

Why for? used in Ulster as an equivalent to 'for what?'

Why but? 'Why not?' (Ulster.) 'Why but you speak your mind out?' i.e. 'Why should you not?' (Kane: Armagh.)

Why then; used very much in the South to begin a sentence, especially a reply, much as *indeed* is used in English:—'When did you see John Dunn?' Why then I met him yesterday at the fair': 'Which do you like best, tea or coffee?' 'Why then I much prefer tea.' 'Why then Pat is that you; and how is *every rope's length* of you?'

Wicked; used in the South in the sense of severe or cross. 'Mr. Manning our schoolmaster is very wicked.'

Widow-woman and widow-man; are used for *widow* and *widower*, especially in Ulster: but *widow-woman* is heard everywhere.

Wigs on the green; a fight: so called for an obvious reason:—'There will be wigs on the green in the fair to-day.'

Will you was never a good fellow, 18, 114.

Wine or wynd of hay; a small temporary stack of hay, made up on the meadow. All the small wynds are ultimately made up into one large rick or stack in the farmyard.

Wipe, a blow : all over Ireland : he gave him a wipe
on the face. In Ulster, a goaly-wipe is a great
blow on the ball with the *camaun* or hurley : such
as will send it to the goal.

Wire. To *wire in* is to begin work vigorously : to
join in a fight.

Wirra ; an exclamation generally indicating surprise,
sorrow, or vexation : it is the vocative of ' Muire '
(*A Mhuire*), Mary, that is, the Blessed Virgin.

Wirrasthru, a term of pity ; alas. It is the phonetic
form of *A Mhuire is truaigh*, ' O Mary it is a pity
(or a sorrow),' implying the connexion of the
Blessed Virgin with sorrow.

Wit ; sense, which is the original meaning. But
this meaning is nearly lost in England while it is
extant everywhere in Ireland :—A sharp Ulster
woman, entering her little boy in a Dublin Infant
School, begged of the mistress to teach him a
little *wut*.

Witch : black witches are bad ; white witches good.
(West Donegal.)

Wish ; esteem, friendship :—' Your father had a
great wish for me,' i.e. held me in particular
esteem, had a strong friendship. (General.) In
this application it is merely the translation of the
Irish *meas*, respect :—*Tá meás mór agum ort* ; I
have great esteem for you, I have a great *wish* for
you, I hold you in great respect.

Wisha ; a softening down of *mossa*, which see.

With that ; thereupon : used all over Ireland. Irish
leis sin, which is often used, has the same exact
meaning ; but still I think *with that* is of old

English origin, though the Irish equivalent may have contributed to its popularity.

'With that her couverchef from her head she braid
And over his litel eyen she it laid.'

(CHAUCER.)

Word ; trace, sign.   (Ulster.)   'Did you see e'er a word of a black-avised (black-visaged) man travelling the road you came?'

Wrap and run : 'I gathered up every penny I could wrap and run,' is generally used : the idea being to wrap up hastily and run for it.

Yoke ; any article, contrivance, or apparatus for use in some work.   'That's a *quare* yoke Bill,' says a countryman when he first saw a motor car.

ALPHABETICAL LIST OF PERSONS

Who sent me Collections of Dialectical Words and Phrases in response to my letter of February, 1892, published in the newspapers.

The names and addresses are given exactly as I received them. The collections of those marked with an asterisk (*) were very important.

Allen, Mary ; Armagh.
Atkinson, M. ; The Pavilion, Weedon.

Bardan, Patrick ; Coralstown, Killucan, Westmeath.
Bentley, William ; Hurdlestown, Broadford, Co. Clare.
Bermingham, T. C. ; Whitechurch Nat. School, Cappoquin, Co. Waterford.
Boyd, John ; Union Place, Dungannon.
Boyd, John ; Dean's Bridge, Armagh.
Brady, P. ; Brackney Nat. School, Kilkeel, Down.
Brady, P. ; Anne Street, Dundalk.
Breen, E. ; Killarney.
Brenan, Rev. Samuel Arthur, Rector; Cushendun, Antrim.
Brett, · Miss Elizabeth C. ; Crescent, Holywood, Co. Down.
Brophy, Michael ; Tullow Street, Carlow.
Brown, Edith ; Donaghmore, Tyrone.
Brown, Mrs. John ; Seaforde, Clough, Co. Down.
Brownlee, J. A. ; Armagh.
Buchanan, Colonel ; Edenfel, Omagh.

Burke, W. S. ; 187 Clonliffe Road, Dublin.
Bushe, Charles P. ; 2 St. Joseph's Terrace, Sandford Road, Dublin.
Burrows, A. ; Grass Valley, Nevada Co., California.
Byers, J. W. ; Lower Crescent, Belfast.
Byrne, James, J.P. ; Wallstown Castle, Castletownroche, Co. Cork.

Caldwell, Mrs. ; Dundrum, Dublin.
*Campbell, Albert ; Ballynagarde House, Derry.
Campbell, John ; Blackwatertown, Armagh.
Cangley, Patrick ; Co. Meath. (North.)
Carroll, John ; Pallasgrean, Co. Limerick.
Chute, Jeanie L. B. ; Castlecoote, Roscommon.
Clements, M. E. ; 61 Marlborough Road, Dublin.
Close, Mary A. ; Limerick.
*Close, Rev. Maxwell ; Dublin.
Coakley, James ; Currabaha Nat. School, Kilmacthomas, Waterford.
Coleman, James; Southampton. (Now of Queenstown.)

Colhoun, James ; Donegal.

Connolly, Mrs. Susan ; The Glebe, Foynes.

Corrie, Sarah ; Monaghan.

Counihan, Jeremiah ; Killarney.

Cox, M. ; Co. Roscommon.

Crowe, A. ; Limerick.

Cullen, William ; 131 North King Street, Dublin.

Curry, S. ; General Post Office, Dublin.

Daunt, W. J. O'N. ; Kilcascan, Ballyneen, Co. Cork.

Davies, W. W. ; Glenmore Cottage, Lisburn.

Delmege, Miss F. ; N. Teacher, Central Model School, Dublin.

Dennehy, Patrick ; Curren's Nat. School, Farranfore, Co. Cork.

Devine, The Rev. Father Pius ; Mount Argus, Dublin.

Dobbyn, Leonard ; Hollymount, Lee Road, Cork.

Dod, R. ; Royal Academical Institution, Belfast ; The Lodge, Castlewellan.

Doherty, Denis ; Co. Cork.

*Drew, Sir Thomas ; Dublin.

Dunne, Miss ; Aghavoe House, Ballacolla, Queen's Co.

Egan, F. W. ; Albion House, Dundrum, Dublin.

Egan, J. ; 34 William Street, Limerick.

Fetherstonhaugh, R. S. ; Rock View, Killucan, Westmeath.

FitzGerald, Lord Walter ; Kilkea Castle, Co. Kildare.

Fleming, Mrs. Elizabeth ; Ventry Parsonage, Dingle, Kerry.

Fleming, John ; Rathgormuck Nat. School, Waterford.

Flynn, John ; Co. Clare.

Foley, M. ; Killorglin, Kerry.

Foster, Elizabeth J. ; 7 Percy Place, Dublin.

G. K. O'L. (a lady from Kilkenny, I think).

Garvey, John ; Ballina, Co. Mayo.

Gilmour, Thomas ; Antrim.

Glasgow, H. L. ; ' Midland Ulster Mail,' Cookstown, Co. Tyrone.

Glover, W. W. ; Ballinlough Nat. School, Co. Roscommon.

Graham, Lizzie F. ; Portadown.

Greene, Dr. G. E. J. ; The Well, Ballycarney, Ferns, Co. Wexford.

Hamilton, A. ; Desertmartin, Belfast.

Hannon, John ; Crossmaglen Nat. School, Armagh.

Harkin, Daniel ; Ramelton, Donegal.

*Harrington, Private Thomas ; 211 Strand, London, W.C. (For Munster.)

Haugh, John ; Co. Clare.

Haughton, Kate M. ; Lady's Island Nat. School, Wexford.

*Healy, Maurice, M.P., 37 South Mall, Cork.

Henry, Robert ; Coleraine.

*Higgins, The Rev. Michael, c.c. ; Queenstown, Cork.

Hunt, M.; Ballyfarnan, Roscommon.

*Hunter, Robert; 39 Gladstone Street, Clonmel.

Irwin, A. J., B.A.; Glenfern, Ballyarton, Derry.

*Jones, Miss; Knocknamohill, Ovoca, Co. Wicklow.

*Joyce, W. B., B.A.; Limerick.

*Kane, W. Francis de Vismes; Sloperton Lodge, Kingstown, Dublin. (For Ulster.)

Keegan, T.; Rosegreen Nat. School, Clonmel.

Kelly, Eliza, Co. Mayo.

Kelly, George A. P., M.A.; 6 Upper Pembroke Street, Dublin. (For Roscommon.)

Kennedy, J. J.; Faha Nat. School, Beaufort, Killarney.

Kenny, The Rev. M. J., P.P.; Scarriff, Co. Clare.

Kenny, Charles W.; Caledon, Co. Tyrone.

Kilmartin, Mary; Tipperary.

Kilpatrick, George; Kilrea, Derry.

*Kinahan, G. H.; Dublin. (Collection gathered from all Ireland.)

Kingham, S. H.; Co. Down.

*Knowles, W. J.; Flixton Place, Ballymena.

Knox, W.; Tedd, Irvinestown.

Lawlor, Patrick; Ballinclogher Nat. School, Lixnaw, Kerry.

Linn, Richard; 259 Hereford St., Christchurch, New Zealand. (For Antrim.)

Lynch, M. J.; Kerry.

*MacCall, Patrick J.; 25 Patrick St., Dublin.

McCandless, T.; Ballinrees Nat. School, Coleraine.

McClelland, F. J.; Armagh.

McCormac, Emily; Cnoc Aluin, Dalkey, Dublin.

MacDonagh, Mr.; Ward Schls., Bangor, Co. Down.

McGloin, Louisa; Foxford, Mayo.

MacSheehy, Brian, LL.D., Head Inspector of Nat. Schools, Dublin.

McKenna, A.; Clones, Co. Monaghan.

McKeown, R.; Co. Tyrone.

McNulty, Robert; Raphoe.

Maguire, John; Co. Cavan

Maguire, M.; Mullinscross, Louth.

Mason, Thos. A. H.; 29 Marlborough Road, Dublin.

Mason, Thos.: Hollymount, Buxton Hill, Cork.

Montgomery, Maggie; Antrim.

*Moran, Patrick; 14 Strand Road, Derry, Retired Head Constable R. I. Constabulary, native of Carlow, to which his collection mainly belongs.

•Morris, Henry; Cashlan East, Carrickmacross, Monaghan.

Murphy, Christopher O'B.; 48 Victoria St., Dublin.

Murphy, Ellie; Co. Cork.

Murphy, J.; Co. Cork.

Murphy, T.; Co. Cork.

Neville, Anne; 48 Greville Road, Bedminster.

Niven, Richard ; Lambeg, Lisburn.

Norris, A. ; Kerry.

O'Brien, Michael ; Munlough Nat. School, Cavan.

O'Connor, James ; Ballyglass House, Sligo.

O'Donnell, Patrick ; Mayo.

*O'Donohoe, Timothy ; Carrignavar, Cork. ('Tadg O'Donnchadha.')

O'Farrell, Fergus ; Redington, Queenstown.

O'Farrell, W. (a lady). Same place.

O'Flanagan, J. R. ; Grange House, Fermoy, Cork.

O'Hagan, Philip ; Buncrana, Donegal.

O'Hara, Isa ; Tyrone.

O'Leary, Nelius ; Nat. School, Kilmallock, Limerick.

O'Reilly, P. ; Nat. School, Granard.

O'Sullivan, D. J. ; Shelburne Nat. School, Kenmare.

O'Sullivan, Janie ; Kerry.

Reen, Denis T.; Kingwilliamstown, Cork.

Reid, George R.; 23 Cromwell Road, Belfast.

Reid, Samuel W. ; Armagh.

*Reilly, Patrick ; Cemetery Lodge, Naas, Co. Kildare.

Rice, Michael ; Castlewellan, Co. Down.

Riley, Lizzie ; Derry.

*Russell, T. O'Neill ; Dublin. (For central counties.)

Ryan, Ellie ; Limerick.

Scott, J. ; Milford Nat. School, Donegal.

*Scott, S. ; Derry.

*Simmons, D. A. ; Nat. School, Armagh.

Simpson, Thomas ; Derry.

Skirving, R. Scot ; 29 Drummond Place, Edinburgh.

Smith, Owen ; Nobber, Co. Meath.

*Stafford, Wm. ; Baldwinstown, Bridgetown, Wexford.

Stanhope, Mr. ; Paris.

Supple, D. J.; Royal Irish Constabulary, Robertstown, Kildare. (For Kerry.)

Thompson, L.; Ballyculter, Co. Down.

Tighe, T. F. ; Ulster Bank, Ballyjamesduff, Co. Cavan.

Tobin, J. E.; 8 Muckross Parade, N. C. Road, Dublin.

Tuite, Rev. P., P.P. ; Parochial House, Tullamore.

Walshe, Charlotte ; Waterford.

Ward, Emily G. ; Castleward, Downpatrick.

White, Eva ; Limerick.

White, Rev. H. V. ; All SS. Rectory, Waterford.

White, John Davis ; Cashel, Co. Tipperary. (Newspaper Editor.)

Weir, Rev. George ; Creeslough, Donegal.

Weir, J. ; Ballymena.

Wood-Martin, Col.; A.D.C. ; Cleveragh, Sligo.

*Woollett, Mr. Marlow ; Dublin.

WORKS

BY

P. W. JOYCE, M.A., LL.D., T.C.D.;

M.R.I.A.

ONE OF THE COMMISSIONERS FOR THE PUBLICATION OF THE
ANCIENT LAWS OF IRELAND;

LATE PRESIDENT OF THE ROYAL SOCIETY OF ANTIQUARIES, IRELAND

LATE PRINCIPAL, MARLBOROUGH STREET (GOVERNMENT)
TRAINING COLLEGE, DUBLIN.

Two Splendid Volumes, richly gilt, both cover and top.
With 361 Illustrations. Price £1 1s. net.

A SOCIAL HISTORY OF ANCIENT IRELAND,

Treating of the Government, Military System, and Law;
Religion, Learning, and Art; Trades, Industries, and Commerce;
Manners, Customs, and Domestic Life
of the Ancient Irish People.

A Complete Survey of the Social Life and Institutions of Ancient
Ireland. All the important Statements are proved home by references
to authorities and by quotations from ancient documents.

PART I.—**Government, Military System, and Law.**—Chapter I. Laying
the Foundation—II. A Preliminary Bird's-eye View—III. Monarchical
Government—IV. Warfare—V. Structure of Society—VI. The Brehon
Laws—VII. The Laws relating to Land—VIII. The Administration of
Justice.

PART II.—**Religion, Learning, and Art.**—Chapter IX. Paganism—
X. Christianity—XI. Learning and Education—XII. Irish Language and
Literature—XIII. Ecclesiastical and Religious Writings—XIV. Annals,
Histories, and Genealogies—XV. Historical and Romantic Tales—
XVI. Art—XVII. Music—XVIII. Medicine and Medical Doctors.

PART III.—**Social and Domestic Life.**—Chapter XIX. The Family—
XX. The House—XXI. Food, Fuel, and Light—XXII. Dress and Personal
Adornment—XXIII. Agriculture and Pasturage—XXIV. Workers in Wood,
Metal, and Stone—XXV. Corn Mills—XXVI. Trades and Industries con-
nected with Clothing—XXVII. Measures, Weights, and Mediums of
Exchange—XXVIII. Locomotion and Commerce—XXIX. Public Assemblies,
Sports, and Pastimes—XXX. Various Social Customs and Observances—
XXXI. Death and Burial. List of Authorities consulted and quoted or
referred to throughout this Work. Index to the two volumes.

Second Edition. One Vol., Cloth gilt. 598 pages, 213 Illustrations.
Price 3s. 6d. net.

A SMALLER SOCIAL HISTORY OF ANCIENT IRELAND.

Traverses the same ground, Chapter by Chapter, as the larger work
above; but most of the quotations and nearly all the references to
authorities are omitted in this book.

Second Edition. Cloth gilt. 188 pages. Price 1s. 6d. net.

THE STORY OF ANCIENT IRISH CIVILISATION.

Third Edition. Thick Crown 8vo. 565 pages. Price 10s. 6d.

A SHORT HISTORY OF IRELAND

FROM THE EARLIEST TIMES TO 1608.

Cloth gilt. 528 pages. Price 3s. 6d.

Published in December, 1897 : now in its 80th Thousand.

A CHILD'S HISTORY OF IRELAND,

WITH

Specially drawn Map and 160 Illustrations,

Including a Facsimile in full colours of a beautiful Illuminated
Page of the Book of Mac Durnan, A.D. 850.

Besides having a very large circulation here at home, this book has
been adopted by the Australian Catholic Hierarchy for all their Schools
in Australia and New Zealand ; and also by the Catholic School Board
of New York for their Schools.

Cloth. 160 pages. Price 9d.

OUTLINES OF THE HISTORY OF IRELAND

FROM

THE EARLIEST TIMES TO 1905.

50th Thousand.

"This little book is intended mainly for use in schools; and it is accordingly written in very simple language. But I have some hope that those
of the general public who wish to know something of the subject, but who
are not prepared to go into details, may also find it useful. . . . I have put
it in the form of a consecutive narrative, avoiding statistics and scrappy
disconnected statements."—*Preface.*

Cloth. 312 pages. 16th Edition : 24th Thousand. Price 2s.

A CONCISE HISTORY OF IRELAND

FROM

THE EARLIEST TIMES TO 1908.

With Introductory Chapters on the Literature, Laws, Buildings, Music,
Art, &c., of the Ancient Irish People.
Suitable for Colleges and Schools.
New and enlarged Edition, bringing Narrative down to 1908.